THE CONSTITUTION OF IRELAND

This book provides a contextual analysis of constitutional governance in Ireland. It presents the 1937 Constitution as a seminal moment in an ongoing constitutional evolution, rather than a foundational event. The book demonstrates how the Irish constitutional order revolves around a bipartite separation of powers. The Government is dominant but is legally constrained by the courts, particularly in their interpretations of the fundamental rights protected by the Constitution. In recent decades, the courts have weakened the constitutional constraints on the Government. Political constraints imposed by opposition parties in parliament and new accountability institutions (such as the Ombudsman) have moderately strengthened but the Government remains by far the most powerful political actor. There is a risk that such executive dominance could lead to democratic decay; however, the referendum requirement for constitutional amendment has prevented Governments from accumulating greater constitutional power.

The book begins with an overview of Irish constitutional history leading to the enactment of the 1937 Constitution, before exploring the foundational decisions made by the Constitution in relation to territory, people and citizenship. Particular attention is paid to the constitutional relationship with Northern Ireland, currently unsettled by the decision of the United Kingdom to leave the European Union. The book details the key institutions of state (Government, Parliament, President and courts), before analysing how different constitutional actors exercise their respective powers of governance, contestation and oversight. A thematic approach is taken to the courts' interpretation of fundamental rights, showing how judicial attitudes have markedly changed over time. Further attention is paid to both formal amendment and informal constitutional change. The Constitution today is markedly different from 1937: it is non-committal on national reunification, less influenced by Roman Catholic natural law teaching, and generally more permissive of Government action. It is perhaps these developments, however, that explain its continued success or, at least, its longevity.

Pictorial Narrative

Ireland's national tricolour flag frames the picture, with the tonal variation of orange and green with white. An architectural juxtaposition of three state buildings in Dublin is at the heart of the composition; it comprises the four columns of the Prime Minister's Office, the triangular façade of the Parliament and the dome of the Four Courts. The same edifice also serves as an allegory of the separation of powers, the principle underpinning the constitution. The structure is bathed in a beam of intense yellow 'laser light' representing the spotlight of accountability, a more recent focus of the Irish constitutional system. The year 1937 on white parchment and the inscription 'WE THE PEOPLE of ÉIRE' is a reminder of the enactment of the Constitution of Ireland and the consolidation of independence from the United Kingdom. The use of the word 'Éire' even in the English version of the constitutional text itself speaks to the contentiousness of what could be called 'Ireland' in 1937. Underneath the resonating phrase rests the portrait of the statesman Éamon de Valera, famous as founder of Fianna Fáil, architect of the Constitution, Taoiseach, and national President. This is just above the image of Mary Robinson, Ireland's first female President and later UN Human Rights Commissioner. The composition is counter balanced with a portrait of Countess Markievicz celebrated as a revolutionary nationalist suffragette and socialist and W B Yeats, the Nobel Prize winning poet, who also served two terms as Senator. In his poem 'In Memory of Eva Gore-Booth and Con Markievicz', Yeats would recall 'Two girls in silk kimonos, both / Beautiful, one a gazelle.' Deconstructed elements of political party emblems are in the foreground, reflecting the constitutional significance of political parties: FF for Fianna Fáil, a star for Fine Gael and a twisted orange and green ribbons for Sinn Féin. The influence of Roman Catholicism on the constitution is represented by a cross in a circle. The Irish Harp, prominently placed on the top right is the national emblem of Ireland.

Putachad
Artist

Oran Doyle
Author

Constitutional Systems of the World
General Editors: Benjamin L Berger, Rosalind Dixon, Andrew Harding, Heinz Klug, and Peter Leyland

In the era of globalisation, issues of constitutional law and good governance are being seen increasingly as vital issues in all types of society. Since the end of the Cold War, there have been dramatic developments in democratic and legal reform, and post-conflict societies are also in the throes of reconstructing their governance systems. Even societies already firmly based on constitutional governance and the rule of law have undergone constitutional change and experimentation with new forms of governance; and their constitutional systems are increasingly subjected to comparative analysis and transplantation. Constitutional texts for practically every country in the world are now easily available on the internet. However, texts which enable one to understand the true context, purposes, interpretation and incidents of a constitutional system are much harder to locate, and are often extremely detailed and descriptive. This series seeks to provide scholars and students with accessible introductions to the constitutional systems of the world, supplying both a road map for the novice and, at the same time, a deeper understanding of the key historical, political and legal events which have shaped the constitutional landscape of each country. Each book in this series deals with a single country, or a group of countries with a common constitutional history, and each author is an expert in their field.

Published volumes

The Constitution of the United Kingdom; The Constitution of the United States; The Constitution of Vietnam; The Constitution of South Africa; The Constitution of Japan; The Constitution of Germany; The Constitution of Finland; The Constitution of Australia; The Constitution of the Republic of Austria; The Constitution of the Russian Federation; The Constitutional System of Thailand; The Constitution of Malaysia; The Constitution of China; The Constitution of Indonesia; The Constitution of France; The Constitution of Spain; The Constitution of Mexico; The Constitution of Israel; The Constitutional Systems of the Commonwealth Caribbean; The Constitution of Canada; The Constitution of Singapore; The Constitution of Belgium; The Constitution of Taiwan; The Constitution of Romania; The Constitutional Systems of the Independent Central Asian States; The Constitution of India; The Constitution of Pakistan; The Constitution of Ireland

Link to series website

www.bloomsburyprofessional.com/uk/series/constitutional-systems-of-the-world

The Constitution
of Ireland

A Contextual Analysis

Oran Doyle

•HART•

OXFORD • LONDON • NEW YORK • NEW DELHI • SYDNEY

HART PUBLISHING

Bloomsbury Publishing Plc

Kemp House, Chawley Park, Cumnor Hill, Oxford, OX2 9PH, UK

HART PUBLISHING, the Hart/Stag logo, BLOOMSBURY and the Diana logo are
trademarks of Bloomsbury Publishing Plc

First published in Great Britain 2018

A catalogue record for this book is available from the British Library.

Library of Congress Cataloging-in-Publication data

Names: Doyle, Oran, author.

Title: The Constitution of Ireland : a contextual analysis / Oran Doyle.

Description: Oxford [UK] ; Portland, Oregon : Hart Publishing, 2018. | Includes index.

Identifiers: LCCN 2018025063 (print) | LCCN 2018026009 (ebook) | ISBN 9781509903443 (Epub) |
ISBN 9781509903436 (pbk. : alk. paper)

Subjects: LCSH: Constitutional law—Ireland. | Constitutions—Ireland. | Delegation of powers—Ireland. |
Civil rights—Ireland. | Federal government—Ireland.

Classification: LCC KDK1225 (ebook) | LCC KDK1225 .D69 2018 (print) |
DDC 342.417—dc23

LC record available at https://lccn.loc.gov/2018025063

ISBN: PB: 978-1-50990-343-6
        ePDF: 978-1-50990-345-0
        ePub: 978-1-50990-344-3

Typeset by Compuscript Ltd, Shannon

To Áilín and Barry

Acknowledgements

I wrote this book primarily while an associate professor in Trinity College Dublin, but also during visits to the Academia Sinica Taipei, Bocconi University Milan, and Keio University Tokyo. I am grateful to each institution for its support. The book is an attempt to make sense of Ireland's Constitution, the role it has played in structuring the Irish State, how it has changed over time, and how it may change in the future. My views on all of these issues have evolved through teaching constitutional law students, but also through countless conversations with my colleagues in Trinity and further afield. I am grateful to them all – students and colleagues alike – for creating the intellectual environment in which I could reflect on these dimensions of the Irish Constitution. I owe a particular debt of gratitude to Donal Coffey, Patricia Doran, Áilín Doyle, Melissa English, Sharon Finnegan, Scott FitzGibbon, Aileen Kavanagh, David Kenny, Kieran Mooney and Rachael Walsh who provided insightful comments on various drafts of the book. It has been a pleasure to work with the Series Editors at Hart, in particular Ros Dixon and Peter Leyland; their feedback has immeasurably improved the book. One of the most enjoyable aspects of the process was discussing with Putachad possible images for inclusion on the front cover. She has created an excellent and engaging painting that caused me to think further about some of the themes in the book. Thanks to my husband George for his love and support of this writing project. I first developed my interest in the workings of the Irish State many years ago during heated discussions over family dinners. I dedicate the book to my parents, Áilín and Barry, who started me on this road.

Oran Doyle
11 May 2018

Table of Contents

Glossary of Irish Language Terms

Ceann Comhairle	Speaker/Chairperson of the Dáil
Cumann na nGaedheal	Party of the Gaels (political party)
Dáil	Assembly (lower house of Oireachtas)
Éire	Ireland
Fianna Fáil	Soldiers of Destiny (political party)
Fine Gael	Family of the Gaels (political party)
Garda Síochána	Police service/police officer
Oireachtas	Parliament
Seanad	Senate (upper house of Oireachtas)
Sinn Féin	We Ourselves (political party)
Tánaiste	Deputy Prime Minister
Taoiseach (Taoisigh)	Prime Minister(s)
Teachta (Teachtaí) Dála (TD)	Dáil Deputy(ies)

Table of Cases

Table of Legislation, Agreements and Treaties

1

Beginnings, Influences and Evolution

Irish Constitutional History – The Irish Free State – Drafting the 1937
Constitution – Overview of the 1937 Constitution – Constitutional
Ideology – Constitutional Balance of Power

I. INTRODUCTION

THE CONSTITUTION OF Ireland was enacted by plebiscite in 1937,
the completion of a process that secured legal independence
from the United Kingdom. Referencing the Gaelic word for
Ireland, it begins in ringing terms: 'We, the people of Éire, … hereby
adopt, enact and give to ourselves this Constitution'. But this simple declaration conceals a whole host of constitutional difficulties. Who were
the Irish people? Why did they think they had the capacity to give themselves this Constitution? What territory would the Constitution apply
to? The answers to these questions can only be found if we situate the
1937 Constitution as a seminal event in the evolution of constitutional
relations between the United Kingdom and Ireland. Many features of
the current Constitution, in particular the relationship with Northern
Ireland, are explained by the precise way in which Ireland secured its
independence from the United Kingdom. More generally, the 1937
Constitution can best be understood as an attempt to continue some
traditions of Westminster government, notably the model of responsible
government (whereby the Government is not directly elected by the
people but is rather elected by and accountable to Parliament), while
distinguishing Ireland in other ways.

Those distinguishing features, principally its emphasis on the national
distinctiveness of the new State and its reliance on the rich intellectual
heritage of Roman Catholic social teaching, are sometimes presented as

the most significant aspects of the 1937 Constitution.[1] However, any characterisation of the 1937 Constitution as narrowly nationalistic or sectarian
is hard to square with its continued effectiveness. Across a range of metrics,
the Constitution of 1937 has proved remarkably successful and resilient.
Ginsberg, Elkins and Melton have calculated the average lifespan of written constitutions since 1789 as 17 years, but the Irish Constitution has
lasted for over 80 years.[2] The 2016 democracy ranking of the Economist
Intelligence Unit ranks Ireland as the sixth most democratic country in
the world.[3] The freedom ranking for 2015 accords Ireland a number one
grade for its freedom rating, political rights and civil rights. Ireland is a
country with many problems but the Constitution seems to have successfully performed its most basic task: the establishment and continuation of
a stable democratic system of government that respects minority rights and
personal freedoms. As much as its failures, its successes must be in some
way attributable to the choices of those who wrote it. In this chapter, I shall
trace Irish constitutional history prior to the enactment of the Constitution,
but with a particular focus on the constitutionally turbulent years of the
Irish Free State from 1922 to 1937. I shall conclude by sketching the outlines
of the Constitution and highlighting the main themes and trends that have
informed constitutional evolution in the subsequent 80 years.

II. IRISH CONSTITUTIONAL HISTORY: 1782 TO 1922

For much of its history, the constitutional story of Ireland was the story
of English influence and control in Ireland. Although Henry II of England
invaded Ireland in the twelfth century, the island did not fall completely
under English control until 1603. An Irish Parliament had existed since
the fourteenth century but, through Poyning's Law of 1494, had limited
its own right to initiate legislation without English approval. The English
Crown secured legal control of Ireland through the use of royal prerogatives and the distribution of peerages to ensure a compliant Parliament.

---

[1] R Foster, *Modern Ireland: 1600–1972* (London, Penguin, 1998) 544. Foster notes that
the fundamental rights in the Constitution 'were much influenced by papal encyclicals
and current Catholic social teaching' but does not trace the other influences. Writing in
1971 (without access to the relevant archival material), JH Whyte focused on the religious
influences on the fundamental rights provisions. JH Whyte, *Church and State in Modern
Ireland* (Dublin, Gill and Macmillan, 1971), 51–6. These accounts may have contributed to
a public perception of the 1937 Constitution as predominantly influenced by religion, but
this would be a mistaken impression. We return to this in ch 9.
[2] Z Elkins, T Ginsburg, and J Melton, *The Endurance of National Constitutions*
(Cambridge, Cambridge University Press, 2009).
[3] https://www.eiu.com/topic/democracy-index (visited 26 August 2017).

The Declaratory Act 1719 asserted the entitlement of the Westminster Parliament to make laws for Ireland, although this was seldom exercised. The Penal Laws, which since the early seventeenth century had imposed a wide range of civil disabilities on Catholics, precluded Catholics from being members of the Irish Parliament and from voting for members of the House of Commons.

In 1782, responding to demands from both the Irish Parliament and other groups within Ireland, Westminster granted full legislative independence to the Irish Parliament, repealing the Declaratory Act.[4] The Irish Parliament amended Poynings' Law and in 1783, Westminster passed the Irish Appeals Act renouncing its right to legislate for Ireland. However, Catholics – more likely to hold nationalistic sentiment – remained precluded from membership of the Parliament. The overall result was a politically unstable situation, not dissimilar to that which pertained in North America at the time, whereby Ireland had legislative independence but was subject to executive control by the English Crown. Moreover, while responsible government had more or less taken hold in Britain, where the Ministers of the Crown had to have the support of Parliament, the Government in Ireland did not have the support of a majority of the Irish House of Commons. It therefore continued to govern Ireland in much the same way as it had before legislative independence: through royal prerogative and patronage.

Given the threat posed by revolutionary and then Napoleonic France, a politically unstable Ireland posed a significant geopolitical risk to Britain. The 1798 Insurrection heightened this sense of risk. A violent rebellion, centred on the southeast of the country, was put down in June. Two months later, a small French invasion force joined Irish forces and gained some success in the west of the country, before also being defeated. The Insurrection allowed the British Prime Minister, William Pitt the Younger, to gather support for a policy of union between Great Britain and Ireland to which he had most probably already been committed. At its most positive, union was presented as a framework that would restructure Ireland's place within the British Empire. Having diminished from a kingdom to a colony, Ireland would be better served by a union that would give it an identity of interest with Britain. Moreover, Catholic emancipation, without which Ireland would be unstable, could only be tolerated within a United Kingdom in which Catholics would never achieve a majority position.[5] The Catholic majority in Ireland could not

---

[4] See generally Foster (n 1) 247–55.

[5] P Geoghegan, *The Irish Act of Union* (Dublin, Gill & Macmillan Ltd, 2001) 7. Pitt resigned in 1801, ostensibly on the ground that George III would not agree to

be permitted to elect a Catholic Parliament that might agitate for Irish independence. These slightly noble concerns neatly supported a solution that would also protect Britain from a French-sponsored attack through Ireland.

In 1799, a Bill to establish a union between Britain and Ireland was defeated by the Irish Parliament. Following increased levels of Crown patronage, the Irish Parliament approved the Act for the Union of Great Britain and Ireland in 1800. The Westminster Parliament then approved the complementary Act of Union (Ireland) Act 1800. The focus of the Acts was on the legislative union of the two countries and fiscal matters. Ward argues that little attention was paid to the future character of Irish administration, with the result that it was unclear where executive power resided. In particular, the powers of the Lord Lieutenant, the pre-existing representative of the Crown in Ireland and a member of the House of Lords, waxed and waned commensurately with the powers of the Chief Secretary, a member of the House of Commons and ultimately a member of the Cabinet. This constitutional confusion continued until Irish independence in 1921.[6] The Westminster Parliament voted for Catholic Emancipation in 1829, but the Irish Protestant Ascendancy continued to dominate the Irish administration until Independence. Notwithstanding its incongruence in a supposedly united kingdom, the separate administration of Ireland also survived several attempts to absorb it into the British governing machinery.

Despite the Union, Ireland remained a separate, restive part of the United Kingdom. A nationalist movement emerged, dedicated to the repeal of the Acts of Union.[7] In the latter half of the nineteenth century, the constitutional ambitions of Irish nationalists advanced alongside 'the land war', which sought to improve the situation of tenant farmers and to redistribute land from landlords to tenants.[8] Ireland had been granted 100 seats in the House of Commons. The Irish representatives used this power to advance the cause of limited self-government for Ireland, known as 'home rule'. The essence of home rule was the devolution of certain legislative powers to an Irish parliament in Dublin

emancipation for Catholics. For an analysis of this question, see CJ Fedorak, 'Catholic Emancipation and the Resignation of William Pitt in 1801' (1992) 24 *Albion* 49.

[6] A Ward, *The Irish Constitutional Tradition: Responsible Government and Modern Ireland 1782–1992* (Dublin, Irish Academic Press, 1994) ch 2.

[7] Foster (n 1) 296–310.

[8] The Westminster Parliament passed Land Acts in 1870, 1881, 1903 and 1909 designed to address the grievances of Irish tenant farmers. The land war can also be characterised as a class struggle within Ireland rather than a nationalistic project. See Paul Bew, *Land and the National Question in Ireland, 1858–82* (Dublin, Gill & Macmillan, 1979).

while Westminster would retain powers considered essential for the State as a whole. Between 1870 and 1916, the Irish Parliamentary Party on a number of occasions used its voting bloc at Westminster to ally with Liberal administrations in return for support for home rule.[9] These plans came to nought due first to Liberal defections in the House of Commons and later to the opposition of the House of Lords. Only with the eradication of the House of Lords' veto by the Parliament Act 1911, did home rule become obtainable.

By this point, however, the strength of opposition to home rule by unionists in the northeast of Ireland was intense. The religious-demographic make-up of this part of Ireland was markedly different, reflecting the success of plantations in Ulster of British Protestants some 250 years previously.[10] The province of Ulster consisted of nine counties, four with a large Protestant majority, two with a narrow Catholic majority and three with a large Catholic majority. Between 1911 and 1914, discussions took place in London over the temporal or permanent exclusion of some or all of Ulster from the provisions for home rule. However, due to legislative overreach by the House of Lords (seeking the permanent exclusion of all of Ulster), the Liberal Government eventually used the Parliament Act to force through the Government of Ireland Act 1914, establishing home rule for the entirety of Ireland. If the Government of Ireland Act 1914 had been implemented, it would likely have led to civil war. In 1912, the vast majority of Ulster Protestant males had pledged themselves to repudiate the authority of any Parliament forced upon them.[11] In 1913, the paramilitary Ulster Volunteer Force had been established to use all means which might be found necessary to stop Home Rule.[12] However, by this point, World War I had commenced. Prime Minister Asquith presented a Suspensory Act for royal assent at the same time as the Government of Ireland Act. This deferred implementation of home rule until after the end of the war, alongside a political promise that some solution would be found for Ulster.

Easter 1916 witnessed a violent rebellion in Dublin, led by revolutionaries who proclaimed an Irish Republic. Having subdued the Rising, the British forces executed its leaders. This likely caused public opinion in nationalist Ireland to harden, moving support away from the Irish Parliamentary

---

[9] Foster (n 1) 422.

[10] J Bardon, *A History of Ulster*, 2nd edn (Belfast, The Blackstaff Press, 2001) ch 5.

[11] JJ Lee, *Ireland 1912–1985: Politics and Society* (Cambridge, Cambridge University Press, 1989) 6.

[12] Bardon (n 10) 439.

Party and towards Sinn Féin.[13] In the UK General Election of 1918, Sinn Féin candidates won 73 of the 105 Irish seats in the House of Commons.[14] Among their number was Countess Markievicz, whose death sentence had been commuted after the 1916 Rising and who now became the first woman to be elected to the Westminster Parliament. Rather than take up their seats in Westminster, however, they assembled in Dublin in January 1919, adopted the Constitution of Dáil Éireann (Assembly of Ireland) and formed their own Parliament. Between 1919 and 1921, the Irish Republican Army fought a war of independence against Britain. In 1920, Westminster established separate Parliaments for Northern Ireland and Southern Ireland through the Government of Ireland Act 1920. On 6 December 1921, the British Government agreed with several Irish representatives a settlement commonly referred to as the Anglo-Irish Treaty. The Treaty granted self-governing dominion status to most of Ireland, similar to that of Canada, while two thirds of the Province of Ulster remained in the United Kingdom. The exclusion of those six counties of Ulster left a southern Ireland that was overwhelmingly Roman Catholic.

The Treaty prompted a significant division in Irish politics, approved by the Dáil by a vote of 64 to 57 in January 1922 and separately by the only-ever meeting of the Parliament for Southern Ireland.[15] Both the Dáil and the Southern Irish Parliament were dissolved and elections held to a new Parliament, which was, depending on one's perspective, the successor to either the second Dáil or the Southern Irish Parliament, or both. This ambiguity over the constitutional lineage of the third Dáil was to remain an issue in Irish constitutional politics for decades. The Treaty supporters won a majority in those elections; the Treaty opponents in Sinn Féin boycotted the new Parliament. A vicious civil war ensued between the former comrades but concluded after about one year, with the pro-Treaty side in control of the fledgling State.

III. THE IRISH FREE STATE: 1922–1937

The Parliament elected in 1922 sat as a constituent assembly and adopted the Constitution of the Irish Free State Act 1922.[16] This Act

---

[13] JJ Lee (n 11) 24–38.

[14] For an account of the period between 1918 and the 1922, see generally JJ Lee (n 11) 38–55.

[15] This was required by the terms of the Treaty.

[16] This method of enactment followed the approach adopted for most other European constitutions adopted between 1919 and 1921: those in Germany, Czechoslovakia, Estonia,

also entrenched the provisions of the Anglo-Irish Treaty, immunising it from constitutional change. The Westminster Parliament then enacted the Irish Free State Constitution Act 1922, including as a schedule the entirety of the Irish Act and Constitution. However, the UK Act also asserted the continuing power of Westminster 'to make laws affecting the Irish Free State in any case where, in accordance with constitutional practice, Parliament would make laws affecting other self-governing Dominions'. The Irish Free State therefore lacked the constitutional autonomy of an independent State and rested on a constitutional document of mixed parentage. These constitutional ambiguities would contribute to its demise.

The 1922 Constitution followed the Westminster model of responsible government, with a close nexus between the Executive and the Lower House of Parliament, especially on financial matters. But it was significantly different from the Constitutions of other countries that had emerged from the control of Westminster. Its most noteworthy innovation was its commitment to the protection of fundamental rights, enforceable through judicial review by the courts. No other Dominion Constitution at the time contained a judicially enforceable Bill of Rights. In this respect, the Constitution of the Irish Free State drew its inspiration from continental European Constitutions adopted in the aftermath of World War I. Cahillane notes that the Committee charged with drafting the Constitution was impressed by the 'enthusiasm for democratic ideals and popular sovereignty which permeated the post-war constitutions'.[17]

Ultimately, three inter-related features would lead to the downfall of the Irish Free State Constitution, in turn explaining features of the current Constitution that replaced it. First, as explained above, the Irish Free State Constitution could be said to derive its authority from an Act of the Westminster Parliament. This undermined its credibility as an Irish Constitution for the Irish people. Secondly, the constitutional order of the Irish Free State made the terms of the Anglo-Irish Treaty unamendable; many of these unamendable provisions, which preserved constitutional connections to the United Kingdom, were deeply objectionable to the

Austria, Poland and the Kingdom of the Serbs, Croats and Slovenes. See DK Coffey, *Constitutionalism in Ireland 1932–1938: National, Commonwealth, and International Perspectives* (London, Palgrave Macmillan, 2018) ch 4.
   [17] L Cahillane, *Drafting the Irish Free State Constitution* (Manchester, Manchester University Press, 2015) 83.

Irish. Thirdly, the Constitution was to prove ineffective for the protection of fundamental rights.

The first problem was a common one for countries that emerged from Westminster control. Any measure of independence that depended on a grant from Westminster could – at least in theory – be revoked by Westminster. The terms of the Constitution itself were ambiguous on this front. On the one hand, the Act that contained the Constitution recited that Dáil Éireann proclaimed the establishment of the Irish Free State, noting that all lawful authority comes from God to the people. Reflecting this, Article 2 of the Constitution recorded that all powers of government in Ireland derived from the people of Ireland. However, these provisions were difficult to square with section 2 of the Act and Article 50 of the Constitution, which precluded any amendments that were inconsistent with the terms of the Anglo-Irish Treaty. Moreover, there was the embarrassing fact that, at least as far as UK constitutional law was concerned, the Constitution secured its authority from an Act of Westminster, section 4 of which reserved the power of the Westminster Parliament to make laws affecting the Irish Free State. From an Irish perspective, the Constitution was contaminated by the potential claim that it was really just a Westminster Act that could be repealed at any moment by Westminster.

The second problem was the content of the unamendable provisions that preserved constitutional connections with the United Kingdom. Article 17 required each member of the Oireachtas (the Parliament) to swear that she would be faithful to His Majesty King George V, his heirs and successors by law. (This requirement led members of Sinn Féin to refuse to take their seats in the Oireachtas.) Legislation passed by the Oireachtas could not have the force of law until it received the King's Assent from the Governor General. The Governor General was empowered to withhold Assent or to reserve the Bill for the consideration of the King, although he was required to act in accordance with Canadian law, practice, and constitutional usage in this matter. Constitutional practice on this point was evolving in Canada, but the very existence of the office of Governor General was controversial in Ireland. Finally, Article 66 provided a right of appeal to the Privy Council in London against decisions of the Irish Supreme Court, undermining the judicial autonomy of the Irish Free State.

The third problem was that the Constitution proved, due to its ease of amendment, ineffective for the protection of constitutional rights. Article 50 of the Constitution allowed amendments by way of ordinary legislation for the first eight years; thereafter a referendum would be required.[18] Article 50 was not itself entrenched against change, save insofar as it provided that the Constitution could only be amended in a manner consistent with the Anglo-Irish Treaty. In 1929, the Oireachtas (Parliament) amended Article 50 to extend the period for amendment by ordinary legislation for a further eight years. This essentially meant that the Oireachtas could circumvent the power of judicial review by infringing rights through constitutional amendment rather than ordinary legislation. This strategy is most vividly illustrated by the 17th Amendment to the Constitution in 1931. Article 2A, directed at subversive elements, consisted of draconian crime control provisions. For instance, prescribed offences were to be tried not by judges but by military tribunals authorised to impose a greater penalty (including the death penalty) than that stipulated by law if the Tribunal thought it was necessary or expedient.[19]

In the late 1920s and early 1930s, the British attitude to its former colonies significantly relaxed, partly in response to Irish pressure, culminating in the Statute of Westminster 1931.[20] As applied to Ireland, the implications were that the Oireachtas was now free to make legislation that contradicted Westminster legislation. (This had always been the view of the Irish, who did not accept the validity of the limitations in the Constitution Act passed by Westminster in 1922.) Moreover, Westminster would no longer exercise its right to legislate for Ireland, unless Ireland requested and consented to the enactment, which was inconceivable.

In 1926, Éamon de Valera had left the Sinn Féin party and formed a new party Fianna Fáil – the Republican Party. Fianna Fáil did not continue with Sinn Féin's policy of refusing to take up parliamentary seats on account of the oath of faithfulness to King George V. They entered the Dáil as the principal opposition party in 1927. Five years later, they formed a government for the first time.[21] De Valera took advantage of the constitutional amendment power, still vested in the Oireachtas, to dismantle the constitutional connections between Ireland and the UK.

---

[18] Hugh O'Kennedy, one of the drafters of the 1922 Constitution and later Chief Justice, wrote in 1932 that the original purpose of this provision had been to allow for minor textual amendments. H O'Kennedy, 'Preface' to L Kohn, *The Constitution of the Irish Free State* (London, Allen and Unwin, 1932) xiii.

[19] The provisions of Article 2A were activated or deactivated by Government Order, leading Hanna J to characterise it as creating a kind of intermittent martial law cloaked under the harmless name of a 'constitutional amendment'. *State (O'Duffy) v Bennett* [1935] IR 70, 98.

[20] See generally DW Harkness, *The Restless Dominion: The Irish Free State and the British Commonwealth of Nations, 1921–31* (London, Macmillan, 1969).

[21] Lee (n 11) 150–7, 168–74.

Although de Valera maintained that the right to amend the Constitution derived from the Irish people, it was the Statute of Westminster that made it more difficult for the British to mount a legal objection. In 1933, the Oireachtas removed the requirement that amendments to the Constitution not breach the provisions of the Anglo-Irish Treaty. In the same Act, the Oireachtas removed the right of appeal to the Privy Council, an affront to Irish nationalists but seen by many Protestants as an important safeguard of the interests of the minority community.[22] The Oireachtas then removed the oath to the British Monarch required of Dáil Deputies. Later that year, the Oireachtas deleted the provision allowing the Governor General refuse the King's Assent to laws passed by the Oireachtas.

The Irish Supreme Court, however, questioned the constitutionality of this approach. In *State (Ryan) v Lennon*, the Supreme Court considered a challenge to the new Article 2A of the Constitution.[23] A majority of the Supreme Court commented obiter that it was not permissible to amend the Constitution in a manner inconsistent with the Anglo-Irish Treaty. In the Supreme Court's view, the Irish Free State Constitution had been enacted by a constituent assembly: the unamendable provisions were – quite simply – unamendable. This fundamentally challenged de Valera's strategy of constitutional decoupling from the United Kingdom. Six months after the judgment in *Ryan*, however, the Privy Council in London in *Moore v Attorney General of the Irish Free State* came to the opposite conclusion about the competence of the Oireachtas to amend the Irish Free State Constitution.[24] In its view, the Westminster Parliament had made the Irish Free State Constitution; the Statute of Westminster subsequently made it permissible for Dominion legislatures to act in breach of an imperial statute. Accordingly, the Oireachtas was free to amend the Irish Free State Constitution, including those provisions that required compliance with the terms of the Anglo-Irish Treaty. This presented an unusual predicament for de Valera. His strategy of using legislation to amend the Irish Free State Constitution and sever the constitutional connections between Ireland and the United Kingdom could only be implemented under a legal theory that accepted the Westminster

---

[22] T Mohr, *Guardian of the Treaty: The Privy Council Appeal and Irish Sovereignty* (Dublin, Four Courts Press, 2016) 137–8.

[23] [1935] IR 170.

[24] *Moore v Attorney General of the Irish Free State* [1935] IR 73. The UK Attorney General argued that the Irish Free State could not abrogate the terms of the Treaty. The Irish Government refused to recognise the proceedings, and indeed prevented the official court papers from being transmitted to London. The Privy Council ultimately rejected the argument of the British Government. See Mohr (n 22) 142–5.

Parliament, not the Oireachtas sitting as a constituent assembly of the Irish people, as the ultimate source of constitutional authority.

Ryan is also important as sounding the death knell of human rights protection under the Free State Constitution. The majority, while clearly disapproving of the content of Article 2A, held that it had been passed in a procedurally valid manner and could not be struck down with reference to broader constitutional or natural law values.[25] De Valera had employed Article 2A to deal with the Blueshirts, a conservative movement that bore mostly superficial similarities to the fascist movements of continental Europe, and the IRA, which posed a much more serious threat to the nascent State. Seán Lemass, a Government Minister and future Taoiseach (Prime Minister), commented that 'there has been a tendency in many countries towards a militarisation of politics, which it is very necessary to arrest if democratic institutions are going to be preserved'.[26] Despite its utility for the Government, however, de Valera was unsettled by the Supreme Court's conclusion in *Ryan* that the Oireachtas had an unfettered power to circumvent the human rights provisions of the Constitution.

Ryan and *Moore* established a number of propositions about the constitutional order of the Irish Free State that led to its demise. First, it was possible as a matter of UK law for Ireland unilaterally to dismantle the constitutional settlement embodied in the Anglo-Irish Treaty. The clearest example of this was when, the morning after the abdication of King Edward VIII, the Oireachtas amended the Constitution to remove all direct references to the Crown and to abolish the office of Governor General. Secondly, the Supreme Court had declared obiter that it was not possible to effectuate that dismantling through the amendment process prescribed by the Irish Free State Constitution. As the post-abdication amendments show, de Valera seemed content just to ignore these dicta; nevertheless, they cast a significant shadow on the legality of his constitutional project. Thirdly, the fact that the Oireachtas had enacted and the Supreme Court upheld the validity of Article 2A demonstrated that the Constitution could not function to protect fundamental rights from legislative abridgement. Fourthly, Coffey has recently argued that these flaws reflect a more general failure of the pro-Treaty Government from

<hr/>

[25] For discussion, see A Kavanagh, 'Unconstitutional Constitutional Amendments from Irish Free State to Irish Republic' in E Carolan (ed), *The Irish Constitution: Perspectives and Prospects* (Dublin, Bloomsbury, 2012).

[26] Lee (n 11) 180, quoting M Manning, *The Blueshirts* (Dublin, Gill & Company, 1970) 123.

1922 to 1932 and the British to facilitate a culture of political constitutionalism that might have accommodated the constitutional aspirations
of Fianna Fáil. Instead, the pro-Treaty Government acted to the full
extent of its legal powers while the British refused concessions such as
the removal of the oath to the British monarch.[27] Fifthly, even if these
issues had not arisen, there remained the foundational problem that the
Constitution could still trace its authority to an Act of Westminster.
Although the constitutional connections with the UK had largely been
removed, the 1922 Constitution was viewed – most importantly by de
Valera himself – as insufficiently Irish, an English imposition. In his
radio address on the publication of the draft Constitution in April 1937,
de Valera observed that the 1922 Constitution 'suffered from the fatal
defects that it was framed not altogether by Irish hands and that it was
made subject to a treaty admittedly imposed by the threat of force. Such
a Constitution could have but one fate'.[28]

IV. DRAFTING A NEW CONSTITUTION

In May 1934, de Valera established a constitutional review committee
with two tasks: first, to identify which of the provisions of the 1922
Constitution should be regarded as fundamental in the sense that they
safeguarded democratic rights; secondly, to submit a recommendation
as to how these could be especially protected from change. In 1935,
however, de Valera settled on a more ambitious project: the drafting
of a new Constitution. It seems that what finally pushed de Valera to
drafting a new Constitution was the decision in *State (Ryan) v Lennon*
about the basis of constitutional authority for the Irish Free State and the
consequent entrenching of the Treaty provisions against constitutional
change.[29]

   Under the overall supervision of de Valera, the new Constitution
was drafted in private by a small group of civil servants, most notably
John Hearne, then legal adviser to the Department of External Affairs.
It was subsequently circulated to Government Departments before being
presented to the Dáil for approval before a plebiscite. It was therefore

---

[27] Coffey (n 16) ch 1.
   [28] G Hogan, *The Origins of the Irish Constitution* (Dublin, Royal Irish Academy,
2012) 534.
   [29] DK Coffey, 'The Need for a New Constitution: Irish Constitutional Change 1932–1935'
(2012) 47(2) *The Irish Jurist* 275.

very much an elite-driven process. Many of the provisions of the 1922 Constitution were simply carried over into the new text. The principal structural innovations of the new Constitution were the introduction of a popularly elected President and a new amendment process. The President more or less assumed the responsibilities previously exercised by the Governor General, although was not formally vested with the executive power.[30] Of greater significance, the Constitution solved the ease-of-amendment problem that had afflicted the 1922 Constitution. After an unextendable three-year period, amendments could be made by referendum only, mirroring the proposed method of enactment for the new constitution: a plebiscite. By removing the power of amendment from the Oireachtas, the new Constitution would significantly empower the courts, given their continuing power of judicial review.[31]

Although the Constitution largely carried over the liberal democratic guarantees of the 1922 Constitution, many of its provisions were marked by a more religious tone. The Preamble opens in the same way as a Christian prayer, 'In the Name of the Most Holy Trinity'. Article 44 provides that the Homage of public worship is due to almighty God. Articles 41 and 42 (family and education), Article 43 (property) and Article 45 (directive principles of social policy) were clearly influenced by scholastic natural law theory, particularly as presented by Roman Catholic social teaching of the 1930s. The Family is the 'natural primary and fundamental unit group of Society' and a moral 'institution possessing inalienable and imprescriptible rights, antecedent and superior to all positive law'. The State recognises woman's 'life within the home'. Parents have an 'inalienable right and duty' to provide for 'the religious and moral, intellectual, physical and social education of their children'. Private property rights are protected on the basis that 'Man, in virtue of his rational being, has the natural right, antecedent to positive law, to the private ownership of external goods.' Although most of these references would not have been considered problematic by members of other religions in Ireland in 1937, their sectarian intellectual lineage was to become a source of contention as Irish society later secularised.

Much of the textual inspiration for these provisions came from religious figures, particularly the Jesuits and the then Headmaster of

[30] The influence of other models on the powers of the Presidency is further explored in ch 4.
[31] See ch 10 for a discussion of how the amendment process affects the constitutional balance of power.

Blackrock College, later Archbishop of Dublin, John Charles McQuaid, all of whom corresponded directly with de Valera during the drafting process. The religious influences should not be overstated, however. First, many of the Constitution's provisions – even in the fundamental rights section – reflected no religious influence whatsoever. Secondly, Ireland was not unusual for constitutions of its time – and indeed later – for introducing provisions of this type.[32] Thirdly, through intense diplomacy directly with the Vatican, de Valera sidestepped the more extreme demands of the Irish Catholic Hierarchy and instead drafted a provision recognising the special position of the 'the Holy Catholic Apostolic and Roman Church as the guardian of the Faith professed by the great majority of the citizens'. The Constitution then also recognised four other Protestant denominations as well as the Jewish congregations and the other religious denominations existing in the State.[33] In a Europe polluted with anti-Semitism, which was unquestionably shared by many within Irish society, this recognition is greatly to de Valera's credit. Although recognition of the special position of the Roman Catholic Church was later to become contentious and would be cited as evidence that Ireland was a clerical State, at the time it was senior Catholic clergy in Ireland rather than representatives of other churches who were unhappy with the provision.

Nevertheless, the religious influences on the text of the Constitution are real. In the 1920s and 1930s, many (including Nobel Laureate and then Senator WB Yeats) had warned that the increasingly Catholic character of the State would alienate Northern Unionists, rendering more difficult the aim of national reunification. This tendency continued into the 1937 Constitution, reinforced by a national identity that left little room for Unionists. The Preamble refers to our fathers having sustained 'centuries of trial' and an 'unremitting struggle to regain the rightful independence of our Nation' from an unnamed but broodingly present erstwhile oppressor. Article 1 of the Constitution recognises an Irish Nation with an 'inalienable, indefeasible, and sovereign right to choose its own form of Government'. As discussed above, one key provision of the Anglo-Irish Treaty had been that six counties of Ulster would remain in the United Kingdom. At the time of the Treaty split, this was not a particularly contentious issue. The Irish side, putting their faith in a boundary commission that would review the border, believed that only

---

[32] G Hogan, 'De Valera, the Constitution and the Historians' (2005) 40 *The Irish Jurist* 291.
[33] D Keogh, *Ireland and the Vatican: The Politics and Diplomacy of Church-State Relations 1922–1960* (Cork, Cork University Press, 1995) 132–40.

four counties would be left out of the new State and that this would prove unsustainable, leading to reunification.[34] By 1937, however, the existence of Northern Ireland was one of the few remaining operative provisions of the Treaty, alongside the retention by the United Kingdom of control of a number of ports. The British would cede control of the Treaty ports in 1938 but the status of Northern Ireland was addressed in the new Constitution. Article 2 asserted that the 'national territory consists of the whole island of Ireland, its islands and the territorial seas'. Article 3, however, provided that 'pending the reintegration of the national territory' the laws of the new State would have the same territorial scope as had the laws of the Irish Free State. The 'Irishness' of the new State was further emphasised in the new Irish-language titles given to governmental officials. The Prime Minister, previously styled 'President of the Executive Council', was now labelled 'Taoiseach', while the deputy Prime Minister now had the title 'Tánaiste'.

In all these ways, the new Constitution would solve the problems with the Irish Free State Constitution, at least as de Valera perceived them. Requiring referendums for amendment strengthened the power of the courts vis-à-vis the Parliament and by extension the protection of fundamental rights. The constitutional connections with the UK had been removed one-by-one between 1932 and 1936: the new Constitution – particularly with its elected Head of State in place of the Governor General – entrenched all those changes. The Constitution was a far more Irish and religiously influenced document. Although much of this occurred at the level of rhetoric, constitutional rhetoric is important. The new Constitution also addressed the remaining problem of Westminster's lingering authority. Article 15.2 emphasised the demise of Westminster: 'The sole and exclusive power of making laws for the State is hereby vested in the Oireachtas: no other legislative authority has power to make laws for the State.' Whatever the Statute of Westminster said, Ireland could never again request Westminster to legislate. At a more fundamental level, the fact that the Constitution was enacted by a plebiscite (and contrary to the amendment procedures for the Irish Free State Constitution) undercut any claim by Westminster to authority.[35] The Preamble stated, 'We, the people of Éire, ... do hereby adopt, enact,

---

[34] Lee (n 11) 53. Ultimately, the Commission recommended only minor changes to the border. The Governments in Westminster, Dublin and Belfast agreed in 1925 to make no changes to the border, as part of a general financial settlement.

[35] Enactment by plebiscite was a significant innovation; none of the interwar European constitutions had been enacted in this way. Coffey (n 16).

and give to ourselves this Constitution.' It thus claimed its authority directly from the Irish people, in a manner that was legally self-validated. In legal terms, therefore, the 1937 Constitution was a revolutionary act. Although it may not have been so apparent at the time, the 1937 Constitution – with its unequivocal substitution of a new constitutional legislator – marked the definitive establishment of Irish independence.

Other politicians were sceptical of de Valera's new Constitution. The draft Constitution was debated in the existing Dáil prior to it being put to the people on the same date as the general election in June 1937. Reaction to the document divided on partisan lines. It was supported by de Valera's party, Fianna Fáil, and opposed by most others. Much of the opposition was based on the unwarranted suspicion that de Valera aspired to a presidential dictatorship.[36] The constitutional text did not allow for such a possibility: the powers of the President were severely circumscribed; the President could not be a member of the Houses of the Oireachtas, while the Taoiseach had to be a member of the Dáil. Indeed, what is remarkable about the 1937 Constitution is the extent to which de Valera curtailed his own powers. By 1936, de Valera had secured a domestic position of supreme power. His party had a secure majority in the lower House of Parliament that it would hold for the next 10 years. Rival institutions held no equivalent power: the upper House of Parliament had been abolished, as had the Governor General. The courts' power of judicial review had effectively been abrogated by the ease with which the Oireachtas (now a unicameral body completely under the control of the Government) could amend the Constitution. In effect, de Valera had the powers of an elected dictator but was choosing to subject those powers to significant constraint. That his new Constitution was so misunderstood by his opponents as an attempt to create a dictatorship says much for the levels of hostility and mutual distrust between the partisans of the Treaty debate 15 years previously. This partisan perception of the new Constitution is apparent from the plebiscite: on a turnout of 75 per cent, it obtained a majority only of 56 per cent to 44 per cent.

De Valera's explanatory address on the enactment of the 1937 Constitution captures his broad view of the document:

> [I]f the constitution of a country like our own is written down at all it should not only define the character of the legislative, executive, and judicial

---

[36] Lee (n 11) 208.

regime, not only be a compendium of the great axioms of constitutional government ... but should contain as well a statement of some at least of the God-given rights of the individual both as a human being and as a member of society the protection of which by the State means more in the long run to the integrity and continuance of the civil society itself than the organisation of the institutions by which it is ruled.[37]

V. OVERVIEW OF THE 1937 CONSTITUTION

The purpose of this book is to provide a contextual account of the Constitution of Ireland. In the chapters that follow, I will analyse how the constitutional order in Ireland actually functions. As an introduction to that account, however, it is useful to present what might be called the official theory of the Constitution, the impression of the constitutional order that one might glean from reading the constitutional text in isolation. As noted above, the 1937 Constitution is considerably more Irish than its predecessor. It begins with an identification of the Irish Nation, a trans-historical entity that possesses the right of self-determination: the right to enact the 1937 Constitution and create a new State. Article 4 provides that the name of the State is Éire or, in the English language, Ireland. Articles 4–11 establish various features of the State: it is sovereign, independent and democratic. The national language is Irish, although both Irish and English are deemed to be official languages. The State owns natural resources, subject to any pre-existing rights or interests.

Articles 12–14 establish the office of the President. Directly elected by a vote of the people for a term of seven years, with the possible extension of one further term – again by popular vote – the President formally holds many powers: supreme command of the armed forces, the nomination of judges to the superior courts, etc. However, Article 13.9 provides that the President's powers may only be exercised on the advice of the Government, except where the Constitution specifically grants an absolute discretion. In reality, therefore, the President is a ceremonial Head of State. However, as we shall see in chapter four, the informal role of the President has expanded in recent decades.

The Constitution is textually committed to a tripartite separation of powers. Article 6.1 provides that all powers of government, legislative,

[37] University College Dublin Archives Department, P150/2431.

judicial and executive, derive under God from the people. Article 6.2 provides that the powers are exercisable only by the organs of State established by the Constitution. Articles 15–27 establish a bicameral Parliament (the Oireachtas) and provide considerable detail on its composition and functioning. The relationship between the Government and the Oireachtas follows the Westminster model of responsible government, largely a crystallisation of the constitutional conventions that governed Westminster in 1922. Article 34 provides that justice shall be administered in courts established by law by judges appointed in the manner provided for under the Constitution. Article 34.3 grants to the ordinary courts a jurisdiction to determine the constitutional validity of any law. (There is no special constitutional court.) Subject to some judicially developed standing rules (see chapter nine), the constitutionality of laws – and other forms of State action – can be directly challenged in the courts. The President also has an absolute discretion, under Article 26 of the Constitution, to refer a law to the Supreme Court, prior to signing it, in order to test its constitutionality.

Article 38 guarantees a number of rights in or around the criminal process. Articles 40–44 protect rights that broadly reflect two different philosophical traditions: liberal democracy and scholastic natural law. On the one hand, there are protections for values such as equality before the law, personal liberty, freedoms of expression, association and assembly. On the other hand, there is protection for the institution of marriage, the autonomy of families coupled with a strong principle of subsidiarity in terms of relationships between children, parents and the State.

Articles 46 and 47 stipulate that the Constitution can only be amended by way of referendum. The Constitution has been amended 30 times but these amendments have rarely affected the core governance structure. Instead, they have focused on Ireland's membership of international organisations, such as the EU, and a general liberalisation of Irish society on issues such as divorce, abortion and marriage equality for gay couples.

VI. CONSTITUTIONAL IDEOLOGY AND CONSTITUTIONAL BALANCE OF POWER

The 1937 Constitution presents itself as a foundational moment, creating a new constitutional order through a revolutionary act of popular will. However, it is better understood as a seminal moment in an ongoing process of constitutional development that stretched back several centuries and continues to this day. An exclusive focus on that master-text document (and the case law interpreting it) would be both incomplete and misleading. The Constitution of a State is not exhausted by its master-text Constitution. Broadly speaking, constitutions are those sets of laws and practices that constitute and control the governance function of states. In Ireland, the master-text document contains most of the constitutional laws, but it is supplemented and informed by other constitutional laws and practices. The focus of this book is on those other laws and practices as much as it is on the constitutional master-text of 1937. Once we broaden our understanding of constitutions in this way, we can identify seven significant changes to the Irish constitutional order that have occurred since 1937. Two relate to constitutional ideology; five relate to the distribution of constitutional power. The remainder of this book is largely structured around an analysis of these changes, which I shall sketch here.

As we saw above, two of the significant distinguishing features of the 1937 Constitution – as against the 1922 Constitution – were its nationalistic and religious overtones. These were not particularly unusual for interwar constitutions but subsequently differentiated the 1937 Constitution from constitutions adopted after 1945. Since the 1960s, these distinguishing features have been gradually bled out of the Constitution, through a combination of judicial decision-making (considered in chapter nine) and formal constitutional change (considered in chapters two and ten). The result is that the Constitution today is close to agnostic on the question of national reunification and much less religiously influenced (more akin to a generically liberal-democratic constitution) than was the case in 1960.

As noted above, the Constitution purports to commit itself to a tripartite separation of powers. The central argument of this book, however, is that the constitutional structure is built on a bipartite separation of power between the Government and the courts. Although the Government is formally accountable to the lower house of Parliament (the Dáil), the discipline of political parties eliminates institutional accountability. Instead, Parliament merely allows opposition politicians to focus public attention on political controversies. Given the desire of Governments to be re-elected, this creates genuine political constraints. These constraints, however, are far less significant than the legal and constitutional constraints interpreted by the courts, grounding my claim that the separation of powers is fundamentally bipartite.

This raises a question, however, as to how such a system of Government dominance has managed to sustain a competitive democracy. One might have expected political partisans to utilise the powers of Government, once attained, in order to mould the system to their benefit. It is primarily the requirement of referendum approval for constitutional changes that has prevented this from happening. In chapter ten, we shall explore how this method of constitutional change has underpinned the existing constitutional structures, enhancing the importance of judicial decisions and providing a further significant check on the power of Government. This is not to say that the Constitution has never changed, but rather to highlight the limited ability of the Government to secure constitutional change.

There have been five significant changes to the distribution of constitutional power since the 1937 Constitution was enacted. By far the most significant change has been Ireland's accession to the European Communities in 1973 and the subsequent development of those Communities into the European Union (EU). The purpose of this book is not to provide an account of the constitutional structure of the EU, which will already be broadly familiar to most readers. In chapter two, however, I shall explore how the Constitution of Ireland has changed to enable Irish membership of the EU. These changes necessitated by membership of the EU have had remarkably little impact on the domestic distribution of constitutional power.

The second significant change in the distribution of constitutional power involves the relationship between courts and Government that lies at the fulcrum of the bipartite separation of powers. The courts constrain the Government primarily through their interpretation of constitutional rights, but also through the imposition of legal constraints on public administration. The strength of these constitutional and legal constraints largely depends on the courts' own sense of how they should fulfil their role, rather than anything stipulated in the Constitution itself. Over time, the courts' understanding of their own role has changed significantly, prompted partly by Government decisions about whom to appoint to the Supreme Court. From the mid-1960s to the mid-1970s, the courts took a highly activist approach to the interpretation of constitutional rights. Levels of judicial activism then gradually reduced over time. The year 2000 marked a significant judicial retrenchment to a more technocratic role. Given that the core constitutional dynamic is the balance between the Government and the courts, these changing judicial attitudes have fundamentally shaped the constitutional order. I shall explore the political dynamics of the judicial appointment process in chapter eight and the courts' approach to constitutional rights in chapter nine.

The third shift in the constitutional balance of power concerns the emergence of public administration institutions and, relatedly, the development of accountability bodies to check those institutions. As we shall see in chapter six, in recent decades, the Government has frequently used its control of the legislative process to create administrative agencies to exercise administrative power. With this development, the Government's role has become more one of policy formation and less one of day-to-day administration. I argue that public administration remains led by the Government and does not challenge the Government. Nevertheless, the Government's control of statutory agencies is more indirect, somewhat reducing the Government's domination of the constitutional order. Related to this development, I chart in chapter seven the emergence of accountability institutions, such as the Ombudsman, that exercise a mostly non-legal but nonetheless important constraint on administrative agencies. These changes partially compensate for the more limited role now played by the courts.

Fourthly, since 1990, there has developed a much more significant informal role for the President as a leader of civic society. We shall see in chapter four that the President has very few real powers, functioning largely as a ceremonial Head of State. Successive Presidents since Mary Robinson, however, have expanded the remit of the Presidency to lead public debate on important societal issues while generally steering clear of party politics.

The fifth and final shift in the constitutional balance of power is an accidental one attributable to the general election in 2016. The results of this election left the two main political parties, Fine Gael and Fianna Fáil, with almost equal numbers of seats in the Dáil both considerably short of an overall majority and without any viable coalition partners. The result has been a Government led by Fine Gael, dependent on a confidence and supply agreement with Fianna Fáil. Because of this, for the past two years we have seen the Constitution function with a tripartite separation of powers as Article 6 might suggest.[38] The Government

---

[38] This develops the insight of Stephen Gardbaum that electoral systems are as important as the formal separation of constitutional powers to the concentration or dispersal of political power. S Gardbaum, 'Political Parties, Voting Systems, and the Separation of Powers' (2017) 65 *American Journal of Comparative Law* 229. Even with the same electoral system, different election results can effect changes in the constitution.

does not control the legislative process and is truly accountable to the Dáil. Throughout this book, I focus on the Constitution as it functioned prior to the 2016 general election before exploring the implications of the new political dispensation.

VII. CONCLUSION

There is a certain irony in these constitutional developments. Nearly 100 years after independence, the Constitution of Ireland operates in a manner remarkably similar to that in the United Kingdom. The religious influences have largely been bled out of the Constitution. The Constitution is close to agnostic about national reunification, the issue previously of greatest controversy with the United Kingdom. Moreover, the courts' turn from judicial activism has significantly reduced the contestation of the dominant Government.[39] Through all of this, the Irish Constitution has become less prescriptive on fundamental questions of identity and quotidian questions of policy. Although the nationalist and religious elements may have helped to secure popular acceptance of the Constitution in 1937, it is perhaps the dilution of those elements that explains its longevity and continued popular acceptance.

FURTHER READING

Laura Cahillane, *Drafting the Irish Free State Constitution* (Manchester, Manchester University Press, 2015)

Donal K Coffey, *Constitutionalism in Ireland 1932–1938: National, Commonwealth, and International Perspectives* (London, Palgrave Macmillan, 2018)

Donal K Coffey, 'The Need for a New Constitution: Irish Constitutional Change 1932–1935' (2012) 47(2) *The Irish Jurist* 275

Roy Foster, *Modern Ireland: 1600–1972* (London, Penguin, 1998)

Gerard Hogan, 'A Desert Island Case set in the Silver Sea: The State (Ryan) v. Lennon' in Eoin O'Dell (ed), *Leading Cases of the 20th Century* (Dublin, Round Hall, 2000)

Gerard Hogan, *The Origins of the Irish Constitution* (Dublin, Royal Irish Academy, 2012)

---

[39] In almost a mirror image, the United Kingdom constitutional order – particularly but not only through the Human Rights Act 1998 – has introduced much greater power for the courts as a check on government.

Gerard Hogan, 'De Valera, the Constitution and the Historians' (2005) 40 *The Irish Jurist* 291

JJ Lee, *Ireland 1912–1985: Politics and Society* (Cambridge, Cambridge University Press, 1989)

Thomas Mohr, *Guardian of the Treaty: The Privy Council Appeal and Irish Sovereignty* (Dublin, Four Courts Press, 2016)

Alan Ward, *The Irish Constitutional Tradition: Responsible Government and Modern Ireland 1782–1992* (Dublin, Irish Academic Press, 1994)

2

Constitutional Foundations

People and Nation – Identity of the People – Territory – Character of the State – International Relations – The European Union – Continuing Relations with the UK and Northern Ireland

I. INTRODUCTION

A S WE SAW in chapter one, a key concern for Éamon de Valera was to ensure that the 1937 Constitution was sufficiently Irish. Enactment by plebiscite – reflected in the words 'We, the people of Éire, … do hereby adopt, enact and give to ourselves this Constitution' – made clear that the Irish constitutional order did not derive its authority from any Act of the Westminster Parliament.[1] Such claims, typical of preambles, are obviously regressive but construct a foundational narrative and rhetoric. Walter Bagehot famously distinguished between the dignified and efficient parts of the United Kingdom Constitution.[2] This distinction provides a useful way of understanding the way in which the Irish Constitution addresses foundational issues. At a 'dignified' or rhetorical level, the Preamble and early Articles of the Constitution suggest a unitary Gaelic nation, claiming lawful authority over the entire island of Ireland. This completely overlooked the identity of northern unionists and succeeded only because, in 'efficient' or functional terms, the Constitution did something quite different. The plebiscite in the Irish Free State through which the Constitution was enacted (and the referendum requirement for subsequent amendments) actually created a new 26-county people as the locus of constitutional authority and focus of constitutional concern. This move shifted the psychological frame of reference and ultimately legitimated

---

[1] The use of 'Éire' rather than 'Ireland' even in the English-language version of the Constitution probably reflected sensitivity to UK objections to the use of 'Ireland' as the name of the State. Article 4 provides that the name of the State in the English language is 'Ireland', but this was less noticeable and provocative than the opening phrase of the Preamble.

[2] Walter Bagehot, *The English Constitution* (London, Fontana, 1963).

(from the Irish perspective) the existence of Northern Ireland as part of the United Kingdom. Popular approval for the Belfast Agreement peace settlement followed in 1998. However, the United Kingdom's recent decision to leave the European Union has unsettled the assumptions of free movement and integrated markets that underpinned the Northern Ireland peace settlement. As greater consideration is given to the (still unlikely) possibility of Irish reunification, the tension between the Constitution's dignified and efficient approaches to the identity of the Irish people has come into sharper focus.

In this chapter, I commence with an examination of the foundational choices made in 1937 as to the identity of the Irish people and the extent of the territory, including a more detailed examination of how citizenship rules have evolved since 1937. We shall consider the implications of the declaration of a republic in 1949 and assess the extent to which features of the Irish State concentrate power in the Government. The Constitution was enacted on the eve of World War II, in which Ireland was to remain neutral. I shall examine the constitutional position on international relations, reflecting de Valera's commitment to the League of Nations during the 1930s, before outlining how the Irish constitutional order has been reshaped to facilitate membership of the European Union. In conclusion, I shall turn to the constitutional connections between Ireland and the United Kingdom, in light of the Northern Ireland peace settlement. This will allow us to reconsider the foundational questions of identity with which the chapter commences.

II. PEOPLE AND NATION

'We, the people of Éire, ... hereby adopt, enact and give to ourselves this Constitution.' This dignified claim imperfectly reflected an efficient reality. The 1937 Constitution did receive popular approval at a plebiscite in June 1937. Article 62 provided that the Constitution would come into force 180 days 'after its approval by the people signified by a majority of the votes cast at a plebiscite thereon held in accordance with law'. The law in question was the Plebiscite (Draft Constitution) Act 1937, enacted by the Oireachtas of the Irish Free State. This provided that those entitled to vote at general elections for the Dáil would be entitled to vote on the draft Constitution. These provisions reveal a curious dichotomy. On the one hand, Article 62 of the new Constitution clearly had no authority prior to the enactment of the new Constitution. On the other hand, the Plebiscite (Draft Constitution) Act 1937 was clearly unconstitutional under the Constitution of the Irish Free State, since it allowed for the replacement of that Constitution without following the amendment process prescribed in that Constitution.

The violence being done to the 1922 Constitution is apparent from Article 58 of the new Constitution. This required judges, who did not resign, to swear the standard judicial oath in Article 34.5 to uphold the Constitution and the laws. Put another way, if any judges had refused to breach their oath to the old constitution and sign up to the new constitutional order, they would automatically have lost their jobs. Nevertheless, the mode of enacting the new Constitution attracted very little, if any, criticism. There were no judicial resignations and no apparent objection to the egregious interference with judicial tenure and independence effected by Article 58. I have argued elsewhere that this quiescence reflected a general and official acceptance within the 26 counties of southern Ireland that the people who lived in those 26 counties were entitled to create a new constitution for that geographical area.[3] The rhetoric of the Preamble worked because it was already accepted by its principal target audience; the constitutional revolution apparent in Articles 58 and 62 went unremarked because constitutional officials likewise accepted an authority beyond the constitutional order. Viewed in this way, the 1937 Constitution was not a foundational event but rather a seminal event in the evolution of a constitutional order that had been gradually coming into existence since 1922.

As we shall shortly see, the Constitution of 1937 claimed the entire island of Ireland to be part of Ireland. It should follow, one might have thought, that the people of Ireland who made the Constitution would be the people of the entire island. But the people who lived in the six counties of Northern Ireland could not vote on the document that purported to be their fundamental law. This geographical embarrassment reflected an unresolved paradox in the constitutional account of the Irish Nation. The Constitution presents the Irish Nation as a trans-historical entity, possessed of a right of self-determination. The British provide the unspoken antagonist against whom the Irish Nation is defined. The Preamble refers to 'the struggle to regain the rightful independence of our Nation', while Article 1 provides that the Irish nation affirms 'its inalienable, indefeasible, and sovereign right to choose its own form of Government'. The Irish Nation is distinct: it determines its own relations with other nations and it develops its life 'in accordance with its own genius and traditions'. By defining the national territory as consisting of the whole

---

[3] O Doyle, 'Constitutional Transitions, Abusive Constitutionalism and Conventional Constraint' (2017) 35 *National Journal of Constitutional Law* 67.

island of Ireland, Article 2 implicitly included all inhabitants of the island within the Irish Nation. The Gaelic character of the Irish Nation is emphasised by the identification of Irish as the national language and the first official language. English – although even then the first language of the vast majority of citizens across the whole island – is relegated to the status of second official language.

The Constitution thus posited an Irish Nation that was Gaelic in character and defined by its historic struggle to liberate its territory from foreign oppressors. It is impossible to conceive how Northern Unionists could be part of this Nation: Gaelic culture was largely alien to them and they identified with those against whom national self-determination had been asserted. These tensions were not created by the Constitution and it is probably unrealistic to expect that the Constitution could have identified an Irish Nation that would *both* justify the exercise of national self-determination against the United Kingdom *and* remain attractive to those who identified with the United Kingdom. The Constitution can, however, be seen as part of a process whereby these contradictions were largely removed from political debate within the Irish State. The Constitution contained sufficient nationalistic rhetoric to gain popular allegiance. But it also legitimised a State called 'Ireland' that did not occupy the entire island and an entity called 'the People of Ireland' who came only from part of the island. As these arrangements continued through time, the separate existence of Northern Ireland came to be acceptable to this new People of Ireland, ultimately facilitating the Belfast Agreement in 1998.

III. WHO ARE THE PEOPLE?

The people are a constitutional actor of continuing significance. Article 6 refers to all power deriving, under God, from the people. The people have the role to designate the rulers of the State, which they do through elections to the Dáil (the lower House of Parliament), and in final appeal to determine all matters of national policy, which they do primarily through the referendum process for constitutional amendment. The people with the continuing power to amend the Constitution and designate the rulers of the State are determined by Article 16.1. All citizens without distinction of sex who have reached the age of 18 (originally 21, but this was reduced by constitutional amendment in 1972) and have not been placed under any disability or incapacity by the Constitution or by law have the right to vote. In 1983, the people amended the Constitution to allow the franchise for Dáil elections to be extended to UK citizens, responding to a Supreme Court decision that had overturned legislation to that effect.[4] This continues a traditional reciprocity in voting arrangements between the UK and Ireland, although UK citizens are not entitled to vote in constitutional referendums or presidential elections.

The Electoral Act 1992 limits the franchise to eligible voters ordinarily resident in Ireland. This phrase is not statutorily defined but clearly permits only a period of temporary residence outside Ireland. Consistent with this, there is no general system to facilitate voting by those who live abroad. They must physically return to Ireland to cast their ballots. This was one feature of the Marriage Referendum of 2015 and the Abortion Referendum of 2018 – the hashtag #hometovote trended globally on twitter – but such commitment to the democratic process is rare. In 2013, a Constitutional Convention recommended that the franchise for presidential elections be extended to citizens living abroad; in March 2017, the Government committed to holding a referendum to facilitate this but has not published a specific proposal. Convicts were not precluded from voting although the absence of any general postal voting system effectively made it nearly impossible for prisoners to vote. In *Breathnach v Ireland*, the Supreme Court rejected a prisoner's claim that his right to vote was unconstitutionally infringed by this arrangement.[5] The Electoral (Amendment) Act 2006 extended to prisoners the right to register for postal voting, prompted by the judgment of the European Court of Human Rights in *Hirst v United Kingdom (No 2)*.[6]

These legislative restrictions on the franchise do not answer the fundamental, anterior question: who is entitled to be an Irish citizen. Article 9, as it appeared in the original Constitution, granted Irish citizenship to all who had been citizens of the Irish Free State immediately prior to the coming into force of the new Constitution. Thereafter, the future acquisition and loss of citizenship would be determined by law. The Irish Nationality and Citizenship Act 1956 granted Irish citizenship to all who were born in Ireland, north or south (*ius soli*), and to persons whose father or mother was an Irish citizen (*ius sanguinis*). In 1998, several constitutional amendments were passed to give effect to the peace settlement in Northern Ireland. Among these, Article 2

---

[4] *re Article 26 and the Electoral (Amendment) Bill 1983* [1984] IR 268.
[5] *Breathnach v Ireland* [2001] 3 IR 230. The Court had previously rejected a similar argument advanced by a person with a disability that precluded her from leaving home to attend a polling station. *Draper v Attorney General* [1984] IR 277.
[6] *Hirst v United Kingdom (No 2)* [2005] ECHR 681.

was amended to include that it was the birthright and entitlement of any person born on the island of Ireland to be part of the Irish nation. This arguably elevated the *ius soli* citizenship entitlement to constitutional status, a proposition apparently accepted in obiter comments by some members of the Supreme Court.[7] In 2004, the people – motivated by immigration concerns – approved an amendment to foreclose this *ius soli* entitlement to citizenship. Article 9 was amended to provide that the only constitutional entitlement of citizenship was for people born on the island of Ireland who had a parent who was either an Irish citizen or entitled to be an Irish citizen. The Oireachtas subsequently passed the Irish Nationality and Citizenship Act 2004 to provide that children born in Ireland to non-Irish parents are entitled to citizenship if those parents have been living in the State for three of the previous four years.[8]

It is not unusual for constitutions to make foundational references to the people. The Irish references go beyond rhetoric, insofar as the modes of constitutional enactment and amendment both directly involve the populace. Moreover, this constitutional feature has led the courts to develop important doctrines. First, in a series of cases, the courts have refused to engage in any substantive review of constitutional amendment proposals on the basis that the people are sovereign and can amend the Constitution in any way that they see fit. We shall consider these cases further in chapter ten. Secondly, the courts have relied on the notion of popular sovereignty to reject claims on the part of the State for special privileges. In particular, this has contributed to the elimination of royal prerogatives from Irish law, an issue that I explore further below in assessing the powers of the State.

IV. TERRITORY

Article 2 of the Constitution originally made a territorial claim to Northern Ireland: 'The national territory consists of the whole island of Ireland, its islands and the territorial seas.' Article 3 severely limited the implications of this claim: pending the re-integration of the national territory, the acts of the new constitutional organs would have no effect in Northern Ireland. The dignified and efficient treatment of territory thus mirrored the dignified and efficient treatment of 'the people',

---

[7] *O and L v Minister for Justice* [2003] 1 IR 1.
[8] Statute also allows for citizenship through naturalisation and through ancestry (up to two generations). There is no bar on dual citizenship.

considered above. At the dignified level, the Constitution claimed to be made by and for the Irish people inhabiting the entire island of Ireland. At the efficient level, the Constitution was made by the people in the 26 counties of southern Ireland and applied only to that geographical area. This contributed to largely removing the topic of Northern Ireland from ordinary political debate. Over the following decades, Northern Ireland would develop into a sectarian Statelet: the largely Catholic nationalist minority were subject to systematic discrimination practised by the largely Protestant unionist/loyalist government. In the late 1960s, many nationalists turned to civil rights protests and other peaceful means to improve their situation.[9] However, the Provisional IRA also commenced a terrorist campaign, widely opposed on both sides of the border, for Irish reunification. This required the Irish constitutional order to grapple with the implications of the territorial claim to Northern Ireland.

In August 1969, the then Taoiseach, Jack Lynch TD, asked the Irish army to prepare military plans for a limited invasion of Northern Ireland to protect nationalists being forced from their homes by loyalist mobs.[10] The Cabinet decided not to implement the plans, preferring to rely on British commitments to protect Northern nationalists. However, the Government did provide an emergency fund to provide relief to civilians forced from their homes. The Arms Crisis of 1970 centred on allegations that some of these funds had been diverted from humanitarian purposes and were instead used to pay for arms. It led to the trial and acquittal of, among others, two Government Ministers. Lynch sacked the Minister for Finance, Charles Haughey TD, although in 1979 Haughey would replace Lynch as leader of Fianna Fáil and Taoiseach. This incident was the closest that Ireland has come to military embroilment in Northern Ireland.

A more subtle constitutional challenge, however, was posed by attempts to involve the Irish Government in solutions to the Northern Ireland conflict. The basic premise of these initiatives was that the Irish Government could play some role in Northern Irish affairs and thereby act as a guarantor of the interests of Northern nationalists. This was problematic to Northern unionists, who resented any role for – as they saw it – a foreign Government. At a more theoretical level, however,

---

[9] JJ Lee, *Ireland 1912–1985: Politics and Society* (Cambridge, Cambridge University Press, 1989) 411–35.

[10] On the arms crisis generally, see D Ferriter, *Ambiguous Republic: Ireland in the 1970s* (London, Profile Books, 2012), ch 12.

it was also problematic for Irish nationalists because these mechanisms implicitly conceded some legitimacy to the existence of Northern Ireland as part of the United Kingdom. In particular, it was argued that this was prohibited by the territorial claim to Northern Ireland in Article 2. The Supreme Court gave its most focused consideration of this argument in *McGimpsey v Ireland*, a challenge to the Anglo-Irish Agreement of 1985.[11] Ironically, this challenge was taken by two Northern Unionists who adopted the constitutional argument of extreme nationalists (the Agreement unconstitutionally recognised the existence of Northern Ireland) in order to meet their own unionist objective of reducing the Irish Government's role in Northern Ireland. Finlay CJ characterised Article 2 as 'a declaration of the extent of the national territory as a claim of legal right'. The re-integration of the national territory was a constitutional imperative. Nevertheless, the Court upheld the Agreement on the basis that the Government was merely recognising the de facto situation in Northern Ireland without in any way abandoning the claim to the re-integration of the national territory. This judgment aptly captured the constructive ambiguity of Articles 2 and 3: at the level of principle, reunification was an imperative. At the level of practice, the Government could implicitly accept the legitimacy of Northern Ireland. This provided constitutional space in which the territorial dispute could be peacefully resolved a decade later.

V. THE CHARACTER OF THE STATE

Article 5 provides that Ireland is a sovereign, independent and democratic State. As with many of the foundational provisions of the Constitution, this Article gains its resonance from the history of British rule. It is highly doubtful whether such a confident assertion could have been made (let alone accurately made) in the Irish Free State Constitution of 1922. It is noteworthy that the Constitution did not explicitly claim that Ireland was a republic. In 1948 while visiting Canada, Taoiseach John A Costello announced that Ireland would be declared a Republic. The Republic of Ireland Act 1948 declared that the description of the State would be 'the Republic of Ireland'. This did not alter the official name of the State, which, as per Article 4 of the Constitution,

---

[11] *McGimpsey v Ireland* [1990] 1 IR 110. The Supreme Court had previously considered a similar argument in relation to the Sunningdale Agreement of 1974. *Boland v An Taoiseach* [1974] IR 338.

remained 'Ireland' or 'Éire'. The Act also repealed the Executive Authority (External Relations) Act 1936. This Act, passed the morning after the abdication of King Edward VIII, had deleted all references to the Crown in the Irish Free State Constitution, while allowing the Irish Free State to utilise the King for the purposes of the appointment of diplomatic and consular representatives and the conclusion of international agreements. This authorisation was continued in Article 29.4.2° of the current Constitution, allowing the Government for the purposes of external relations to 'avail of or adopt any organ, instrument, or method of procedure used or adopted for the like purpose by the members of any group or league of nations with which the State is or becomes associated for the purpose of international co-operation in matters of common concern'. Although this spectacularly oblique reference to the United Kingdom monarch continues in the Constitution to this day, the Republic of Ireland Act 1948 ended the practice, thereby removing the last constitutional connection with the United Kingdom. The Act granted the President the power to perform those functions on the advice of the Government. It was only at this point that the President was recognised externally as Head of State, thereby fully establishing Ireland as an independent State.

Setting aside the issue of reunification, 1949 marked the achievement of a republic in the sense of separation from the United Kingdom and anti-monarchism. That this could be achieved constitutionally suggests that the 1937 Constitution had established a republic in all but name. However, other characteristics of the State were less clear. During the Supreme Court's period of greatest activism – from the 1960s to the 1980s – it developed a concept of the State subject to law, necessarily with limited powers. In *Byrne v Ireland*, the Supreme Court rejected the claim that the State was internally sovereign, articulating instead a principle of popular sovereignty: the State was subject to the Constitution, which in turn was subject to the People.[12] It is significant that the Court sought to subordinate the State to the law. As we saw in chapter one, the 1937 Constitution was best viewed not as a foundational moment but rather as a seminal moment in an ongoing constitutional evolution. The Constitution did not claim to create a State. In *Byrne*, however, the Court interpreted the Constitution as creating the State. This subordination of State to law had practical significance in limiting the powers of the State.

---

[12] *Byrne v Ireland* [1972] IR 241. The Court distinguished between internal and external sovereignty. Externally, the State is sovereign vis-à-vis other States.

The plaintiff sued the State for personal injuries after she tripped and fell in a trench that had been dug and refilled (not very effectively) by employees of the State. The State sought to rely on the prerogative of immunity from suit. This raised the question of whether any royal prerogatives had survived.

In British constitutional theory and practice, the Crown was (and still is) both the personification of the State and the supreme authority within the State. Over time, certain powers that were deemed to inhere in the Crown came to be exercisable by or on the authority of the executive. Some of these powers were very regal in character, relating to the personality of the Crown as supreme authority. Others, however, could reasonably be seen as necessary powers for any State to have.[13] Article 49 of the 1937 Constitution provides that all royal prerogatives that applied in or in respect of the Irish Free State now belonged to the people and could be exercised by the Government. The Supreme Court in *Byrne*, however, rendered this provision meaningless, by concluding that no Crown prerogatives existed in the Irish Free State and therefore could not have existed in 1936/37 to be carried over by Article 49. In Walsh J's view, the King in the constitutional order of the Irish Free State was purely a creature of the Constitution and had no inherent powers. This depended on a theory of the Irish Free State that would have had few, if any adherents, during the time of that State.[14] Although few would have objected to the elimination of the royal prerogative of immunity from suit, in *Webb v Ireland* the Court followed the same logic to eliminate the royal prerogative of treasure trove.[15] However, the Court avoided the unsavoury prospect of allowing a treasure hunter gain ownership of a priceless early Christian artefact by cobbling together a new doctrine to the effect that the State should own antiquities of importance that are discovered and have no known owner.

Notwithstanding the Court's view in *Byrne* that the State was the subject of the Constitution, the Supreme Court has held that there are inherent powers that the State must hold simply by reason of being a State, irrespective of constitutional silence on the issue. These powers vest in the Government but may be taken over by legislation. Most notably, the Court has consistently held that there is an inherent State power

---

[13] P Leyland, *The Constitution of the United Kingdom: A Contextual Analysis*, 3rd edn (London, Bloomsbury, 2016) 87–8.

[14] For criticism, see J Kelly, 'Hidden Treasure and the Irish Constitution' (1988) 10 *Dublin University Law Journal* 5.

[15] [1988] IR 353.

to control immigration.[16] This executive power has been controlled by legislation but could – in theory – be returned to the Government.[17] Although these powers neither carry a royal warrant nor derive their legal validity in a chain of title from Crown prerogatives, they are remarkably similar to the powers that vest in the UK Crown under that rubric. *Byrne* raised the possibility of a *recthstaat*, a State wholly subject to law. If the Government can only exercise powers conferred by law, there is at least a requirement for the Government to secure public authorisation for its powers through the legislative process. The Court's more recent willingness to identify inherent State powers presumptively vested in the Government, however, concentrates further political power in the Government and reduces the opportunity for political scrutiny and contestation of that power.

VI. INTERNATIONAL RELATIONS

During the 1920s and 1930s, Ireland placed great emphasis on international recognition and the power of diplomacy. De Valera himself had served as President of the Council of the League of Nations in 1932 and was firmly committed to the objectives of that organisation.[18] The Constitution – rather optimistically for 1937 – endorsed these internationalist ideals. Article 29 commits Ireland to a consensual posture in international affairs: 'devotion to the ideal of peace and friendly cooperation amongst nations', 'the pacific settlement of international disputes by international arbitration or judicial resolution', and acceptance of the 'generally recognised principles of international law'.

The Constitution adopts a dualist approach to treaties: international agreements cannot become law without being enacted by the Oireachtas. International agreements (unless merely technical and administrative) must be laid before the Dáil. If they involve a charge on public funds, they do not bind the State unless approved by the Dáil, reflecting the general role of the Dáil in financial governance and accountability. In contrast, customary international law is not treated in a dualist manner although, as we shall see below, the deference paid by the courts to the

---

[16] See, for instance, *Re Article 26 and the Illegal Immigrants (Trafficking) Bill 1999* [2000] 2 IR 360 and *Laurentiu v Minister for Justice* [1999] 4 IR 26.

[17] See ch 6.

[18] For de Valera and the League of Nations, see D Ferriter, *Judging Dev* (Dublin, Royal Irish Academy, 2007) 128–9.

Government in the realm of foreign affairs makes it all but impossible for a litigant successfully to invoke customary international law against the State.

Article 29.4 vests the executive power of the State in relation to foreign affairs in the Government. Although the Constitution does not explicitly grant the courts any power to review how the Government exercises the executive power, the Supreme Court has identified a judicial power to intervene where the Government acts 'in clear disregard' of the powers and duties conferred on it by the Constitution.[19] In *Crotty v An Taoiseach*, a narrow majority of the Supreme Court held that it was a clear disregard of the Constitution for the Government to sign up to Title III of the Single European Act, a treaty commitment that essentially required Ireland to endeavour to formulate and implement a European foreign policy.[20] Walsh J reasoned that the Government was unconstitutionally fettering its own power to conduct foreign policy.[21] *Crotty* has cast a long shadow over Ireland's conduct of international affairs. Although no subsequent treaty has been struck down on the basis of *Crotty*, amendments to the treaties governing the EC and the EU have (as we shall see in the next section) generally been put to referendums. It has also been questioned whether the logic of *Crotty* renders Ireland's membership of the United Nations unconstitutional.[22] This doubt has led Ireland to rely on its obligations as an EU Member State to implement UN sanctions, rather than doing so on the basis of an authority in national law.[23]

The more recent case of *Pringle v Government of Ireland*, however, may signal a less exacting approach than that evident in *Crotty*.[24] Mr Pringle challenged the European Stability Mechanism (ESM) Treaty, arguing in particular that participation in the ESM impinged on and diminished Ireland's budgetary, economic and fiscal sovereignty. In rejecting this claim, a majority of the Supreme Court took at least a minimalist interpretation of *Crotty*. The broad range of treaty-making powers in the Constitution indicated that it was permissible for Ireland to enter into

---

[19] *Boland v An Taoiseach* [1974] IR 338. For further discussion, see ch 8.
[20] *Crotty v An Taoiseach* [1987] IR 713.
[21] ibid 783.
[22] For an account of this debate, see D Fennelly, '*Crotty's* Long Shadow: the European Union, the United Nations and the Changing Framework of Ireland's International Relations' in E Carolan (ed), *The Constitution of Ireland: Perspectives and Prospects* (Dublin: Bloomsbury Professional, 2012) 405–11.
[23] ibid 415–20.
[24] *Pringle v Government of Ireland* [2012] IESC 47.

binding international commitments that constrained future freedom of action. What would be problematic was a treaty that carved out a policy-making function and transferred that power to another body. Although Ireland was signing up to make a significant sum of money available to the ESM, this was not problematic since the maximum sum was specified in the Treaty itself.

This latitude for the treaty-making power is more consistent with a general attitude of deference displayed by the courts to other exercises of the executive power in the context of foreign affairs. For instance, in *Horgan v Ireland*, the High Court rejected a challenge to the State's provision of Shannon airport as a stopover for US military aircraft en route to the Persian Gulf.[25] Although Kearns J was prepared to accept that customary international law rules on the conduct of militarily neutral countries could be part of Irish law by reason of Article 29.3 of the Constitution, he also held that the Government had been given a wide discretion in relation to the conduct of foreign affairs and this could not be fettered by any principle of international law.

VII. THE EUROPEAN UNION

Ireland was not a founding member of the EEC but joined with the first wave of accession States alongside the UK and Denmark on 1 January 1973. Ireland's membership rests on an interaction of statutory and constitutional provisions. The people amended the Constitution to authorise Ireland to join the European Communities. This was not sufficient for Ireland to meet its obligations of membership, however, since it would not afford supremacy and direct effect to Community law, as required by Community law. To address this issue, section 2 of the European Communities Act 1972 provided that the Treaties forming the European Communities and the existing and future Acts adopted by the institutions of those Communities would be binding on the State and part of the domestic law of the State under the conditions laid down in those treaties. This provision would clearly have been unconstitutional; Article 29.4 was therefore also amended to include a statement that 'no provision of this Constitution invalidates laws enacted, acts done or measures adopted' by the State that 'are *necessitated by* the obligations

---

[25] *Horgan v Ireland* [2003] 2 IR 468.

of membership' of the European communities.[26] This provision essentially immunises section 2 of the 1972 Act from constitutional challenge.

The phrase 'necessitated by the obligations of membership' does not provide any authorisation for Ireland to sign up to further or deeper European integration, since the EU treaties do not oblige Member States to accept changes to those treaties. Nevertheless, in *Crotty v An Taoiseach* the Supreme Court held that the original constitutional authorisation to join the European Communities further authorised the State to join in subsequent amendments, so long as such amendments did not alter the essential scope or objectives of the Communities.[27] The Court held that three aspects of the Single European Act did not alter the essential scope and objectives of the original treaties: the creation of the Court of First Instance, to hear some cases previously heard by the European Court of Justice (ECJ); the explicit grant of competence in some areas to the Communities; the change in voting method on some issues in the European Council from unanimity to qualified majority voting. The latter two changes were of considerable constitutional significance. Although the ECJ had taken an expansive interpretation of existing competences, textually enumerating those competences rendered them more secure and potentially broadened the range of powers from which the ECJ could infer further competences.[28] Moreover, the introduction of qualified majority voting removed Ireland's veto-power over certain developments. That the Supreme Court was prepared to uphold these developments might have suggested that there were few constitutional constraints on Ireland's ability to sign up to further rounds of European integration. However, as we saw above, a majority of the Court took a different attitude to Title III of the Single European Act, holding that it amounted to an abdication of the Government's power to conduct foreign relations.[29] In the view of the majority, this did alter the essential

---

[26] Emphasis added.

[27] *Crotty v An Taoiseach* [1987] IR 713.

[28] For a discussion of the ECJ's approach to competences, see TC Hartley, *The Foundations of European Union Law*, 7th edn (Oxford, Oxford University Press, 2010) 112–4.

[29] A quirk of *Crotty* is that the one-judgment rule required the Supreme Court to deliver only one judgment in respect of that portion of the Single European Act (SEA) that was implemented by statute, while allowing each member of the Court to deliver his own judgment in respect of Title III, which was implemented by executive action alone. It seems likely that the stronger majority judges on Title III (Walsh and Henchy JJ) may have disagreed with the Court's decision on the other aspects of the SEA, making it even more difficult to discern a clear ratio.

scope and objectives of the original Treaties because a common foreign and security policy was a feature of a political, rather than an economic, union.

The difficulty of reconciling the majority judges' attitude to Title III with the Court's attitude to the other aspects of the Single European Act has led Governments to adopt a cautious approach to subsequent European treaties, putting all significant amendments to the EC Treaties to a referendum. The Single European Act itself was approved by 70 per cent of the people in the referendum that followed *Crotty*. The Treaty of European Union (Maastricht) was approved by 69 per cent in 1992. The Treaty of Amsterdam was approved by 62 per cent in 1996. The Treaty of Nice was originally rejected by 54 per cent of the people in 2001, but subsequently ratified by 63 per cent a year and a half later. Somewhat similarly, the Treaty of Lisbon was rejected by 54 per cent of the people in 2008 but subsequently ratified by 67 per cent of the people a year and a half later. To a certain extent, the Nice and Lisbon votes can be understood as a protest against deepening European integration notwithstanding the Irish people's general satisfaction with their membership of the EU (see below). The second Lisbon vote took place during the financial crisis, which undoubtedly affected many voters about the wisdom of a further protest. All that said, a feature of the Nice and Lisbon votes was a significantly increased voter turnout for the second referendum, following a more assertive campaign on the part of the Government. Although the initial rejections of the Nice and Lisbon treaties are significant, their ultimate approval is also important in assessing Irish attitudes to the EU. Finally, in 2012 60 per cent of the people ratified, at the first time of asking, the Fiscal Compact Treaty. This series of referendums cumulatively amounts to the biggest changes in the Irish constitutional order since 1937, and arguably since 1922.

Irish people view the European Union favourably. In the 2017 Eurobarometer poll, 59 per cent of Irish respondents reported that they viewed the EU fairly or very positively; 80 per cent were fairly or very positive about the future of the EU.[30] In both cases, this was the highest number in any Member State. There is a common narrative that the EU helped the founding Member States move beyond the enmity of World War II, many Mediterranean States to leave dictatorship behind, and central and eastern European States to complete their emergence from communism. A similar narrative exists about the EU's existential

---

[30] Available at http://ec.europa.eu/commfrontoffice/publicopinion/index.cfm/Survey/get SurveyDetail/instruments/STANDARD/surveyKy/2143.

importance for Ireland, namely that it allowed Ireland to become a truly independent State not dominated by its much larger neighbour. In turn, this allowed the development of a much healthier relationship between Ireland and the United Kingdom as equal members of the EU. On the one hand, this facilitated the constitutional settlement in relation to Northern Ireland. On the other hand, it is inconceivable that Ireland might follow the UK's decision to leave the EU, even to preserve that constitutional settlement. It is to these issues that we now turn.

VIII. CONTINUING RELATIONS WITH THE UK AND NORTHERN IRELAND

We saw at the start of this chapter how the 1937 Constitution dealt with the issue of Northern Ireland. The dignified part of the Constitution emphasised the claims of Irish nationalists to legitimate authority over the whole island of Ireland. The efficient part of the Constitution, however, treated Northern Ireland and its inhabitants as an irrelevance: the Constitution would not apply to Northern Ireland (pending reintegration of the national territory); the population of Northern Ireland had no role in enacting the Constitution, amending the Constitution or electing representatives. This constitutional sleight of hand likely played a significant role in removing the issue of Northern Ireland from day-to-day politics, at least until the start of the terrorist campaigns. This in turn allowed Irish nationalism to avoid the unresolved contradictions in the notion of the Irish people. As time passed, Northern Ireland became less like an arbitrary imposition and more an accepted political fact of life. This provides the constitutional context, from the Irish perspective, in which the 1998 peace settlement was agreed.

The settlement involved three strands of relationships: within Northern Ireland; between Ireland and Northern Ireland; and between Ireland and the United Kingdom. These were captured in two mutually referring agreements: the Belfast Agreement between the parties in Northern Ireland, the Irish Government and the British Government; and the British-Irish Agreement between the two sovereign States. The Agreements were approved in simultaneous referendums held on both sides of the border. In Ireland, 95 per cent voted to allow ratification of the British-Irish Agreement and to make a number of important constitutional changes. The most significant change was the abandonment of Ireland's territorial claim to the entire island of Ireland. The Agreement provided that the replacement of Articles 2 and 3 was only to take effect upon a declaration by the Irish Government that it was satisfied that other aspects of the Agreement were being implemented. The Government issued this declaration in 1999, thereby formally effecting the constitutional change. As a result, Article 2 no longer refers to territory but instead refers to the birthright of every person born on the island of Ireland to be part of the Irish nation. Article 3 refers to the 'firm will of the Irish Nation, in harmony and friendship, to unite all the people who share the territory of the island of Ireland, in all the diversity of their identities and traditions'. It explicitly states that reunification can only occur through peaceful means, with the consent of a majority of people – democratically expressed – in both jurisdictions. The United Kingdom is similarly committed to ensuring Irish unity in those circumstances. In essence, the Agreement confirms the territorial settlement of the Anglo-Irish Treaty of 1922. By locating the decision-making power for Northern Ireland with the people who live in Northern Ireland, it accords a legitimacy to that political entity that had never before been conceded by Ireland. In these ways, the Constitution is now close to agnostic on the question of national reunification, a significant change from 1937.

At the same time, the Agreement seeks to diminish the importance of territory in a number of ways. First, as already noted, Article 2 recognises the birthright of all people born on the island of Ireland to be part of the Irish nation. Secondly and more concretely, Article 3 was amended to allow for the creation of institutions with executive powers and functions shared between Ireland and Northern Ireland. This allowed for the creation of a North/South Ministerial Council to include representatives of the Irish Government and the Northern Ireland Executive. The Council meets in plenary format twice a year: the Irish Government is led by the Taoiseach while the Northern Ireland representation is led by the First Minister and Deputy First Minister, representing the two different political traditions in Northern Ireland. The Council also meets in specific sectoral formats, with each side represented by the appropriate Minister. The Council works through co-operation and agreement and oversees six areas of policy co-operation, such as agriculture and tourism, and six North-South implementation bodies, addressing areas such as inland waterways and food safety promotion. In legal and constitutional terms, the North/South Ministerial Council is not of great significance. Given that it must work through agreement, its importance derives from its role in facilitating discussion and joint action. Nevertheless, in terms of improving relations between Northern Irish and Irish politicians, the requirement to meet and discuss non-constitutional issues is important and may well have contributed to the noteworthy improvement in relations.

In a similar vein, the Agreements also establish a British-Irish Council, consisting of representatives of the British and Irish Governments, the devolved administrations in Northern Ireland, Scotland and Wales and representatives of the Isle of Mann and the Channel Islands. The British-Irish Council also operates through agreement to facilitate discussion on issues of mutual interest. It has done work on issues such as digital inclusion, energy and the environment. Again, the British-Irish Council is of limited constitutional significance, except insofar as it facilitates the development of relationships between politicians in Britain and Ireland. It is less powerful than the North/South Ministerial Council in that it has no bodies with any executive power – and as such is not specifically referenced anywhere in the Irish Constitution. However, from the perspective of Unionists in Northern Ireland, it does place the north-south relations in a more palatable context of deepening relations between all the people who inhabit the islands off the northwest coast of Europe.

At the time of writing, this constitutional settlement is under pressure on two fronts. On the one hand, the power-sharing institutions in Northern Ireland are suspended due to a political dispute between the largest unionist and nationalist parties, the Democratic Unionist Party and Sinn Féin. As a result, the North/South Ministerial Council is also suspended. The dispute originated over quotidian allegations of political incompetence or corruption but reflects a broader and deeper level of mistrust between the parties on identity issues.[31] On the other hand, the decision of the United Kingdom to leave the European Union reverses assumptions about open borders and shared markets that underpinned the removal of Ireland's territorial claim to Northern Ireland in 1998. The status of Northern Ireland as a constituent part of the United Kingdom is far less objectionable to Northern nationalists, particularly those living close to the border, if that border is effectively invisible. These difficulties are exacerbated by political attitudes to Brexit within Northern Ireland. Although Northern Ireland voted for the UK to remain within the EU by a margin of 56 per cent to 44 per cent, research suggests that 85 per cent of Catholics and 90 per cent of self-described nationalists voted to remain,

[31] '"Cash for ash": the energy scandal surrounding DUP leader Arlene Foster', *The Independent* 13 June 2017.

while 60 per cent of Protestants and 66 per cent of self-described unionists voted to leave.[32]

There is thus a significant sectarian division in attitudes to Brexit
itself. Unsurprisingly, Brexit was most opposed by those for whom, given
their ideological preferences, it had the most adverse consequences.
That unionists, in contrast, voted for Brexit accentuates the concerns
of nationalists and makes it difficult for Northern Ireland politicians to
adopt a cross-community approach to the management of Brexit. This
picture is further complicated by the fact that the Democratic Unionist
Party, which has a confidence and supply agreement with the minority
Conservative Government at Westminster, holds the view that the United
Kingdom should leave both the Customs Union and the Single European
Market. The UK and Irish Governments are committed to continuing the
Common Travel Area between Ireland and the UK, which will allow UK
and Irish citizens move freely between the two countries. However, if the
UK leaves the Customs Union and the Single European Market, goods
crossing the border between Northern Ireland and Ireland will need to
be monitored in some way in order to ensure the integrity of the customs
and regulatory regime on either side of the border.

The purpose of this book is not, of course, to speculate about the
terms on which the UK will leave the EU. Nevertheless, the erection of
a visible and experienced border seems likely to undermine nationalist
support for the constructive ambiguities of the 1998 peace settlement.
This picture is further complicated by the backdrop of significant demographic changes in Northern Ireland. The census of 1926 showed that
34.9 per cent of Northern Ireland's population were Catholics while
66.3 per cent were Protestants. By 2011, 40.8 per cent of the population
were Catholics and 42.4 per cent were Protestants. Moreover, 49.2 per cent
of children under the age of four were Catholics, while 36.4 per cent
were Protestants.[33] One needs to be very careful with such figures. Not all
Catholics are nationalists (far from it) and not all self-described nationalists would necessarily support reunification in a plebiscite. Nevertheless,
the demographic change is in itself destabilising, making unionists feel
less secure and altering the political incentives for Sinn Féin to operate
the power-sharing institutions agreed in 1998. The immediate response
to the suspension of the Northern Irish institutions is direct rule from

[32] John Garry, 'The EU referendum Vote in Northern Ireland: Implications for our understanding of citizens' political views and behaviour' available at https://www.qub.ac.uk/
brexit/Brexitfilestore/Fileupload,728121,en.pdf, visited 7 January 2017.
[33] 'Catholic Population Set to Dwarf Protestants in Years Ahead', *News Letter*
18 March 2017.

Westminster. Indefinite direct rule, however, is opposed by all nationalist parties in Northern Ireland and the Irish Government, rendering it a politically unstable solution. There seems to be little prospect of securing agreement among the Northern parties to a new political settlement. The only alternative – increased involvement of the Irish Government in the governance of Northern Ireland – is anathema to unionists. All told, demographic change, Brexit, and political pressures have combined to make the constitutional status of Northern Ireland more uncertain than at almost any time since 1922. While reunification remains unlikely, the ability of the Irish Constitution to manage reunification is now worthy of academic consideration.[34]

The original wording of Article 3 clearly implied that the geographical scope of the Constitution could be extended to include Northern Ireland in some point at the future, quite possibly without the need for any constitutional amendment. Article 15.2 allows the Oireachtas to create subordinate legislatures, apparently intended to allow for a devolved assembly for Northern Ireland. However, there is no equivalent provision in relation to the Government and the executive power, suggesting that a unitary government would need to apply to the entire island. This would make it difficult, if not impossible, to continue the consociational elements of current governance in Northern Ireland. The electoral system for the Dáil, which we shall explore further in the next chapter, of multi-seat constituencies elected by PR-STV might well be appropriate for representing the diversity of political beliefs in Northern Ireland. Given that the Constitution requires a ratio of representatives to politicians of no lower than 1:30,000, a significant increase in the size of the Dáil would be necessary.

The efficient part of the Constitution appears adequate to absorb Northern Ireland into a unitary Irish State, if that were desired. Whether those who had historically identified as unionists would feel adequately represented in such a State is another question. Significant difficulties follow from the dignified part of the Constitution. As discussed at the start of this chapter, the Constitution assumed a largely homogeneous Irish people, committed to Irish self-determination over the entire island of Ireland. The rhetoric and symbolism of the Constitution reflect these assumptions. We further saw in the last chapter how Roman Catholic teaching significantly influenced many of the provisions of the Constitution. However, I also noted in the last chapter that these two areas

---

[34] My understanding of these issues has been informed by an unpublished paper of Dr David Kenny, for which I am grateful.

have been the subject of the greatest ideological change in the Constitution, through both formal amendment and judicial decision-making. Having explored those trends through the course of this book, I will return in the concluding chapter to the ability of the Irish Constitution to accommodate reunification. This question has two dimensions: whether Northern Unionists could feel accommodated by this constitutional order and whether citizens of this constitutional order would want to accommodate Northern Unionists.

IX. CONCLUSION

In this chapter, I have explored the foundations of the Irish constitutional order. National identity was to the forefront for the constitutional framers in 1937. The whole point of the 1937 Constitution was to establish a definitive rupture with the United Kingdom. The Irish Nation is defined with reference to its struggle for independence, an identity closely linked to the particular geographic entity that is the island of Ireland. There was a fundamental problem with this account of national identity, however. A large portion of the people living on that island, particularly concentrated in one part of the island, did not identify with this struggle for independence. Quite the contrary: they identified with those responsible, as the Constitution viewed it, for denying Ireland's rightful claims to self-determination. Article 3 provided a legal fix for this problem: pending the re-integration of the national territory, the laws passed by the new constitutional institutions would not apply to Northern Ireland. This was probably as good a solution as was possible in 1937.

Over time, this rather exclusive national identity has softened. The Supreme Court deftly sidestepped attempts to use Articles 2 and 3 to preclude an accommodation with Northern Unionists. Constitutional references to 'nation' and 'people' were relevant to the ordering of constitutional power within 26-county Ireland rather than the making of claims outside Ireland. The constitutional commitment to the pacific settlement of international disputes reflected and contributed to a culture in which military conflict over Northern Ireland was virtually inconceivable. The Irish people voted repeatedly to support greater European integration, a process that facilitated improved relations with the United Kingdom. The culmination of these developments was a radical relaxation of national identity in 1998. The island of Ireland remained central to Irish identity but membership of the Irish nation became optional – a matter of self-definition rather than imposition. As a result of these changes, the Constitution has replaced a very clear sense of Irishness with a much less distinctive one. The status of Northern Ireland is now a matter of diplomacy and consensus, rather than a claim of legal right. A side-effect of this is to make the Constitution less relevant to public debate. Nevertheless, if national reunification becomes a real possibility, the Constitution's understanding of Irishness will again come to the fore of public debate.

FURTHER READING

Gavin Barrett, 'The Evolving Door to Europe: Reflections on an Eventful Forty Years for Article 29.4 of the Irish Constitution' (2012) 47(2) *Irish Jurist* 132

James Casey, '*Crotty v An Taoiseach*: A Comparative Perspective' in James O'Reilly (ed), *Human Rights and Constitutional Law: Essays in Honour of Brian Walsh* (Dublin, Round Hall Press, 1992)

Maria Cahill, 'Constitutional Exclusion Clauses, Article 29.4.6, and the Constitutional Reception of European Law' (2011) 34 *Dublin University Law Journal* 74

Maria Cahill, 'Judicial Conceptions of Sovereignty' in Eoin Carolan (ed), *The Constitution of Ireland: Perspectives and Prospects* (London, Bloomsbury, 2012)

Desmond M Clarke, 'Nationalism, The Irish Constitution, and Multicultural Citizenship' (2000) 51 *Northern Ireland Law Quarterly* 100

Kevin Costello, 'The Expulsion of the Prerogative Doctrine from Irish law: Quantifying and Remedying the Loss of the Royal Prerogative' (1997) 32 *Irish Jurist* 145

David Fennelly, '*Crotty's* Long Shadow: the European Union, the United Nations and the Changing Framework of Ireland's International Relations' in Eoin Carolan (ed), *The Constitution of Ireland: Perspectives and Prospects* (Dublin: Bloomsbury Professional, 2012)

David Fennelly, *International Law in the Irish Legal System* (Dublin, Thomson Reuters Round Hall, 2014)

Diarmaid Ferriter, *Ambiguous Republic: Ireland in the 1970s* (London, Profile Books, 2012), ch 12

John Kelly, 'Hidden Treasure and the Irish Constitution' (1988) 10 *Dublin University Law Journal* 5

JJ Lee, *Ireland 1912–1985: Politics and Society* (Cambridge, Cambridge University Press, 1989)

Niall Lenihan, 'Royal Prerogatives and the Constitution' (1989) 24 *Irish Jurist* 1

Julien Sterck, 'The Nation's Own Genius: A European View of Irish Constitutional Identity' (2014) 37 *Dublin University Law Journal* 109

3

Government and Oireachtas

Party Politics – The Government – Coalition Governments – The Dáil
Electoral System – Preserving a Fair Electoral Process – The Senate –
The Internal Organisation of the Houses of the Oireachtas

I. INTRODUCTION

IN CHAPTER TWO, I analysed the foundations of the Irish constitutional order: nation, people, State and territory. In this chapter,
I commence an exploration of how that State is governed. Article 6
speaks of all powers of government, legislative, judicial and executive,
deriving, under God, from the people. This wording suggests a tripartite
division of power along the lines suggested by Montesquieu. Consistent
with this, Article 15 assigns the legislative power to the Oireachtas
(National Parliament), Article 28 assigns the executive power to the
Government, and Article 34 assigns the judicial power to the courts.
This impression of a tripartite separation of powers, however, is deeply
misleading. The political power to act is concentrated almost exclusively
in the Government, legally checked by the courts. The separation of
powers in the Constitution is therefore fundamentally bipartite.

The Constitution adopts the Westminster model of responsible
government, with the Government accountable to the lower House of
Parliament, the Dáil. In general elections, the people choose Teachtaí
Dála (TDs, Dáil Deputies) who then elect a Taoiseach for appointment
by the President. The Taoiseach secures her election not through the
spontaneous and shifting association of like-minded individuals, but
rather through the disciplined coordination of whipped political parties.
As a result, a Government is typically guaranteed a majority in the Dáil.[1]

---

[1] The current political situation is a notable exception, with the Government dependent
on a confidence-and-supply arrangement with the principal opposition party. In this and
subsequent chapters, I will present the Constitution as it operated prior to 2016 before
highlighting the ways in which it currently operates differently.

This ensures that the Government controls the legislative process and is at no real risk of being removed from office by the Dáil. The politics of the constitutional relationship between Dáil and Government concentrate political power in the Government, albeit that coalitions experience internal contestation that somewhat checks the power of the Government to act.

In this chapter, we explore the constitutional relationships between Oireachtas and Government that lead to this concentration of political power. In particular, we shall explore how political parties compete for seats in the Dáil, which in turn determines the election of a Taoiseach. We shall consider how the Government relates to the civil service, before identifying some specific features of coalition governments. Having completed this consideration of the Government, we shall explore the two Houses of the Oireachtas, the Dáil and Seanad, in greater detail. The electoral system for both Houses, the implications of these for the way in which Government functions, and the measures that have been taken to preserve the fairness of those electoral processes will all be analysed. We shall then consider the internal organisation of the Houses of the Oireachtas, before concluding the chapter with two further constitutional officers, the Attorney General and the Director of Public Prosecutions.

II. PARTY POLITICS

Although political parties are nowhere mentioned in the Constitution, they play a central role in the operation of the constitutional order. Prior to Independence, Irish politicians had disparaged the whip-bound discipline of political parties at Westminster.[2] The aspiration for the political system of the new State to be different did not long survive. The bitter Civil War divide translated into parliamentary politics once Fianna Fáil decided to take its seats in 1927. Within 10 years of establishment, therefore, the Oireachtas was dominated by whip-bound parties with a confrontational rather than consensual style.[3] Political parties serve important democratic functions. They allow for a more effective presentation of options to the electorate and for voters to choose a coherent policy programme, particularly on economic and budgetary issues. Political parties therefore allow for choice and accountability in

[2] L Cahillane, 'Anti-party Politics and the Irish Free State Constitution' (2012) 35 *Dublin University Law Journal* 34.
[3] M Manning, 'Houses of the Oireachtas: Background and Early Development' in M MacCarthaigh and M Manning (eds), *The Houses of the Oireachtas: Parliament in Ireland* (Dublin, Institute of Public Administration, 2010) 23–5.

the delivery of political programmes.[4] Although party leaders exercise a considerable degree of control within political parties, Gallagher argues that parliamentary parties exercise a real constraint on the Ministers from that party.[5] They are powerful veto players who can prevent the adoption of policies with which they disagree, even if they cannot initiate policies themselves.[6]

Since the foundation of the State, Governments have been led by one of two political parties, Fianna Fáil or Fine Gael.[7] In terms of ideology, Fianna Fáil and Fine Gael are both broadly centrist parties, veering from slightly left-of-centre to centre-right over time, Fine Gael generally but not always being more right-wing than Fianna Fáil.[8] While the right is broadly dominant, political debate in Ireland has rarely been structured around a left-right political cleavage. This somewhat unusual state of affairs has been attributed to the fact that at important formative moments the left-right cleavage was not the most salient in Irish politics.[9] As the franchise was extended in the late nineteenth century, the principal political division was between Irish nationalists and unionists. Following the 1916 Rebellion, the Irish Parliamentary Party lost nearly all its support to Sinn Féin, which won the vast majority of seats (outside what is now Northern Ireland) in the 1918 election to the Westminster Parliament. As we saw in chapter one, Sinn Féin did not take up its seats in Westminster but instead formed a new assembly in Dublin, the first Dáil. After Independence, this nationalist grouping then fractured along the lines of Civil War allegiance, revolving around support for the compromises in the Anglo-Irish Treaty, rather than any class or left-right split. Fine Gael, as a successor of Cumann na nGaedheal, was the party of those who had supported the Anglo-Irish Treaty. Fianna Fáil was the party of those who had opposed the Treaty but now sought to operate the institutions of the new State.[10] Sinn Féin continued in existence but with the very limited support of those who entirely rejected the 1922 settlement.

---

[4] E Daly and T Hickey, *The Political Theory of the Irish Constitution: Republicanism and the Basic Law* (Manchester, Manchester University Press, 2015) 104.

[5] Political parties of course have both a parliamentary and non-parliamentary component. Given the subject of this book, the focus is on parliamentary political parties.

[6] M Gallagher, 'Parliamentary Parties and the Party Whips' in MacCarthaigh and Manning (eds) (n 3) 148.

[7] In the Irish Free State, Cumann na nGaedhal, the forerunner of Fine Gael, led the Government from 1922 to 1932.

[8] See L Weeks, 'Parties and the Party System' in Coakley and Gallagher, *Politics in the Republic of Ireland*, 5th edn (London, Routledge, 2011) 142–3.

[9] ibid 137–40.

[10] For a discussion of this early period, see P Mair, *The Changing Irish Party System* (London, Pinter Publishers, 1987) ch 1.

Although important policy differences exist between Fianna Fáil and Fine Gael at any particular point in time, it is difficult to identify any ideological distinction that has existed diachronically.[11] Traditionally Fianna Fáil took a more nationalistic approach than Fine Gael to Northern Ireland, but this difference between the parties has virtually disappeared since the Northern Ireland peace settlement of 1998. Political competition between Fianna Fáil and Fine Gael is intense, although antagonism between their partisans has diminished as the Anglo-Irish Treaty receded into the past and they came to adopt similar approaches to Northern Ireland. Present allegiance to political parties probably derives from historical or family allegiance, the popularity, perceived competence and integrity of party leaders, and the attractiveness of individual policy proposals.[12] As important as political pull factors are the push factors associated with each political party. Fianna Fáil members were heavily involved in a number of corruption scandals that came to light in the 1990s and 2000s (see chapter seven) and were subsequently seen as responsible for the financial crisis, having governed the country for 11 years leading up to the crisis. Fine Gael is often seen as a party of the wealthy, cocooned from the concerns of ordinary working people. Labour is seen as overly concerned with social-moral issues (such as abortion) at the expense of socio-economic issues, as well as having reneged on promises it made before forming a Government with Fine Gael in 2011. Sinn Féin is for many tainted by its association with the provisional IRA.

Fianna Fáil, founded by Éamon de Valera, was the largest party continuously between 1937 and 2011, leading the Government for 56 of those 74 years. It originally refused to form coalition governments, thereby periodically allowing other parties an opportunity to coalesce in Government. Since 1989, however, Fianna Fáil has formed coalitions with a number of smaller parties: the economically right wing Progressive Democrats from 1989 to 1992; the left-wing Labour Party from 1992 to 1994; the Progressive Democrats again from 1997 to 2007; the environmentalist Green Party from 2007 to 2011. In order to form successive governments, Fianna Fáil sought to establish ideological common ground with several partners. After the general election that

[11] Writing in 1987, Mair argued that in the period between 1961 and 1982, Fianna Fáil followed a corporatist identity while Fine Gael (and Labour) followed a social democratic ideology. But this ideological division does not hold up for the following 35 years. ibid 140–1.
[12] For a detailed discussion, see K Cunningham and M Marsh, 'Voting Behaviour' in J Coakley and M Gallagher (eds), *Politics in the Republic of Ireland*, 6th edn (London, Routledge, 2017).

followed the collapse of its coalition with the Progressive Democrats in 1992, a senior adviser prepared a comparison of Labour and Fianna Fáil party policies. This allowed Fianna Fáil to respond to Labour's over-tures within one hour, after Labour's negotiations with Fine Gael broke down.[13] Nearly 15 years later, a year prior to the 2007 general election, Taoiseach Bertie Ahern prepared for a possible coalition with the Green Party (replacing the Progressive Democrats) by talking about environ-mental issues that overlapped with Fianna Fáil policies.[14] For Fianna Fáil, ideological direction was often secondary to retaining power. The other 18 years saw coalition governments led by Fine Gael, usually in coali-tion with the left-wing Labour Party and sometimes in conjunction with other smaller parties. The left-right ideological flexibility of Fianna Fáil and the fact that the centre-right Fine Gael generally coalesced with the centre-left Labour Party has tended to produce centrist government. One consequence of this, as we shall see in chapter eight, is that ideologi-cal considerations have seldom been a factor in judicial appointments.

The financial and economic crisis post 2008 resulted in a significant realignment of support for political parties at the 2011 and 2016 general elections. Fine Gael replaced Fianna Fáil as the largest party in 2011, a position that it narrowly held against a somewhat resurgent Fianna Fáil in 2016. Labour briefly became the second largest party in 2011, only to be nearly eliminated at the General Election of 2016. Support for Sinn Féin has grown fairly steadily since the mid-1990s, to the extent that it is now the third largest party. Far larger than the Labour Party, Sinn Féin draws its support primarily from working class voters, many of whom might have supported Fianna Fáil or Labour in the past. Sinn Féin is the most nationalistic of the political parties, firmly committed to national reunification and operating in both Northern Ireland and Ireland. There is no significant far right or anti-immigrant right wing political party in Ireland. Other parties of the right and left have emerged at various times. Some have argued that Ireland's rules on political funding (see below) have created a cartel system which makes it increasingly difficult for any new party to break through.[15]

The 2016 General Election produced a balkanised Dáil, with no obvi-ous political configuration capable of forming a majority Government.

---

[13] A Reynolds, *My Autobiography* (London, Transworld Ireland, 2009) 175–6.

[14] B Ahern, *The Autobiography* (London, Arrow Books, 2010) 323–5.

[15] E O'Malley and J FitzGibbon, 'Everywhere and Nowhere: Populism and the Puzzling Non-Reaction to Ireland's Crisis' in H Kriesi and TS Pappas (eds), *European Populism in the Shadow of the Great Recession* (Colchester, ECPR Press, 2015) 292.

Fine Gael received 50 seats on a vote share of 25.5 per cent; Fianna Fáil received 44 seats on a vote share of 24.3 per cent; Sinn Féin received 23 seats on a vote share of 13.8 per cent; Labour received seven seats on a vote share of 6.6 per cent. An alliance of far-left parties received six seats on a vote share of 3.9 per cent; the Social Democrats received three seats on a vote share of 3 per cent; the Green Party received two seats on a vote share of 2.7 per cent; the remaining 23 seats went to non-aligned candidates.[16] This illustrates a remarkable fragmentation in party support. The two parties that had dominated Irish politics for the previous 80 years received barely 50 per cent of the vote. In the short run, this political fragmentation has led to even less ideological politics, with a Fine Gael minority Government dependent on a confidence and supply arrangement with Fianna Fáil. As a result, the current Government does not control the legislative process and is meaningfully accountable to the Dáil. The last general election, therefore, has resulted in a significant change in how the Constitution operates, moving it much closer to the tripartite separation of powers presented by Article 6. This goes further than Stephen Gardbaum's claim that electoral systems are as important as the formal separation of constitutional powers to the concentration or dispersal of political power. Even with the same electoral system, different election results can effect changes in the constitution.[17] In this and subsequent chapters, I shall present the constitutional relationships and processes as they operated prior to 2016, before assessing how the current dispensation differs.

The status of political parties in the Dáil depends on whether they support the Government. The Government has its own rights in the Dáil in terms of the introduction of legislation, and allocation of speaking time. Non-Government parties must be organised as groups. A registered political party with five or more TDs is automatically a group. Smaller political parties and/or non-party TDs may join together to form 'technical groups'. Membership of technical groups is an essential pre-requisite to gaining access to the time of the Dáil. The rules in relation to technical groups have been somewhat relaxed: previously, there could only be one technical group and it required seven members. The changes mean that technical groups can be more ideologically cohesive, perhaps allowing them to have a greater impact in the Dáil.

---

[16] 'Results Hub' *The Irish Times* http://www.irishtimes.com/election-2016/results-hub (visited 22 April 2016).

[17] S Gardbaum, 'Political Parties, Voting Systems, and the Separation of Powers' (2017) 65 *American Journal of Comparative Law* 229.

III. THE GOVERNMENT

The Taoiseach is the political leader of the country and must use her formal and informal powers to exercise that leadership role.[18] As Taoiseach, she both chooses who serves in the Cabinet and sets the agenda for the Cabinet. As leader of the largest single support grouping in the Dáil, usually holding a majority in the Dáil, she has the power to set the agenda in the Dáil. She has significant powers of patronage that can be used to retain the support of other influential members of her political party. However, her power will be less where she has formed a coalition government, making herself dependent on the continued support of another political party. Moreover, her position within her own party will become insecure once she becomes seen as an electoral liability.

The Constitution allows the Government to consist of between seven and 15 members, although in recent decades 15 members have always been appointed. The President appoints Government Ministers on the nomination of the Taoiseach, who retains the absolute right to dismiss members of the Government. Apart from the Taoiseach, Government Ministers gain political power based on the importance of their Department and/or their political support within their party. The Taoiseach, Tánaiste (Deputy Prime Minister) and Minister for Finance must all be members of the Dáil. The Taoiseach may nominate members of the Seanad as Government Ministers, but no more than two members of the Seanad can be members of the Government. Only two Senators have served as members of the Government since 1937. Given the power of the Taoiseach to nominate 11 members of the Seanad, this provides a route for non-politicians to be appointed to Government but this has only been utilised on one occasion since the introduction of the 1937 Constitution. The Irish political system thus has little provision for and almost no practical experience of external Ministers. As members of the Dáil who will most likely seek re-election, Government Ministers remain understandably concerned with their local constituency. The Irish electoral system of PR-STV and multi-seat constituencies ensures that there are very few, if any, safe seats in the Dáil. With Government Ministers and party leaders at risk of electoral defeat,[19] it would be a foolish Government Minister who failed to pay attention to constituency issues.

---

[18] See E O'Malley, 'The Apex of Government: Cabinet and Taoiseach in Operation' in E O'Malley and M MacCarthaigh (eds), *Governing Ireland: From Cabinet Governance to Delegated Government* (Dublin, Institute of Public Administration, 2012) 43–6.

[19] Weeks (n 8) 106.

Article 28.4 provides that the Government must meet and act as a collective authority, responsible to the Dáil for the Departments of State administered by the members of the Government. Given that the Government will usually have the support of a majority in the Dáil, this responsibility is more theoretical than real. As with many aspects of Ireland's constitutional structure, however, the current minority Government represents a significant exception in this regard. For instance, in November 2017, faced with an opposition motion of no confidence in the Tánaiste and Minister for Justice, Taoiseach Leo Varadkar was compelled to allow the resignation of the Tánaiste rather than face a general election.[20]

The Supreme Court inferred a general rule of cabinet confidentiality from the requirement of collective authority.[21] In 1997, the people approved a referendum that placed the requirement of cabinet confidentiality in the constitutional text, while making certain exceptions to allow the High Court determine that disclosure should be made in the context of court proceedings or a tribunal of inquiry. Cabinet confidentiality is routinely breached, however, the media frequently reporting on what was discussed at Cabinet. When relations between cabinet members are fraught, the revelations are more detailed. In 2011, for example, a number of Labour Government Ministers provided the details for a newspaper story on how ineffective the Labour Party leader was in his Cabinet contributions.[22] The rule on cabinet confidentiality largely serves to protect Government Ministers from having to answer difficult questions rather than to protect the integrity of collegial decision-making.

Since 1994, a particularly problematic practice has emerged of Governments designating one junior minister who is not a member of the Cabinet but who attends Cabinet meetings. This originally allowed the smallest party in a three-party coalition government to have an additional member attending cabinet meetings. However, it has become a standard practice for all governments, circumventing the constitutional limitation of 15 members of the Government.[23] Whatever its constitutionality in 1994, the passage of the cabinet confidentiality referendum has almost certainly rendered the practice unconstitutional. It is inconsistent with

---

[20] 'Frances Fitzgerald resigns "to spare unnecessary election"', *The Irish Examiner* 28 November 2017.

[21] *Attorney General v Hamilton (No 1)* [1993] 2 IR 250.

[22] 'Dithering Gilmore fails to deliver at Cabinet', *The Irish Independent* 5 September 2011.

[23] P Leahy, *The Price of Power: Inside Ireland's Crisis Coalition* (Dublin, Penguin Ireland, 2013) 94.

confidentiality to invite a stranger to listen to all of one's discussions. Nevertheless, the practice is politically convenient and therefore persists; more Ministers means fewer disgruntled backbenchers. Meetings of the Cabinet are also attended by the Attorney General, who cannot be a Member of the Government, and by the Secretary General to the Government, a civil servant who takes the minutes. The Chief Whip attends and sits beside the Taoiseach, although does not speak because she is not a member of the cabinet.[24]

Article 28.2 of the Constitution provides that the organisation of and distribution of business among Departments of State shall be regulated in accordance with law.[25] The law in question dates from the Irish Free State: The Ministers and Secretaries Act 1924. This Act established 11 Departments of State, since increased to 15. In law, a Minister is not merely the Head of the Department but personifies the Department as a corporation sole. Statutory powers are assigned to the Minister who is responsible in law for every action of the Department. Although this is not legally required, each Member of the Government (a constitutional position) is also a Minister who heads one of the Departments. The 1924 Act allows for the appointment of Ministers of State to assist the Minister at the head of the Department or Departments to which they are assigned. Some Ministers of State are given well-defined areas of responsibility within a Department or the task of coordinating a policy area between Departments. Ministers of State are not members of the Government although – as noted above – some are allowed to attend cabinet meetings. The Taoiseach is supported by the Department of the Taoiseach.

Although the Constitution requires that the Government is collectively responsible to the Dáil, Hogan and Morgan assert that a convention of individual ministerial responsibility also exists.[26] Consistent with this, a Minister must answer Dáil questions in respect of all matters that arise in her own Department. Although a Minister is accountable for her Department to the Dáil in this sense, the Minister's responsibility is for policy while the permanent civil service is responsible for the implementation of that policy. The dividing lines here are not entirely clear and as a political crisis develops, a Minister may become directly involved

---

[24] M Gallagher (n 6) 151.
[25] See generally G Hogan and DG Morgan, *Administrative Law in Ireland*, 4th edn (Dublin, Round Hall, 2010) ch 3.
[26] ibid para 3-05.

in attempts to resolve the crisis. Individual responsibility notionally requires the resignation of Ministers who fail to perform their functions properly. However, it is difficult to discern any strict observance of this convention. A Government that commands a majority within the Dáil will be able to defeat any motion of no confidence in one of its Ministers. Any Ministerial resignation will therefore be at the behest of the Taoiseach, although the Taoiseach will of course be cognisant of the broader political difficulties of a Minister continuing in office.

Each Government Department is staffed by permanent Civil Servants, as are other constitutional institutions (such as the Oireachtas). The election of a new Government does not cause any change in civil service personnel, although Government Ministers will usually each appoint a small number of special advisers. Secretaries General lead the Civil Service, heading each Department of State. Their three main functions are administration of the Department, policy advice to the Minister, and Accounting Officer for their Department. They must be appointed and removed by the Government as a whole, rather than simply by the Minister who heads their Department as is the case with all other Civil Servants. The Public Service Management Act 1997 introduced (although it may just have mirrored existing political practice) a distinction between the 'determination of matters of policy' and (broadly speaking) the management of the Department. The Minister retained responsibility for the former while the Secretary General of the Department was recognised as having responsibility for the latter. This cannot displace the Government's constitutional responsibility to the Dáil but it does reflect the obvious reality that no Government Minister could be the manager of her Department. As we shall see in chapter seven, the Houses of the Oireachtas (Inquiries, Privileges and Procedures) Act 2013 allows Oireachtas committees to require Secretaries General to attend before committees. Secretaries General can be questioned on the management of their Departments but the precise dividing line with ministerial accountability remains unclear. Where this line is drawn will always be a function of politics.

IV. COALITION GOVERNMENTS

Between 1937 and 1989, there were coalition governments for 15 years and single-party governments (sometimes narrowly in a minority) for 37 years. Since 1989, all governments have been coalition governments. This shifts the dynamics in constitutional governance. The fundamental difference is that there are two or more discrete blocs of Ministers who may have different views and incentives about the direction and continuation of the Government. Of course, there may well be significant divergence even within a political party, but its members have strong incentives to resolve their differences. Conversely, members of opposing political parties – even if joined in coalition – may have incentives to carve out distinctive positions, particularly as the next election looms into view. There is thus a standing possibility at all times that the relationship will end and that the bonds of collective responsibility will dissipate. In a coalition government, each party-leader can usually terminate the Government by withdrawing her party's support, thereby eliminating the Government's majority in the Dáil and removing the Taoiseach's absolute right to dissolve the Dáil.[27] Depending on how harmonious the political relationships are, this can introduce considerable instability. During the Fine Gael – Labour coalition of 2011–2016, there were frequently differences between the two parties over how to cut expenditure and raise taxes in a way that would meet Ireland's budgetary commitments to the Troika of international lenders that had funded the bailout. The Government nearly collapsed in 2013 before the Labour Ministers agreed to accept a compromise proposal on taxation.[28] This illustrates that, regardless of their respective strengths, a coalition government depends equally on the continued involvement of all parties, significantly enhancing the role of smaller parties. For this reason, each party provides an important political constraint on the actions of the other party. This internal contestation somewhat diminishes the power of the Government vis-à-vis other constitutional actors.

Reflecting the political reality that each party is an equal partner in Government, a convention has more or less emerged that each party leader has the authority to nominate and terminate the appointment of her own Government Ministers, notwithstanding that only the Taoiseach can formally exercise those powers.[29] Coalition parties will have negotiated a programme for Government that determines how many Ministers

---

[27] As we shall see in ch 4, the President may refuse a dissolution to a Taoiseach who no longer retains the support of a majority in the Dáil.

[28] E Gilmore, *Inside the Room: the Untold Story of Ireland's Crisis Coalition* (Kildare, Merrion Press, 2016) 138.

[29] An exception to this was when, shortly prior to the general election of 2011, Taoiseach Brian Cowen sought to appoint six new Ministers for transparently electoral reasons. The Green Party (the junior coalition party) objected to this plan and refused to support the appointment of new Ministers. 'Greens "vetoed" Cowen's plan to appoint Ministers', *The Irish Times* 20 January 2011.

each party will have, reflecting their respective numbers in the Dáil but also sometimes a perception as to which was the winner in the general election.[30] This division of spoils is always a source of contention. Following the general election of 2011, the Labour Party only agreed to having five Government Ministers (one third of the Cabinet) after it was also offered a super-junior ministry and the right to nominate the Attorney General, formally the prerogative of the Taoiseach.[31] The Tánaiste (Deputy Prime Minister) is generally, though not always, the leader of the second biggest party in the coalition. Article 28.9.4° requires that a Minister must resign if requested by the Taoiseach to do so. In a coalition government, however, each party leader will determine if her own Ministers should resign. If the Taoiseach were unilaterally to exercise her constitutional prerogative formally to request the resignation of a Minister from another political party, that would cause the other party to withdraw its support from the Government. Similarly, if one party were to join a Dáil motion of no-confidence in a Minister of another party, that would rupture the collective responsibility of the Government signalling that the Taoiseach no longer had the support of a majority in the Dáil. In that circumstance, Article 28.10 requires the resignation of the Taoiseach unless the Taoiseach requests (and the President grants) a dissolution of the Dáil. Either of these events could happen, but it would signal that the fundamental relationship of trust between the parties necessary to sustain the Government had already broken down. In short, since each party in a coalition will usually have the means to terminate the Government, its continued existence depends not on constitutional rules or the prerogative of the Taoiseach but rather on the extent to which the parties involved are able or even wish to manage their differences and preserve their relationship.[32]

V. THE DÁIL ELECTORAL SYSTEM

The composition of the Government depends on elections to the Dáil, the lower House of the Oireachtas. The Constitution limits the term

---

[30] In the Fianna Fáil – Labour Government of 1992–1994, the Labour Party held six of 15 cabinet positions, despite Fianna Fáil having more than twice as many Dáil seats. In the view of Bertie Ahern, then Minister for Finance and later Taoiseach, this reflected the fact that Labour were the obvious 'winners' in the election, significantly increasing their vote while the vote of Fianna Fáil had declined. Ahern (n 14) 150.

[31] Gilmore (n 28) 86.

[32] We shall consider coalition relationships in more detail in ch 6.

of each Dáil (and by extension the Seanad) to seven years, but allows for legislation to prescribe a shorter period. In practice, legislation has always specified a period of five years. There is now, in my view, a constitutional convention limiting the life-span of the Oireachtas to five years. The Dáil is elected by a system of proportional representation single transferable vote through a number of multi-seat constituencies (PR-STV). In 1958 and 1968, referendum proposals to change to a First-Past-the-Post system were rejected. In 2002, an All Party Oireachtas Committee rejected any changes to the system of PR-STV, emphasising the power that it gives to the individual voter. In 2013, a Constitutional Convention – consisting of 66 randomly selected citizens and 33 elected politicians – recommended retention of the PR-STV system. We noted above the way in which this electoral system ensures that there are few if any safe seats, with the result that Government Ministers and leading politicians remain keenly attuned to local interests. Complaints that this is an unhelpful distraction from national issues have not gained traction with the general population.

Article 16.2 establishes a number of constitutional parameters for the electoral process. The ratio between the number of members to be elected for each constituency and the population of each constituency can be no less than 1:20,000 and no more than 1:30,000. At present, there are 158 members of the Dáil, close to the 1:30,000 limit. The ratio must, so far as it is practicable, be the same throughout the country. In *O'Donovan v Attorney General*, the High Court declared unconstitutional a set of constituency boundaries that produced significant disparities in representation.[33] Rural constituencies, particularly in the West, tended to get higher representation than urban constituencies, particularly Dublin. Budd J rejected arguments that the geography of the west of Ireland, its distance from the capital, and the allegedly less demanding nature of voters in Dublin could justify this disparity. In his view, equality of representation was the constitutional requirement: although precise mathematical equality might not be possible, it would be practicable to achieve a more even distribution. The Oireachtas immediately passed the Electoral (Amendment) Bill 1961, which the President referred to the Supreme Court under Article 26.[34] The Supreme Court took a somewhat more relaxed approach than had Budd J in *O'Donovan*, holding that courts should only interfere with the judgment of the Oireachtas

---

[33] *O'Donovan v Attorney General* [1961] IR 114.
[34] *In re Article and the Electoral (Amendment) Bill 1961* [1961] IR 169.

where there was a 'manifest infringement' of Article 16.2. The Court specifically held that it was permissible for the Oireachtas to seek to adhere to geographical or well-known political or cultural boundaries in drawing constituencies.

The fact that the Constitution vests the power to draw constituency boundaries in the Oireachtas allows politicians to influence boundaries for personal or partisan advantage. The precise drawing of constituency boundaries and the choice of three-, four-, or five-seat constituencies can have a significant effect on how votes cast translate into party representation. In 1974, the Minister for Local Government under the then Fine Gael-Labour coalition attempted an ambitious gerrymander to suppress the representation of the main opposition party, Fianna Fáil, at the next general election. This was to be achieved by establishing a large number of three-seat constituencies in the Dublin area.[35] This backfired, however, when Fianna Fáil's support rose sufficiently that it actually gained an overrepresentation from the division of constituencies, allowing it to return to Government with an overall majority in 1977.

Perhaps chastened by this experience, the Oireachtas based its next constituency division in the Electoral (Amendment) Act 1981 on the recommendations of an independent commission, chaired by a Supreme Court judge. This practice continued on an ad hoc basis for the next 15 years. The Electoral Act 1997 provides a statutory basis for this arrangement, requiring the relevant Government Minister to establish an independent Constituency Commission following each national census. The Act lays down a number of criteria that the Commission must follow. For instance, only three-, four- and five-seat constituencies are permissible; breaching of county boundaries must be avoided as far as possible; constituencies must consist of contiguous areas. The Commission must be chaired by a High Court or Supreme Court judge. The other members are the Ombudsman, the Secretary General of the Department of Local Government (the Department responsible for elections), the Clerk of the Dáil and the Clerk of the Seanad. The Commission presents a report to the Clerk of the Dáil, which is then laid before both Houses of the Oireachtas. The Report has no formal legal or constitutional status. Nevertheless, the reports of the Commission have always been implemented by the Oireachtas. This constitutional convention has successfully depoliticised the drawing of constitutional boundaries, providing a significant safeguard against democratic backsliding.

---

[35] D Ferriter, *Ambiguous Republic: Ireland in the 1970s* (London, Profile Books, 2012) 40–1.

The PR-STV electoral method has implications both for party support within the Dáil and the sort of individuals who seek election. First, the voting system of PR-STV produces a notable seat bonus for the larger parties, as the results of the 2016 general election set out above illustrate. PR-STV is more proportional than a First-Past-the-Post system but less proportional than a PR list system.[36] Secondly, the fact that all TDs are elected directly from multi-seat constituencies rather than from party lists or from single-member constituencies has implications for who makes a viable electoral candidate. Although political parties are themselves largely top-down organisations in which elites control much of the agenda,[37] candidate selection must be sensitive to local party concerns: it is not uncommon for a local party official, refused a place on the party ticket, to leave the party and successfully stand for election as a non-party candidate. Even apart from this risk, candidates must be attractive to their own local electorate. Because every constituency has at least three seats, many political parties will run more than one candidate. This reduces, but does not eliminate, the importance of party affiliation and increases the importance of a politician's local profile. It is exceptionally rare for a candidate to be elected for a constituency other than one in which she had lived for an appreciable period of time.

The general election of 2016 was the first held following the introduction of gender quotas. Under the Electoral (Amendment) (Political Funding) Act 2012, political parties stood to lose 50 per cent of their State funding if they did not select at least 30 per cent female and 30 per cent male candidates. For the 2016 election, 30 per cent of the candidates were women.[38] This increase in the number of women candidates has significantly increased the number of women TDs, an issue on which Ireland has long lagged behind other comparable countries. 22 per cent of TDs are now women, a six-percentage point increase on the previous situation. There has been no systematic study of the previous employment or social class of the members of the current Dáil, although some insights can be gleaned from the information each provided about her occupation for the ballot paper.[39] The two most commonly cited occupations are teachers (approximately 15 per cent)

---

[36] A Lijphart, *Electoral Systems and Party Systems: A Study of Twenty-Seven Democracies, 1945–1990* (Oxford, Oxford University Press, 1994) 160–2.

[37] Weeks (n 8) 113.

[38] For discussion see F Buckley, Y Galligan and C McGing, 'Women and the Election: Assessing the Impact of Gender Quotas' in M Gallagher and M Marsh (eds), *How Ireland Voted 2016: the Election that Nobody Won* (Dublin, Palgrave Macmillan, 2016) ch 8.

[39] Gallagher and Marsh (eds) (n 38) appendix 2.

and farmers (approximately 10 per cent). Beyond that, there is a reasonable number of both employees and owners of what would appear to be small businesses (for instance, auctioneers and management consultants) and professionals (particularly lawyers and accountants). This is broadly consistent with more systemic studies of previous parliaments, which show domination by middle class, middle-aged men. Impressionistically, the range of occupations is fairly reflective of middle-class Irish society, with the exception of people who work for large multinational corporations. One factor that appears to affect success is coming from a family with a political background and experience of contesting elections.[40]

An extreme level of personal intra-party competition at the local level coheres with large degrees of party cohesion and discipline in the Dáil.[41] Within the Oireachtas, the party whip is closely observed, party cohesion being higher in Ireland than the European average. The strong party whip allows TDs to pursue common projects with like-minded individuals but also protects them from the pressures that can be exerted by local- or issue-interest groups.[42] There are frequently complaints that TDs are overly focused on their local constituency work to the detriment of their responsibility to focus on national issues. This concern may be overstated, however, relying on a platonic ideal of the politician's role that few, if any, political systems achieve. Academics generally now characterise the local role of a TD as one of brokerage rather than clientelism. TDs have little if any power to distribute State benefits but they do have a special access to the State bureaucracy and help their constituents navigate an often obscure system.[43] Consistent with this, TDs on average spend more than half their time on constituency work and less than 40 per cent on legislative duties.[44] Their primary role is as intermediaries between people and government rather than active shapers of that government.

The system facilitates the election of non-party candidates, making the formation of governments more difficult, as illustrated by the 2016 general election. 23 seats were won by non-party candidates. By definition, they do not share a common political agenda and, unlike

[40] Weeks (n 8) 120.

[41] R Sinnott, 'The Electoral System' in Coakley and Gallagher (eds) (n 8) 127.

[42] M Gallagher, 'The Oireachtas: President and parliament' in Coakley and Gallagher (eds) (n 8) 202–3.

[43] M Gallagher, 'The Constituency Role of Dáil Deputies' in Coakley and Gallagher (eds) (n 8) ch 8.

[44] M MacCarthaigh, 'The Role of the Houses of the Oireachtas: Theory and Practice' in MacCarthaigh and Manning (eds) (n 3) 46.

small political parties, cannot promise a cohesive bloc of support in the election of the Taoiseach in return for policy commitments. That said, the current minority Government is supported by a number of non-party TDs, several of whom have been appointed Government Ministers. Their support, combined with the abstention of Fianna Fáil, has allowed the Dáil to elect the leader of Fine Gael as Taoiseach. Although there have been minority governments in the past, their support levels in the Dáil were close to that of a majority, making them clearly the dominant grouping. Not only does the current Government lack a legislative majority, it faces an alternative legislative majority within the Dáil. For the first time in the history of the State, a Government may be forced to implement legislation with which it disagrees and which it cannot have repealed. Moreover, the Taoiseach will cease to retain the support of a majority in the Dáil *either* if a small number of non-party TDs withdraw support *or* Fianna Fáil ends its confidence and supply arrangement. This is one of the significant changes in the constitutional balance of power that I identified in chapter one. Without any new laws, let alone a formal amendment of the Constitution, a novel distribution of party-political support at a general election produced a fundamental change in the way in which the Constitution operates. At present, the actual constitutional structure more closely resembles the structure presented in Articles 6, 15 and 28: a tripartite separation of powers, with the Oireachtas controlling the legislative power and the Government meaningfully accountable to the Dáil. It is too early to say definitively whether this has facilitated healthy consensual politics or political paralysis.

VI. PRESERVING A FAIR ELECTORAL PROCESS

A conundrum of democratic governance is that a democratically elected assembly can adopt measures that lead to democratic decay. Specifically, it can make decisions to privilege the interests of current members or to manipulate future elections in favour of the current majority. We have already observed how the Oireachtas observes two constitutional conventions that counteract this tendency: never extending its own term beyond five years and delineating constituency boundaries in accordance with the recommendations of an independent commission.[45] The Oireachtas

---

[45] By constitutional convention, I mean a shared practice on the part of constitutional actors, perceived by them to be of normative significance, not to exercise their constitutionally explicit powers to their full extent.

has passed further legislation that protects the electoral process from partisan politics. Most fundamentally, the administration of elections is assigned to the Department of Local Government and conducted in a strictly non-partisan manner.

Over the last 20 years, a complicated system of political funding has developed that aims to reduce the scope for corruption in politics. The funding regime is partially a response to the findings of a tribunal of inquiry in 1997 that a leading business man had paid over £1.3 million to the former Fianna Fáil leader and Taoiseach, Charles Haughey, as well as smaller sums to a leading Fine Gael politician, Michael Lowry. The State provides funding for politics in Ireland, while also constraining the freedom of political actors to raise their own funds. The scheme of restrictions was introduced in 1997, but has been amended in a number of respects since then, most notably in 2012. The overall trajectory has been towards stricter regulation, achieved through lowering the disclosure threshold, lowering the level of donation that can be made, making donations from corporate donors more difficult, and linking the funding of political parties to the meeting of gender quotas. However, there are no general limits on expenditure.

The Electoral Act 1997 provides that State funding will be provided to registered political parties that received 2 per cent or more of the first preference votes at the previous general election. Each party receives a baseline sum of €127,000 and a portion of a larger sum, prorated according to the percentage of first preference votes. As noted above, the Electoral (Political Funding) Act 2012 would have reduced the State funding of political parties by 50 per cent if they failed to nominate 30 per cent women (or 30 per cent men) candidates for the 2016 General Election. As and from the first General Election held after 2023, the requirement will rise to 40 per cent women candidates and 40 per cent men candidates. The Electoral Act 1997 also allows for the reimbursement of expenses, up to a maximum limit, of candidates for election who were elected or who received one quarter of the quota required to be elected.

The Oireachtas (Ministerial and Parliamentary Offices) (Amendment) Act 2014, adjusting a scheme that commenced in 1938, provides a further allowance on the basis of the number of TDs and Senators elected. An amount is paid per TD and Senator, with the per-head amount decreasing the greater the number of representatives. If a party forms part of a Government, the allowance is reduced by one third to recognise the support effectively provided by the Civil Service. Money provided under this scheme cannot be used for any electoral purpose.

The Electoral (Political Funding) Act 2012 limits TDs, Senators and MEPs (as well as candidates for these offices) to receiving no more than €1,000 from a particular person in a particular year. Political parties can receive no more than €2,500 from a particular person in a particular year. There is a general limit of €200 on cash donations from any particular person in a particular year. Anonymous donations cannot exceed €100. Similarly, corporate entities can give no more than €200 unless they are registered on the register of corporate donors and provide a statement confirming that the donation was properly approved. The Standards in Public Office Commission maintains the register of corporate donors; a donor must register for each year in which it makes a donation. The Register of Corporate Donors for the past few years shows that no more than 15 donors register each year, the majority of which are trades unions.[46] The 2012 Act requires political parties to disclose any donation greater than €1,500. Individuals must disclose any donation greater than €600.

The Electoral Act 1997 also limits the amount of money that may be spent during Dáil election campaigns. The amount varies depending on whether the candidate is standing in a three-seat, four-seat or five-seat constituency. A candidate may transfer up to half her allowed expenses to the political party for which she is a candidate, thereby allowing that party to spend money on a national campaign. However, these limits only apply during the formal election campaign – the time between the dissolution of the Dáil and the General Election. Political parties may spend money in advance of the campaign that is clearly geared towards the campaign.

The Ethics in Public Office Act 1995 requires Members of the Houses of the Oireachtas to file an annual statement of their interests. The Second Schedule to the Act provides a very wide definition of registrable interests, from money and employment to interests in land and travel assistance provided to the Member. The Clerk of each House establishes a register of members' interests, which is publicly available. The Act also requires Members to declare their interest in any matter in the House on which they propose to speak or vote. Members of the public may make a complaint to a Committee of Members Interests to allege that a Member has breached her duty to register or declare her interest.

Whereas the Department of Local Government organises elections, the Standards in Public Office Commission is responsible for regulating

---

[46] http://www.sipo.ie/en/Reports/Register-of-Corporate-Donors/.

the funding of political parties and the political process. It also has responsibilities under the Ethics in Public Office Act 1995 in relation to alleged misconduct by public officials, including elected representatives. For the last 20 years, there have been proposals to establish a permanent Electoral Commission that could provide more unified regulation of matters relating to elections. In January 2016, a joint committee of the Oireachtas published a report calling for the establishment of such a Commission. That Dáil was dissolved shortly after the publication of this report. It remains to be seen whether the current Oireachtas will legislate to establish the Electoral Commission.

On occasion, the courts have also intervened to use constitutional principles to protect democratic processes from political action and inaction. As seen above, in *O'Donovan v Attorney General*, the High Court declared a set of constituency boundaries to be unconstitutional. In *Doherty v Government of Ireland*, the High Court declared that the Dáil could not unreasonably delay directing the Chairperson of the Dáil to move the writ for a by-election. The Government, which controlled the Dáil, had a clear incentive to delay moving the writ: it was likely to lose the seat in question thereby reducing its already slender majority.[47] The decision of the Court forced the Government's hand and led the Oireachtas to enact the Electoral (Amendment) Act 2011 to impose a six-month limit for moving the writ to fill a casual vacancy. The courts have sometimes intervened to protect the interests of candidates for election. In *Kelly v Minister for the Environment*, the High Court held that it was unconstitutional, in assessing the election expenses of Dáil candidates, to exclude the office expenses of sitting TDs, Senators and MEPs.[48] This effectively outlawed a practice whereby existing representatives could spend more than new candidates on their election campaigns, breaching a fundamental norm of fairness that governed the electoral process.

VII. SEANAD ÉIREANN

It is somewhat surprising that the Constitution includes a bicameral Parliament. The Irish Free State Constitution had established a Seanad, largely as a protection for the rights of Southern Unionists (ie, those who had wished to retain the Union with the United Kingdom). It had limited powers but could delay the passing of legislation and exercised

---

[47] [2010] IEHC 369.
[48] [2002] IESC 73.

this power to slow down de Valera's dismantling of the constitutional connections between the Irish Free State and the UK in the 1930s. In 1936, the Oireachtas amended the Constitution to abolish the Seanad. Nevertheless, de Valera included a Seanad in the new Constitution enacted just one year later. The ultimate constitutional design of the Seanad largely adopted the recommendations of a Commission, formed on the abolition of the old Seanad.[49] This was one of the few instances of public consultation in relation to the new Constitution.

The method of election to the Seanad is very different from that which applies to the Dáil. A general election for the Seanad must be held within 90 days of the dissolution of the Dáil. Typically, a general election for the Seanad takes place after the general election for the Dáil, facilitating unsuccessful Dáil candidates to run for the Seanad. The Seanad consists of 60 members. 11 are nominated by the Taoiseach who is appointed next after the reassembly of the Dáil following a general election.[50] This assists the Taoiseach in ensuring a Government majority in the Seanad while raising the profile of future party prospects. However, several Taoisigh have also nominated a number of non-aligned Senators, often drawn from outside the world of politics.[51] Of the 49 elected members, three are elected by the graduates of Trinity College, University of Dublin and three are elected by the graduates of the National University of Ireland. In 1937, these were the only two universities in the State. Allowing the graduates of Trinity College to elect Senators effectively ensured Protestant representation in the Oireachtas, given that Catholics traditionally did not attend that university. In 1979, the people amended the Constitution to allow for legislation to alter the parameters of university representation, for instance by the inclusion in the electorate of graduates of other third level institutions. However, no legislation has ever been passed in this regard.

The other 43 elected members are elected from five vocational panels of candidates having knowledge and experience of the following areas: culture, agriculture, labour, industry and commerce, public

---

[49] See generally G Hogan, *The Origins of the Irish Constitution 1928–1941* (Dublin, Royal Irish Academy, 2012) 192–209.

[50] This means that where a new Dáil cannot elect a Taoiseach, the caretaker Taoiseach cannot make nominations to the new Seanad. This is the only constitutional function of the Taoiseach that cannot be exercised by the caretaker Taoiseach.

[51] For instance, Taoiseach Albert Reynolds nominated Gordon Wilson, a Northern Ireland peace campaigner, to the Seanad following the 1992 general election. Taoiseach Enda Kenny nominated Fiach MacConghail, then director of the Abbey Theatre, following the 2011 general election.

administration. This reflects Roman Catholic theories of vocationalism, prevalent in the 1930s, that the State should be representative of different interest groups in society.[52] Article 19 of the Constitution allows for legislation to provide for the direct election of Senators by functional or vocational groups. This option has never been exercised, however. Legislation instead grants this franchise to elected politicians: the members of the Dáil elected at the most recent general election, the members of the Seanad, and the members of every County Council in the country.[53] The electorate of professional politicians has a far greater influence on the composition of the Seanad than the panels of expertise from which the candidates are notionally drawn. The overall composition of the Seanad broadly reflects that of the Dáil. Most nominees are party candidates, who either aspire to be members of the Dáil or who have retired from membership of the Dáil.[54] The university constituencies, although almost impossible to justify in principle, have tended to elect a more diverse range of Senators appropriate to the limited legislative role of the Upper House.

In 2013, the people rejected a referendum to abolish the Seanad.[55] The campaign for abolition focused on the alleged €20 million annual running costs, the desire to reduce the overall number of politicians, the lack of any clear role played by the Seanad and – from the left – an attack on the elitist character of the electorate. The proposal was opposed on the basis that it was a power grab by the Government, eliminating the Seanad in favour of a unicameral Parliament necessarily dominated by the Government. Although conceding many of the criticisms of the Seanad, opponents to the proposal argued that the electoral processes and powers of the Seanad should be reformed so that it could exercise a more meaningful constitutional role in a more democratically acceptable way. Despite much consideration of possible reforms, both before and after the defeat of the abolition proposal, the Seanad remains unreformed. The Seanad cannot be blamed for its inability to reform itself; reform can

---

[52] DK Coffey, '"The Union Makes us Strong": *National Union of Railwaymen v Sullivan* and the Demise of Vocationalism in Ireland' in L Cahillane, J Gallen and T Hickey (eds), *Judges, Politics and the Irish Constitution* (Manchester, Manchester University Press, 2017) 183–4.
[53] Seanad Electoral (Panel Members) Act 1947.
[54] M Laver, 'The Role and Future of the Upper House in Ireland" (2002) 8 *Journal of Legislative Studies* 49, 52.
[55] For an account of this campaign, see D Kenny, 'The failed referendum to abolish the Ireland's Senate: defending bicameralism is a small and relatively homogenous country' available at tcd.academia.edu/davidkenny.

only occur with the support of the Dáil and Government. The continued existence of a weak Seanad well serves the interests of the professional politicians in the Dáil: the Seanad cannot challenge their powers but does helpfully provide a crèche, convalescent home and retirement community for professional politicians, who have not managed to be elected to the real seat of power, the Dáil.

VIII. THE INTERNAL ORGANISATION OF THE HOUSES OF THE OIREACHTAS

Article 15.10 of the Constitution empowers each House to make its own rules and standing orders: the majority of these are carried forward from one Dáil and Seanad to the next. The chairperson of the Dáil is the Ceann Comhairle, who is automatically re-elected to the next Dáil. In 2016, the Dáil made new standing orders to provide for a secret ballot in the election of the Ceann Comhairle, ending the situation whereby the Government effectively chose the Ceann Comhairle by nominating its own candidate and whipping its party members to vote for that candidate. After the General Election of 2016, it was unclear which parties – if any – would be in a position to form a Government. All the major parties, with the exception of Fine Gael, nominated a single candidate for the position of Ceann Comhairle. This practice of party-nomination seems at odds with the spirit of the change to a secret ballot. The refusal of Fine Gael, the largest party, to nominate a candidate may not have been so much out of a commitment to an open process as a recognition that losing a member to the position of Ceann Comhairle would render it more difficult for them to form a Government.

The Oireachtas does much of its work through four types of committee: standing committees, joint committees, select committees and special committees. Standing committees continue from one Oireachtas to the next. For instance, the Business Committee agrees the weekly agenda for the business of the Dáil; the Committee of Public Accounts reviews the way in which public money is spent. Joint committees of the two Houses generally have a remit that mirrors that of Government Departments. They are therefore reinstituted in every Oireachtas, taking account of any reallocation of governmental responsibility. Some joint committees have a broader remit. For instance, the Committee on European Union Affairs considers important EU developments and initiatives that affect Ireland and scrutinises EU legislation and proposals. Select committees are committees of either House that perform functions that are constitutionally assigned to a particular House. For instance, the TDs on the Joint Committee on Justice and Equality will form themselves as the Dáil Select Committee on Justice and Equality for the purpose of considering a Bill in that domain. Finally, the Dáil and Seanad may appoint a Special Committee to address a particular issue. In 2017, the Oireachtas formed a Special Committee to consider the report of the Citizens' Assembly into the 8th Amendment to the Constitution.[56] As with all aspects of the Oireachtas, committees have tended to be dominated by the Government. They are not particularly powerful relative to committee systems in other legislatures.[57] That said, there has been a general trend towards more powerful committees.

IX. THE ATTORNEY GENERAL AND DIRECTOR OF PUBLIC PROSECUTIONS

Article 30 of the Constitution provides for an Attorney General who is the 'adviser of the Government in matters of law and legal opinion'. Similarly to Government Ministers, the Attorney General is appointed by the President on the nomination of the Taoiseach. The Taoiseach can also require the Attorney General to resign. The Attorney General is precluded from being a member of the Government although attends all meetings of the Cabinet. She leads the Office of the Attorney General, which provides advice to the Government and drafts legislation on behalf of the Government. She also has responsibility, under the Ministers and Secretaries Act 1924, for the Chief State Solicitors Office which manages the day-to-day litigation of the State. In *McLoughlin v Minister for Social Welfare*, the Supreme Court emphasised that the Attorney General, and her related offices are independent of the Government.[58] Prior to independence, the Attorney General had a role in the assertion or defence of public rights or interests. This role, although not mentioned in the Constitution, has continued.

The Attorney General defends the constitutionality of all legislation in litigation, whether in the context of an Article 26 reference by the President or a litigant-initiated case. Because of the obligation on the Oireachtas not to enact legislation that is unconstitutional, the Government cannot propose legislation that it believes to be unconstitutional. Such a belief

---

[56] See ch 10.
[57] S Martin, 'The Committee System' in MacCarthaigh and Manning (eds) (n 3) 301.
[58] *McLoughlin v Minister for Social Welfare* [1958] IR 5.

will necessarily be formed based on the advice of the Attorney General. This gives the Attorney General something approaching a veto power on the passage of legislation. We shall consider this further in chapter five.

Article 30.3 of the Constitution requires that all non-summary offences be prosecuted by the Attorney General or some other person authorised in accordance with law to act for that purpose. The Prosecution of Offences Act 1974 created a Director of Public Prosecutions who assumed most of the prosecutorial functions of the Attorney. The Director of Public Prosecutions exercises broad discretion in terms of deciding whether to prosecute an alleged offence and, as we shall see in chapter eight, deciding in which court certain offences should be tried. She is independent in the exercise of her functions. This is perhaps the only example in the constitutional order of an official or institution that can exercise a power of initiative (as distinct from a power to check or constrain) independently of the Government.

X. CONCLUSION

In this chapter, we have commenced our exploration of the distribution of constitutional power. Although several provisions in the Constitution suggest that there is a tripartite separation of powers, the Constitution fundamentally operates on the basis of a bipartite distribution of powers between the Government and the courts. At the start of the chapter, we saw how the Westminster model of responsible government combined with tightly whipped political parties ensures that the Dáil is subservient to the Government, rather than the Government accountable to the Dáil. As well as removing the accountability check of the Dáil, this ensures (given the relative weakness of the Seanad) that the Government controls the legislative process, to which we will return in chapter five.

Aside from this fundamental separation of powers, however, the institutional framework explored in this chapter allows for a number of important political constraints on the Government. The electoral system has produced a succession of coalition governments for the past 30 years. This results in compromise and contestation within the heart of the Government. Each governing party is, to some extent, a check on the instincts of the other. The Oireachtas respects two highly significant constitutional conventions: limiting Dáil terms to five years (two less than the constitutionally stipulated maximum) and deferring to an independent constituency commission in the drawing of boundaries for legislative districts. Moreover, the courts have intervened to ensure that the Government cannot unreasonably delay the holding of by-elections. As a result, the TDs of the Government parties know that they will face re-election in highly competitive multi-seat constituencies in less than five years, and that they cannot benefit from the Government's dominance to arrange constituency boundaries to suit themselves. The near universal desire of politicians to be re-elected means that public accountability can generate real political constraint. Legislation must be approved in a public forum, again generating political constraints. Even though the Dáil is unlikely to exercise its constitutional power to remove the Government, opposition parties can use the accountability mechanisms of the Dáil to focus public attention on alleged government incompetence or corruption. We shall explore these processes in chapter seven. The general election of 2016 produced an even more dramatic change, rendering the Government truly accountable to the Dáil and depriving the Government of its typical ability to control the legislative process. As a result, at the time of writing, the Constitution operates along the lines of a tripartite separation of powers as suggested by Article 6.

FURTHER READING

David M Farrell and Richard Sinnott, 'The Electoral System' in John Coakley and Michael Gallagher (eds), *Politics in the Republic of Ireland*, 6th edn (London, Routledge, 2017)

Michael Gallagher, 'The Oireachtas: President and Parliament' in John Coakley and Michael Gallagher (eds), *Politics in the Republic of Ireland*, 6th edn (London, Routledge, 2017)

Michael Gallagher and Michael Marsh eds, *How Ireland Voted 2016: the Election that Nobody Won* (Dublin, Palgrave Macmillan, 2016)

Gerard Hogan and David Gwynn Morgan, *Administrative Law in Ireland*, 4th edn (Dublin, Round Hall, 2010) ch 3.

Muiris MacCarthaigh and Maurice Manning eds, *The Houses of the Oireachtas: Parliament in Ireland* (Dublin, Institute of Public Administration, 2010)

Jim O'Callaghan, 'Seanad Éireann – An Opportunity for Real Political Reform' in Eoin Carolan (ed), *The Constitution of Ireland: Perspectives and Prospects* (London, Bloomsbury, 2012)

Eoin O'Malley and Muiris MacCarthaigh eds, *Governing Ireland: From Cabinet Governance to Delegated Government* (Dublin: 2012, Institute of Public Administration)

4

The President

Election and Removal of the President – Roles of the President –
Evolution of the President's Role

I. INTRODUCTION

O NE OF THE principal innovations of the 1937 Constitution was
the introduction of an elected presidency. Article 12.1 describes
the President as taking 'precedence over all other persons in
the State'. Although the President's internal status as Head of State was
secured by the Constitution, the King of England continued to accredit
ambassadors and conclude international agreements on behalf of
Ireland until 1949. As we saw in chapter two, it was only with Ireland's
departure from the Commonwealth and the Republic of Ireland Act
1948 that the President became recognised externally as Ireland's Head
of State. Consistent with the model of responsible government, the
President has few significant powers. She largely functions as a ceremonial Head of State, mostly exercising the sorts of powers that would be
exercised by the Queen in the United Kingdom or governors general in
Canada, Australia or New Zealand. However, the President has a small
number of roles that are more consistent with European Heads of State
in the interwar years. Moreover, the fact that Presidents have an electoral
mandate allows them to play a more active role in public than one would
typically expect of a governor general. In recent decades, successive
Presidents have played a more interventionist role.

In chapter three, I argued that the fundamental separation of powers
in the Constitution is bipartite, between the Government on the one
hand and the courts on the other hand. However, the Government is
subject to a number of important political constraints, which we shall
explore further in chapter seven. The President is a further mild source
of political constraint on the Government. First, the President holds
a small number of discretionary powers that constrain the powers of
the Oireachtas and Government. Secondly, even where the President

must act on the advice of the Government or Taoiseach, her involvement dignifies the function in a way that creates a moral check on the Government. Governments sometimes engage in politically sharp practice, but it would be unseemly to involve the President in such practice. Thirdly, the way in which successive Presidents have enhanced their informal role has allowed them to speak to political issues, while not getting involved in party politics. Because the President's values may differ from those of the Government, this provides a counterweight of rhetorical power.

II. THE ELECTION AND REMOVAL OF THE PRESIDENT

The President is directly elected by proportional representation – single transferable vote. The electorate is the same as for the Dáil, except that British citizens are not entitled as such to vote. To be eligible to stand for election as President, a citizen must be 35 years old. In 2015, the people rejected a referendum proposal to reduce this age threshold to 21, the same as applies for election to the Dáil or Seanad. The term of office is seven years; no President can serve more than two terms. The nomination process lies largely in the control of politicians. Although former or sitting Presidents can nominate themselves for a second term, thereby preserving their political neutrality while in office, all other candidates must be nominated either by at least 20 members of the Oireachtas or by four local county councils. No member of the Oireachtas nor County Council can nominate more than one candidate. Until 1997, this effectively meant that a candidate had to have the support of one of the larger political parties to stand for the Presidency. Since then, however, the fracturing of political parties and a general relaxation of political control has opened up the nomination process to a wider range of candidates.

Article 14 establishes a Presidential Commission, consisting of the Chief Justice, the chairperson of the Dáil and the chairperson of the Seanad, to exercise the powers of the President in circumstances in which the President is unable to do so. This could arise because of incapacity, death, resignation, impeachment, or mere absence from the State. Given that the President must ordinarily sign a Bill into law no sooner than the fifth day and no later than the seventh day after its presentation for signature, the Presidential Commission reasonably frequently performs this function. Article 12.10 provides a procedure for the impeachment of the President, which requires a two-thirds majority vote in each House of the Oireachtas. No consideration has ever been given to the exercise of this power.

III. THE ROLES OF THE PRESIDENT

On assuming office, the President takes an oath to maintain the Constitution of Ireland and uphold its laws. In the current constitutional structure, the President has three roles. First, she is the nominal holder of many fundamental constitutional powers. However, these must be exercised automatically or on the advice of another constitutional organ. Secondly, she is the holder of a small number of discretionary constitutional powers, two of which are significant. Thirdly, she has a role – formally recognised in the constitutional text but informally expanded by recent Presidents – of speaking to or on behalf of the Nation. We shall consider each of these in turn.

In relation to nominal powers, the President plays a largely formal role in government formation. As we saw in chapter three, she appoints the Taoiseach on the nomination of the Dáil, and Government Ministers on the nomination of the Taoiseach. Unlike the Queen in the United Kingdom and the Head of State or governor general in some other former dominions, she has no power to request a particular party-leader to seek to form a government. The President accepts the resignation or terminates the appointment of Government Ministers on the advice of the Taoiseach. And she appoints judges on the nomination of the Government. Some constitutional provisions explicitly qualify the grant of power to the President but there is a more general saver in Article 13.9: the powers and functions conferred by the Constitution on the President can only be exercised and performed by her on the advice of the Government, unless explicitly specified otherwise. Thus, even constitutional powers that do not appear to be qualified, such as the vesting of the supreme command of the defence forces in the President, are in fact qualified by the general obligation to act on the advice of the Government. Moreover, although the Oireachtas can confer additional functions or powers on the President, as happened with the Republic of Ireland Act 1948, the Constitution provides that any such powers can only be exercisable on the advice of the Government. The extent to which she is subject to the Government is emphasised by Article 12.9 which precludes the President from leaving the State without the permission of the Government.

The President's discretionary powers must mostly be exercised after consultation with the Council of State, consisting of current constitutional office-holders, all former Presidents, Taoisigh and Chief Justices, and up to seven members appointed by the President. It exercises a purely advisory role in relation to the President's functions, differentiating it significantly from bodies with similar names in continental Europe. The President has discretionary powers in resolving some procedural disputes between the Seanad and the Dáil, which have never been exercised. Under Article 27, the President can decline to sign a Bill where a majority of members of the Seanad and at least one third of the members of the Dáil present a petition that the Bill contains a proposal of such national importance that the will of the people ought to be ascertained. This potentially counteracts the ability of the Dáil to override the Seanad on legislative issues. The President may decline to sign such a Bill, unless and until either it is passed by the people in a referendum or a new Dáil, following an intervening general election, resolves that it should be passed.

The President has two instances of significant constitutional power that have played a role in the operation of constitutional government. Article 13.2.2° allows the President to refuse a dissolution of the Dáil to a Taoiseach who has ceased to retain the support of a majority in the Dáil. This is the sole discretionary power in respect of which the President need not consult with the Council of State, presumably because this might not be possible in a time-pressured situation of high political drama. This power has never been exercised but it did come sharply into focus on two occasions. In January 1982, the Fine Gael Labour coalition fell when it lost a vote on its budget. President Patrick Hillery had anticipated that he was likely to come under pressure from his former political party, Fianna Fáil, to refuse a dissolution. Hillery was of the view that it would be unwise to refuse the Taoiseach's request for a dissolution: it was far from clear that the political alignment in the Dáil would allow the Fianna Fáil leader to be elected Taoiseach; moreover, any intervention would embroil the President in party politics. On the night in question, he deftly directed his aide de camp that he would not accept any phone calls from anyone other than the Taoiseach. Eight phone calls were made by or on behalf of the Fianna Fáil leader who threatened to visit the President's residence in person. Hillery told his staff to bar the gates but this did not prove necessary. The Taoiseach arrived and requested the dissolution of the Oireachtas, which Hillery granted.[1] In 1994, a political crisis led the Labour Party to leave its coalition with Fianna Fáil and instead form a coalition with Fine Gael and the Democratic Left. Had Fianna Fáil Taoiseach Albert Reynolds requested a dissolution, it would have been open to President Mary Robinson to exercise her discretionary power

---

[1] J Walsh, *Patrick Hillery: The Official Biography* (Dublin, 2008, New Island) 473–8.

to refuse the dissolution. There had not been a vote of no-confidence in the Reynolds Government but Reynolds had clearly lost the support of a majority of the Dáil. Robinson let it be known that she would refuse a dissolution if it were requested. Reynolds made no request.[2]

Article 26 allows the President, following consultation with the Council of State, to refer a Bill to the Supreme Court to determine whether any of its provisions are unconstitutional. This is an exception to the general obligation on the President, under Article 25, to sign every Bill (other than a Bill to amend the Constitution) that has been passed by the two Houses of the Oireachtas. Article 26 references are an important feature of the Irish constitutional order. The possibility of Presidential intervention may amount to a check on legislative overreaching. An immediate Presidential reference carries greater political salience than the possibility of a litigant challenge at some point in the future. Moreover, legislation that has been referred by the President and upheld gains a constitutional immunity from future challenge. This contrasts with legislation that is upheld in the course of ordinary proceedings, which gains no such immunity. Perhaps partly as a result of this, the President has referred few Bills but the rate of attrition is high: of only 14 Bills referred since 1937, seven have been held unconstitutional.[3] Seven of the references occurred between 1994 and 2004; there has been none since. The Supreme Court has questioned whether the abstract review of the Article 26 procedure is preferable to an 'action in which specific imputations of unconstitutionality would fall to be determined primarily on proven or admitted facts.'[4] Nevertheless, the fact that only a President can commence a process whereby legislation gains this constitutional immunity is significant.

The President's third role is to speak to and on behalf of the Nation. The Constitution provides the President with a number of public communication powers. Having consulted with the Council of State, she may convene a meeting of the Houses of the Oireachtas, address the Houses of the Oireachtas and address the Nation. Every such message or address, however, must have received the approval of the Government. In more recent years, Presidents have informally expanded this role into

---

[2] G Hogan, 'Ceremonial role by far most important for President', *The Irish Times* 21 October 1997.

[3] G Hogan, D Kenny and R Walsh, 'An Anthology of Declarations of Unconstitutionality' (2015) 54(2) *The Irish Jurist* 1, 16–20.

[4] *In re Article 26 and the Housing (Private Rented Dwellings) Bill 1981* [1983] IR 181, 186.

one of generally speaking on behalf of civil society, without seeking Government approval. This has allowed Presidents to articulate themes for their presidencies, which they can then implement through their choice of engagements.

IV. THE EVOLUTION OF THE PRESIDENT'S ROLE

The picture that emerges from these provisions is largely a textual crystallisation of the powers exercised by a Governor General in British Dominions during the 1930s. Coffey has recently argued that the basis for the office of President was modelled not on the Governor General but instead on continental Heads of State who could exercise a 'suspensive veto'.[5] This allowed the President to suspend an action from taking place until another body determined its suitability. However, not all of these powers survived the drafting process. Both the Article 26 reference and the Article 27 plebiscite could be characterised as involving a suspensive veto, as could the role of the President in relation to constitutional amendments in the first three years of the Constitution under Article 51 (see chapter ten). However, no President has exercised powers under Articles 27 and 51, while Article 26 references to the Supreme Court remain infrequent. Notwithstanding the influence of continental models on the Presidency, therefore, the comparison with Governors General remains instructive.

Nevertheless, the direct election of the President vests her with a popular mandate that a Governor General could never obtain. Although this democratic mandate cannot transcend the constitutional limitations of the office, it has allowed Presidents to develop a role parallel to that strictly envisaged by the Constitution. A review of the Presidents since 1937 illustrates the way in which the role has changed in the last 28 years. The first President (1938–1945) was Douglas Hyde. Significantly, given the overwhelming Catholicity of the nascent State, Hyde was a Protestant. A scholar of the Irish language and a leading figure in the Gaelic Revival of the late nineteenth and early twentieth centuries, Hyde was jointly nominated by all political parties. The next 28 years saw the Presidency held by two retired Fianna Fáil politicians: Seán T O'Kelly (formerly Deputy Prime Minister and Minister for Finance) from 1945 to 1959,

---

[5] DK Coffey, *Drafting the Irish Constitution 1935–1937: Transnational Influences in inter-War Europe* (London, Palgrave Macmillan, 2018) ch 4.

then de Valera himself from 1959 to 1973. Erskine Childers, again a Fianna Fáil nominee, died in office in 1974 and was replaced by Cearbhall Ó Dálaigh. Ó Dálaigh had been Chief Justice and was jointly nominated by all political parties. In 1976, Ó Dálaigh exercised his powers under Article 26 to refer the Emergency Powers Bill to the Supreme Court to test its constitutionality.[6] This Bill formed a significant part of the Government's response to the IRA's terrorist campaign, prompting the Minister for Defence to describe the President as a 'thundering disgrace'. When news of this emerged, the President demanded that the Taoiseach sack the Minister for Defence. The Taoiseach refused and Ó Dálaigh resigned the Presidency, seeing the issue as symptomatic of a general lack of regard for the office of President on the part of the Government.[7] Patrick Hillery, former Fianna Fáil Minister for Foreign Affairs and EEC Commissioner, was then President for the next 14 years.

Apart from the Ó Dálaigh years, Presidents largely assumed an unobtrusive role, impeccably performing the constitutional and ceremonial aspects of their role without intruding into public debate. The election of Mary Robinson as President in 1990 broke this mould. A former human rights lawyer and professor of constitutional law in Trinity College Dublin, Robinson was nominated by the Labour Party and others. She was thus the first non-Fianna Fáil President to be elected. She adopted a notably more expansive version of her role, using the Presidency to highlight issues relating to the Irish diaspora, peace in Northern Ireland and the less privileged. In expanding the role, she was facilitated by the Government significantly increasing the budget of the Presidency.[8] In 1991, the then Taoiseach, Charles Haughey, informed Robinson of Government legal advice to the effect that she constitutionally required government approval prior to giving press interviews or speaking independently of government, as to do so would constitute 'addressing the nation'. Robinson argued for a different interpretation of the constitutional restriction, to which Haughey ultimately acceded, that would require Government approval only for formal addresses.[9] This was crucial in establishing the freedom of the President to become an independent voice.

---

[6] See discussion in ch 9.

[7] D Ferriter, *Ambiguous Republic: Ireland in the 1970s* (2012, Profile Books, London) ch 9.

[8] M Robinson, *Everybody Matters: A Memoir* (London, Hodder and Stoughton, 2012) 147.

[9] ibid 161–2.

The Robinson Presidency changed the public's expectations of the role, which in turn changed the views of political parties on whom to nominate. Not only did political parties realise that their own candidates required a different profile, they also relaxed the party whip in county councils to allow further nominations come forward through that route. 1997 saw the nomination of one Member of the European Parliament, two charity workers, one former winner of the Eurovision song contest and US religious talk show host, and another former law professor from Trinity College Dublin. Mary McAleese, the former law professor, won the Presidency and served two terms. Although nominated by Fianna Fáil, she was in a very different mould from the previous Presidents nominated by that party. She successfully used the Presidency to focus on reconciliation between Protestants and Catholics, particularly in her native Northern Ireland. This process culminated in the highly successful visit of Queen Elizabeth II to Ireland in 2011, the first by a reigning English monarch to an independent Ireland.

2011 again saw a wide range of candidates, the election being won by Michael D Higgins. Although a former member of the Labour Party and Government Minister, Higgins was closer to the profile of Robinson and McAleese than that of previous Presidents. His ministerial portfolio had covered issues related to arts and heritage. A published poet, his public profile hovered somewhere between that of public intellectual and politician. Whereas Robinson and McAleese largely avoided commentary on socioeconomic issues in their Presidencies, Higgins has pushed the boundaries of the office significantly further, offering at times pointed critiques of what he sees as the neoliberalism prevalent in public life, particularly in responses to the financial catastrophe. In a speech to the European Parliament in 2013, Higgins noted the dangers of regarding 'our people as dependent variables to the opinions of rating agencies, agencies unaccountable to any demos'.[10] There is now a popular expectation that the President be a leader of civil society, resolutely removed from party politics and impeccably neutral in the performance of constitutional functions, while engaging public debate on broad themes of public concern. This evolution of the role of the President is one of the five significant changes in the balance of power that have occurred since 1937, which I identified in chapter one. Although the President has not acquired any substantive powers, the profile of the President allows for

---

[10] http://www.thejournal.ie/michael-d-higgins-speech-european-parliament-873314-Apr2013/ (visited 22 August 2017).

significant contestation of public policy choices. Presidents have mostly avoided even indirect conflict with the Government; nevertheless, the evolution of the Presidency has somewhat diminished the Government's domination of the political scene.

V. CONCLUSION

The President in Ireland largely plays a ceremonial role, similar to that exercised by Governors General in former dominions of the United Kingdom. However, reflecting the continental model that influenced the drafting process, the President exercises real power under Article 26, referring potentially unconstitutional legislation to the Supreme Court. The potential of such a reference increases the political significance for the Government of ensuring that the Bills it presents to the Oireachtas are constitutional. The President also exercises an important power where a Taoiseach loses the support of a majority in the Dáil. Nevertheless, the greater importance of the presidency relates to the evolution of its informal role. Since the election of Mary Robinson in 1990, successive Presidents have pushed the informal boundaries of the office, allowing themselves to become significant voices in public discourse. Although they have generally avoided even indirect conflict with the Government, they have transformed the Presidency into an institution from which important contributions can be made to societal debates. Notwithstanding this evolution, however, the Presidency exercises little political power.

FURTHER READING

John Walsh, *Patrick Hillery: The Official Biography* (Dublin, 2008, New Island)
John Coakley, 'An Ambiguous Office? The Position of the Head of State in the Irish Constitution' (2012) 47(2) *Irish Jurist* 43
Donal Coffey, *Drafting the Irish Constitution 1935–1937: Transnational Influences in inter-War Europe* (London, Palgrave Macmillan, 2018) ch 5
Diarmuid Ferriter, *Ambiguous Republic: Ireland in the 1970s* (2012, Profile Books, London) ch 9
Mary Robinson, *Everybody Matters: A Memoir* (London, Hodder and Stoughton, 2012)

5

Legislative Power
and Interpretation

Preparation of Legislation for the Oireachtas – Passage through the Oireachtas – Legislative Debate – Constitutional Limits on the Form of Legislation – The Attorney General and the Legislative Process – The 2016 Oireachtas – Legislative Interpretation

I. INTRODUCTION

L EGISLATION CONSISTS OF general rules laid down in advance, which people can use to guide their own behaviour. In cases of default or disagreement, the general rules can be interpreted by the courts. Article 6 of the Constitution identifies the legislative power as one of the three powers of government, derived from the people. Article 15 assigns the legislative power exclusively to the Oireachtas (Parliament). However, as we noted in chapter three, the Government generally controls the Dáil and (as we shall see in this chapter) the Dáil holds legislative primacy over the Seanad. Notwithstanding the formal separation of constitutional powers, therefore, the constitutional reality is generally that the Government controls the legislative process.

In this chapter, we shall present how primary legislation comes into being, from its preparation by the Government to formal enactment through the Oireachtas.[1] We shall then consider how primary legislation interacts with secondary legislation, a dynamic that in Ireland is regulated by the courts because of a constitutional principle limiting the delegation of legislative power. In chapter three, we identified the Attorney General as a significant constitutional officer, one of whose roles is to ensure the constitutionality of Bills that the Government presents to the Oireachtas. Her interpretation of constitutional constraints therefore plays a significant

---

[1] The slightly different rules that apply to financial legislation will be considered in ch 6 in order to allow a holistic account of the financial governance of the State.

role in determining whether legislation can be enacted. Given that the purpose of legislation is to guide behaviour, we shall conclude with a brief examination of how the courts interpret legislation.

II. PREPARATION OF LEGISLATION FOR THE OIREACHTAS

The Cabinet Handbook, although it has no formal legal status, provides a guide for how Government business should be conducted and therefore a broadly accurate description of those processes.[2] Of particular relevance for this chapter, it details the internal Government procedures for the initiation and processing of legislation. Government must collectively approve draft legislation in the form of a Bill before it can be presented to the Oireachtas. We shall now consider the steps typically taken by Government before it approves a Bill for presentation to the Oireachtas.

Proposals for legislation come from Government Ministers. If the proposed legislation is likely to involve constitutional issues or substantial issues of legal policy, the Government Department must consult with the Office of the Attorney General before circulating a draft scheme of the legislation to relevant Government Departments. The draft scheme of the proposed Bill consists of numbered heads, with instructions for drafting and explanatory notes. This scheme must be circulated to the Department of Finance, the Office of the Attorney General and every other Department that might be concerned with the subject matter of the proposed legislation. The draft scheme should be accompanied by a Regulatory Impact Analysis. Following consultation, which should ordinarily last at least two to three weeks, the Department prepares a memorandum for the Government Agenda, seeking approval to draft the legislation. The consultation period can be abridged in cases of urgency and the Government can authorise prioritised drafting. Competition for drafting time between different Bills is managed by a committee chaired by the Government Chief Whip.

Once the Government has given its approval for drafting, the process continues as a joint work between the relevant Department and the Office of the Parliamentary Counsel to the Government, within the Office of the Attorney General. Consultations may take place with outside bodies, but the text of any Bill should not be disclosed prior to

---

[2] Department of the Taoiseach, *Cabinet Handbook* (2007) available at http://www.taoiseach.gov.ie/eng/Publications/Publications_Archive/Publications_2007/CABINET_HANDBOOK2007.pdf (visited 11 May 2016).

its approval by the Government and its submission to the Houses of the Oireachtas. If unforeseen policy issues emerge, they must be submitted to the Government for its approval. When the Parliamentary Counsel has completed work on the Bill, the relevant Department may arrange for it to be printed on White Paper. Government approval is then sought for the White Paper and its submission to the Oireachtas. These strictures do not apply to Finance Bills, Appropriation Bills and Bills to implement budget proposals, as well as some other categories of legislation that do not raise policy issues.

In 2011, cabinet procedure was amended to allow the Government to publish legislation in draft format. The Standing Orders of the Dáil were then amended in 2013 to make this a requirement of the Dáil rather than a concession of the Government. Standing Order 146A mandates a process known as pre-legislative scrutiny. Prior to its presentation or introduction to the Dáil, the relevant Minister must present the general scheme or draft heads of a Bill to the relevant committee of the Dáil. This must happen unless the Business Committee of the Dáil agrees to waive the requirement.[3] However, the Committee charged with considering the Bill may decide that it is not necessary to consider the Bill. The vast majority of Bills since then have been submitted to pre-legislative scrutiny. The relevant Committee has a broad discretion on how to conduct that scrutiny. It can invite submissions from the general public or from specific groups, hold hearings, and/or request Government officials to make presentations. But it need not do any of these things. At the end of the process, the Committee usually (but not always) publishes a formal report containing its judgment on the General Scheme of the Bill, which it forwards to the Government for its consideration.[4]

The main advantage of the pre-legislative scrutiny procedure is that it allows a more collaborative procedure, through which the more formal input of the Oireachtas into legislation can be obtained while policy is still in formation. Once the Government has adopted the Bill and formally published it, any policy change might be portrayed as a defeat for the Government. As a relatively new development in the Irish legislative process, it is not possible fully to characterise or evaluate the way in which pre-legislative scrutiny operates. Moreover, the current dynamic

---

[3] The Finance Bill and other budget-related Bills are excluded from pre-legislative scrutiny.

[4] See Oireachtas Library and Research Service, 'Pre-legislative scrutiny (PLS) by parliament' (2014) available at http://www.oireachtas.ie/parliament/media/housesoftheoireachtas/libraryresearch/spotlights/Final_Spotlight_PLS_17Dec2014_172050.pdf (visited 25 May 2017).

of a minority government so alters the balance between Government and Oireachtas as to make pre-legislative scrutiny less important, further impeding any attempt to evaluate its effectiveness. Since November 2017, a broadly analogous procedure applies to private members' Bills: these receive 'pre-legislative scrutiny' if they pass the second stage of the legislative process (see below), suggesting that there is a realistic possibility of enactment.

III. PASSAGE THROUGH THE OIREACHTAS

In order for legislation to become law, it must be approved by the Dáil. The Seanad plays a consultative role. Each House of the Oireachtas considers Bills in accordance with its own Standing Orders, which are broadly similar. Bills, with the exception of Money Bills,[5] can be introduced in either House first. Passage through each House of the Oireachtas involves five stages. For Government and to a limited extent for opposition groups, the first stage simply involves presenting the text of the Bill for publication and circulation. The Second Reading involves a debate on the broad policy of the Bill. The Government Minister responsible for the relevant area will introduce the Bill. The procedures on pre-legislative scrutiny, discussed above, envisage that the relevant Committee chair play a key role in this debate. At the conclusion of the debate, the House votes on whether the Bill should progress to the Third Reading. This is known as the Committee Stage and involves – at least in theory – a detailed analysis of each provision of the Bill, rather than a broad debate on its principles. In the Dáil, this Reading usually occurs before a select committee of TDs with responsibility for the subject-area of the Bill. However, the Third Reading can occur before a committee of the entire House, a practice which is more prevalent in the Seanad. This allows all interested members to engage with the detail of the Bill. Significant amendments can be made at the Committee Stage, provided that they relate to the policy of the Bill approved by the full House at the Second Reading.

The Fourth Reading involves the return of the Bill, as amended at Committee Stage, before the full House. At this point, any member may propose amendments, provided these have not already been rejected by a Committee of the whole Dáil. Amendments defeated in a Select Committee may be re-submitted for Report Stage. Once this stage is

---

[5] Bills to amend the Constitution must also be introduced in the Dáil, as we shall see in ch 10.

completed, the House moves – usually immediately – to the Fifth Reading, the final stage. There is rarely further substantive debate at this stage but it culminates with the all-important vote of the House on whether to pass the Bill. If the Bill is passed, it then moves to the other House where it goes through the same process. Once both Houses have passed the Bill, it goes to the President for signature.

Where a Bill, other than a Money Bill, has been passed by the Dáil, it proceeds to the Seanad. Although the Constitution presents the Seanad as having the power to amend and reject legislation, this mischaracterises the real extent of its powers. When the Dáil has passed a Bill, the Seanad has 90 days to consider it, or such longer period as both Houses agree. If the Seanad fails to consider the Bill, rejects the Bill or passes amendments with which the Dáil disagrees, the Dáil has 180 days from the expiration of the 90 days (or longer agreed period) to resolve that the Bill should be deemed to have been passed by both Houses of the Oireachtas in the terms in which it was approved by the Dáil. The net effect of this rather tortuous provision is that the Dáil has the power to override any decision, whether to amend or reject a Bill, made by the Seanad. In terms of raw constitutional power, the Seanad can only delay Bills. For Money Bills, the Seanad has an even more constrained role, reflecting the primacy of the Dáil in financial matters. We shall consider this in chapter six.

IV. LEGISLATIVE DEBATE

Government control of the legislative process is pervasive. The Government, assuming it holds a majority in the Dáil, decides which Bills get debated and how long can be spent debating each Bill. The Government can use its Dáil majority to ensure that its Bills get priority. It can also use its majority to determine that a particular stage come to an end and a vote be taken on whether the Bill proceed to the next stage, a vote which it is guaranteed to win. It is through these mechanisms that the Government Chief Whip ensures the implementation of the legislative dimensions of the Government's programme.

The Government's control of the legislative process, however, does not immunise the Government from the political costs of passing unpopular legislation. Indeed, the Government's clear control of the legislative process probably enhances its political accountability for unpopular or misconceived legislation; poorly judged legislation cannot be blamed on a need for political compromise. Gallagher argues that the legislative process, while not giving a meaningful input to the Oireachtas, does serve the purpose of requiring that legislative proposals be ventilated and subject to opposition scrutiny.[6] As a result, the Government will be subject to political constraint in implementing the legislative dimension of its governance programme. O'Dowd, however, argues that even this purpose is undermined by the availability of a particularly drastic parliamentary procedure. Known as 'the guillotine', this manoeuvre allows the Dáil to determine that the time for debate has elapsed, with the result that all remaining stages of the Bill can be dispensed with on a single vote.[7] Although political parties are closely whipped, Government Ministers have strong incentives to keep their own backbench TDs onside. Individual TDs probably have greater input into the legislative process through the informal network of their own parliamentary party meeting than through formal contribution to Dáil debates.[8]

We saw in chapter three how the allocation of time in the Dáil depends on party groupings. The Government receives the greatest amount of time, reflecting both its majority position and its need to progress its own legislation. The Government and recognised groups are entitled to present Bills, although groups can have no more than one Bill on the order paper of the Dáil at any time. This requires opposition parties to have clear legislative priorities. The Standing Orders for each Dáil provide that any member, including Government backbenchers, may move for leave to introduce a Bill. This motion may be opposed but in practice it rarely is. For an individual Member this is the first stage. Once leave to introduce has been granted, the Bill will be published and circulated. Standing Orders stipulate the sequence in which groups may debate the second stage of Bills, reflecting the overall strength of the groups. The larger the group, the more frequently it gets to debate a Bill. Such Bills can only proceed during private members business. In the current Dáil, four hours each week are set aside for private members business. This is an increase in time on previous Parliaments, reflecting the fact that the Government is in a minority.

O'Dowd has undertaken research that illustrates the stranglehold of the Government on the legislative process.[9] Reviewing a number

---

[6] M Gallagher, 'The Oireachtas: President and Parliament' in J Coakley and M Gallagher (eds), *Politics in the Republic of Ireland*, 6th edn (London, Routledge, 2017) 187.
[7] J O'Dowd, 'Parliamentary Scrutiny of Bills' in M MacCarthaigh and M Manning (eds), *The Houses of the Oireachtas: Parliament in Ireland* (Dublin, Institute of Public Administration, 2009) 325. We shall see below that the minority Government formed in 2016 is unable to implement the guillotine in Dáil debates.
[8] Gallagher (n 6) 187.
[9] O'Dowd (n 7) 326–30.

of Oireachtas sessions from the 1960s, 1970s and 1980s, he tracked the number of amendments tabled and their outcome.[10] In the Dáil, most amendments are proposed either by the Government (effectively adjusting its own Bill) or by the opposition parties. In contrast in the Seanad, government backbenchers and independent Senators move a significant number of amendments. O'Dowd attributes this to the less confrontational nature of the Seanad and the particular role played by the University Senators. However, Government amendments have a far greater chance of success. For his time period, O'Dowd assesses the success rate of Government amendments at 99.2 per cent and the success rate of non-Government amendments at 3.13 per cent. The formal rejection of an amendment, however, does not necessarily imply that the tabling of the amendment was ineffective. The Government will often table its own amendment, supported by the drafting expertise of the Office of the Attorney General, in response to an amendment proposed by an opposition or backbench TD. O'Dowd demonstrates that a significant number of Government amendments are of this type. In assessing the quality of debate, O'Dowd notes that the dynamic is one where other members challenge the Minister on aspects of the Bill. However, these challenges are often not a serious attempt to persuade the Minister to amend the Bill but rather question what the purpose or the effect of the provision will be. Typically, the Minister will give an assurance as to how the provision would be interpreted or applied.[11]

Although the assessment period is somewhat dated, the overall picture has changed little. Gallagher comments that 'the Dáil is still not fundamentally an active participant in the process of making laws, let alone broader policy.'[12] However, the innovation of pre-legislative scrutiny may allow for greater involvement of TDs in the shaping of policy; the dynamics of the current Dáil necessarily allow for greater input into legislation. Some maintain that debate in the Seanad proceeds in a more reflective, constructive and non-party spirit.[13]

Two Bills from 2013 illustrate the different ways in which legislation can pass through the Oireachtas. As part of the financial bailout of the State, the Government provided €30.6 billion in promissory notes to two banks, Anglo Irish Bank and Irish Nationwide, which were

---

[10] There is little to suggest that this ratio has changed substantially in the intervening period, at least prior to the 2016 general election.
[11] O'Dowd (n 7) 331.
[12] Gallagher (n 6) 177.
[13] ibid 184.

subsequently nationalised and merged into the Irish Banking Resolution Corporation. The promissory notes allowed the two banks to borrow from the Central Bank money that had been created by the Government. This process ensured that that the banks remained solvent and bond-holders suffered no losses. However, the Government was under an obligation to repay €3.06 billion each year for 10 years to the Central Bank, which then destroyed the money. The Government was of the view that these annual repayments would make it impossible for the State ever to restore its financial viability. It thus engaged in negotiations with the European Central Bank to adjust the repayment schedule.[14] At 7.30pm on 6 February 2013, the Dáil was debating a motion, tabled by a non-party TD, calling on the Government to declare that Ireland would not pay the €3.06 billion due on 31 March 2013. The Government had tabled an amendment to the motion that effectively replaced all the text with wording that called on the Government to continue its negotiations with the European Central Bank.[15]

At the same time, the Government was preparing a Bill that would liquidate IBRC and deal with the debt in a more sustainable way for the State. When the debate adjourned after two hours, the Government successfully moved a motion that the Dáil should reconvene at 10.30pm, providing a good illustration of how the Government typically controls the allocation of time in the Dáil. The Government also secured Dáil approval for its amended motion. At 10.30pm, the Minister of State at the Department of the Taoiseach successfully moved a motion that the Dáil resume at 11pm. At 11pm, he then moved a motion that the Dáil would consider and vote on all stages of the Irish Bank Resolution Corporation Bill 2013, setting the maximum time allowed for the debate and for the contributions of all party-leaders and finance spokespersons to the debate. Members of the opposition complained that they had just received copies of the Bill and did not have an opportunity to read it. The Government and opposition TDs then agreed to adjourn the Dáil until midnight to allow the opposition consider the Bill. At 2.55am, the Dáil passed the Bill through all remaining stages in one vote, the opposition Fianna Fáil party supporting the Bill on the basis of assurances given by the Minister for Finance that there was no realistic alternative. In the meantime, the Seanad had agreed to resume sitting at 12.30am, which

---

[14] For an account of the political manoeuvring, see P Leahy, *The Price of Power: Inside Ireland's Crisis Coalition* (Dublin, Penguin Ireland, 2013) 225.

[15] For the resumption of this debate, see http://oireachtasdebates.oireachtas.ie/debates%20authoring/debateswebpack.nsf/takes/dail2013020600051?opendocument.

it then adjourned on a number of occasions. The Bill then proceeded through the Seanad in an expedited fashion. The Seanad also passed a motion to concur with the request of the Government that the President sign the Bill into law earlier than the general period of 5–7 days after passage, under Article 25.2.2°. The President signed the legislation the same day.

The Irish Bank Resolution Corporation Act 2013 illustrates the ease with which Government can control the schedule of the Dáil to pass legislation quickly. It was probably warranted, given what would have happened on the financial markets if it was known that liquidation of the bank was about to happen. At the other end of the spectrum lies the Protection of Life in Pregnancy Act 2013. As will be discussed in more detail in chapter ten, the Constitution was amended in 1983 to provide explicit recognition for the right to life of the unborn, with due regard to the equal right to life of the mother. In *Attorney General v X*, the Supreme Court held that a pregnant woman was entitled to a termination of pregnancy where there was a real and substantial risk to her life, including through suicide.[16] This decision was controversial but the people on two occasions rejected constitutional amendments that would have removed the possibility of a termination in cases of feared suicide. In 2011, the European Court of Human Rights held that there was an obligation on Ireland to enact legislation that would give effect to the decision in the *X case*, so that pregnant women could establish whether they were entitled to a termination of pregnancy in Ireland.

In January 2013, the Oireachtas Joint Committee on Health and Children held three days of discussions with interest groups in relation to the issues. In April, the Government published the draft Protection of Life in Pregnancy Bill, which was the subject of pre-legislative scrutiny for a number of days in May. The Committee heard evidence from experts and healthcare professionals before preparing its own report on the draft Bill. The second stage of the Bill in the Dáil was taken over four days, allowing for a wide range of contributions on the Bill. The select Committee considered the Bill over two days before it returned to the Dáil. There was again considerable debate at report stage before the Dáil passed the Bill and it moved for consideration in the Seanad, again over a number of days. The Bill was passed by both Houses on 23 July 2013 and signed into law a week later. The legislation did not proceed at the same breakneck speed as the Irish Bank Resolution Corporation Bill.

---

[16] *Attorney General v X* [1992] 1 IR 1.

In particular, the extensive pre-legislative scrutiny is a welcome development. However, it was still a process marked by Government dominance.
The two Government parties applied the party whip, a particular issue
for the more conservative members of the Fine Gael party. Five Fine Gael
TDs were expelled from the party for voting against the Bill at different stages, including Minister of State for Europe, Lucinda Creighton.
Several of these sought to form a new political party, led by Creighton,
but all lost their seats at the next general election. This illustrates the
strength of party discipline, a key factor in maintaining the Government's
dominance of the Dáil.[17]

V. CONSTITUTIONAL LIMITS ON THE FORM OF LEGISLATION

Article 15.4 precludes the Oireachtas from enacting any unconstitutional
laws and deems such laws invalid. In chapter nine, we shall consider how
constitutional rights limit the permissible content of legislation. In this
chapter, we shall focus on limits to the form of legislation. Article 15.2 of
the Constitution states that the sole and exclusive power of makings laws
for the State is vested in the Oireachtas; no other legislative authority has
power to make laws for the State. As we saw in chapter one, the purpose
of this provision was to assert the legislative authority of the Oireachtas
over Westminster. However, it also appears – on its face – to prohibit
any delegation of legislative power on the part of the Oireachtas. This
is problematic because it is simply not practicable for the Oireachtas to
pass all the legislation to keep up with the demands of a hyper-regulated
modern State. The courts have taken a common-sense approach to this
tension, carving out an exception to the strict injunction in Article 15.2.
In *Cityview Press v An Comhairle Oiliúna*, the Supreme Court held that
it was permissible for the Oireachtas to delegate legislative power to other
entities provided that that the primary legislation specified all matters of
principle and policy, leaving only matters of detail to be regulated by
the secondary legislator.[18] This 'principles and policies' test has never
been strictly applied. Rather than require that primary legislation specifically enumerate principles and policies to bind the secondary legislator,

---

[17] In contrast, neither Fianna Fáil nor Fine Gael applied a party whip to the constitutional amendment proposal in 2018 to remove the right to life of the unborn from the
Constitution.
[18] *Cityview Press v An Comhairle Oiliúna* [1980] IR 381.

the courts are willing to infer principles and policies from the other provisions of the Act. Moreover, the courts have generally upheld legislative delegations of power that specify some principles and policies, even if they allow secondary legislation to develop further principles and policies. Only delegations of power that are devoid of principles and policies have been declared unconstitutional.[19]

The Supreme Court, again relying on Article 15.2, has held that Henry VIII clauses are unconstitutional. A Henry VIII clause is a statutory provision that allows the delegate of legislative power to amend primary legislation, a particular affront to the legislative authority of the Oireachtas. In a number of cases, the courts have opted for a narrow (and sometimes implausible) construction of a statute to ensure that it does not empower a Government Minister to amend a statute.[20]

It is sometimes difficult to identify precisely what values, if any, are served by the courts' non-delegation doctrine. In some cases, there was heightened concern because the legislative power had been delegated to an actor that was not democratically accountable in any sense.[21] However, where, as in most cases, the delegated legislator is a Government Minister, it could be argued that the democratic accountability of the Minister through the Dáil is sufficient. Is there really anything problematic with a Minister for Justice having a wide power to regulate the deportation of non-nationals or to add new drugs to the list of controlled substances? Furthermore, as noted by Carolan, the effect of the doctrine is to shift considerable power to the courts who determine the line between permissible and impermissible delegations of legislative power.[22] The constraint on the Government empowers the courts. On the other hand, if there were no constraint on the delegation of legislative power and Henry VIII clauses, the Government's domination of the Dáil would allow it entirely to hollow out the legislative role of the Oireachtas. The requirement on the Government to pass legislation through the Oireachtas brings greater publicity to proposed laws, allowing for public debate and meaningful

---

[19] In *Laurentiu v Minister for Justice* [1999] 4 IR 26, the Supreme Court declared unconstitutional section 5(1)(e) of the Aliens Act 1935 that baldly empowered the Minister for Justice to make regulations for the exclusion or the deportation and exclusion of such aliens from the State.

[20] See, for instance, *Cooke v Walshe* [1984] IR 710.

[21] *McGowan v Labour Court* [2013] IESC 21, striking down a provision in the Industrial Relations Act 1946 that effectively allowed some employers and trade unions set conditions for all others in the sector.

[22] E Carolan, 'Democratic Control or "High-Sounding Hocus-Pocus"? – A Public Choice Analysis of the Non-Delegation Doctrine' (2007) 29 *Dublin University Law Journal* 111.

opposition by other parties. Political pressure can therefore be brought to bear against unwise or unpopular proposals, even if the Government of the day holds a legislative majority.

The ambiguities of the principles and policies test, however, render it an unclear signal. It is difficult to predict what legislation might be struck down by the courts, leading to a rather crabbed style of legislative drafting, where great care is taken to specify a wide range of types of delegated legislation that could be made by the delegated legislator. This is doubly artificial when one bears in mind that the primary legislation itself is being drafted by and at the instigation of the Government. The dynamic is that of the Government requesting the Oireachtas to ratify a delegation of legislative power back to itself. Behind this drafting process lies the spectre of the courts and a possible strike-down of a grant of legislative power. In general, the style of drafting for statutory instruments largely follows that used for statutes. However, statutory instruments are drafted in-house within each Government Department, rather than by the dedicated Parliamentary Draftsman's Office in the Office of the Attorney General. As a result, the quality of the drafting is arguably less high.

In this regard, it should be borne in mind that 'delegated legislation' is a constitutional law concept rather than a precise legal category. In practice, the most common form of delegated legislation is a statutory instrument made by a Government Minister.[23] The Act that delegates the legislative power will generally stipulate that the Government Minister lay a draft of the delegated legislation before each House of the Oireachtas. In some cases, the approval of each House is required before the regulations can come into force.[24] More commonly, however, each House of the Oireachtas is given a power to annul the regulation by passing a resolution within 21 days.[25] Nevertheless, the general domination of the Dáil and Seanad by the Government ensures that neither of these is a particularly meaningful constraint.

One further significant constitutional case followed on from the non-delegation doctrine. The Supreme Court declared section 5(1)(e) of the Aliens Act 1935 unconstitutional in *Laurentiu v Minister for Justice*.[26] Because the State's immigration control system largely depended on

---

[23] See generally G Hogan and DG Morgan, *Administrative Law in Ireland*, 4th edn (Dublin, Round Hall, 2010) 32–56.

[24] See for instance the Planning and Development Act 2000, s 262.

[25] See for instance the Misuse of Drugs Act 1977, s 38.

[26] *Laurentiu v Minister for Justice* [1999] 4 IR 26.

regulations made under section 5(1), the Court's judgment raised the prospect that the immigration system could collapse. To avoid this possibility, the Oireachtas passed the Immigration Act 1999, section 2(1) of which provided that every such regulation (other than those based on section 5(1)(e) itself) would 'have statutory effect as if it were an Act of the Oireachtas'. This sought to preserve the regulations made under section 5(1) even if other provisions in section 5(1) itself were subsequently found unconstitutional. In *Leontjava and Chang v Director of Public Prosecutions*, the Supreme Court rejected a constitutional challenge to this method of enactment.[27] Keane CJ, delivering the judgment of the Court, noted that the Constitution was silent as to the form of legislation. As a result, the 'choice by the Oireachtas to incorporate the instruments in question by reference rather than by setting out their text *verbatim* in the body of the Act was one which they were entitled to make'. This judgment validates a legislative practice of failing to scrutinise legislation closely. As we saw above, the Third Stage of the legislative process involves a section by section scrutiny of the Bill. Although this cannot – of itself – produce detailed scrutiny of legislative language, there is something to be said for the formal requirement that every legislative clause be at least noted. If one section of a Bill, however, can effectively incorporate a whole other corpus of law, that formal requirement is set at nought.

VI. THE ATTORNEY GENERAL AS A VETO-HOLDER IN THE LEGISLATIVE PROCESS

The Attorney General, as the chief legal adviser to the Government, exercises considerable influence over the legislative process. All government statutes are drafted by the Office of the Parliamentary Counsel within the Office of the Attorney General. The Attorney General also advises the Government on what legislation may permissibly be enacted. Given the constitutional constraints on the legislative power of the Oireachtas and the international human rights obligations that bind the State, this significantly empowers the Attorney General. As noted above, Article 15.4 specifically prohibits the Oireachtas from enacting unconstitutional legislation. By extension, the Government should not present unconstitutional Bills to the Oireachtas. The Government's view

---

[27] *Leontjava and Chang v Director of Public Prosecutions* [2004] 1 IR 591.

of the constitutionality of legislation will be based on the advice of the Attorney General. For this reason, the Attorney General is tantamount to a veto-player in the enactment of legislation, albeit that the veto can only be exercised on limited grounds. The Government is not bound by the advice of the Attorney General but does place heavy reliance on that advice, at least in publicly defending its legislative decisions.

The respect paid by the Government to the Attorney General provides a significant safeguard for human rights, whether protected in the Constitution or elsewhere. However, it has been argued that deference to the Attorney General stifles legislative debate within the Oireachtas. Foley has shown how advice of the Attorney General to the effect that legislation is constitutional functions as a debate-stopper within the Houses of the Oireachtas.[28] Given that the Oireachtas is constitution-ally responsible for passing legislation and given that the Attorney is not accountable to the Oireachtas, it would be preferable for the Oireachtas to consider itself whether legislation is constitutional. There are good reasons not to publish the advice of the Attorney. Given that any doubts expressed in such advice would inevitably fuel constitutional chal-lenges to the legislation in question, the prospect of publication might well discourage the Attorney from providing candid advice in writing. Nevertheless, it would be possible for the Attorney to publish a state-ment of reasons as to why she believes legislation to be constitutional (or not). This could inform legislative debate within the Dáil. That this does not happen further underscores the dominance by the Government of the legislative process.

VII. THE OIREACHTAS ELECTED IN 2016

As noted in the Introduction, the configuration of the current Dáil has resulted in a minority Government. This means both that the Govern-ment cannot be certain that its own legislation will be passed and that the combined Opposition forces may secure the enactment of legislation with which the Government disagrees. Although it is too early to offer any definitive assessment of how this has altered the legislative process, it has unleashed a number of identifiable dynamics. First, it has become easier to pass private members legislation. Previous Governments, even if they agreed with the substance of an Opposition Bill, were likely to

---

[28] B Foley, 'Presuming the Legislature Acts Constitutionally: Legislative Process and Constitutional Decision-Making' (2007) 29 *Dublin University Law Journal* 141.

vote it down and later introduce a Government Bill on the same issue. It has been reported that no private members Bills were passed between 1954 and 1989, and only one between 2002 and 2008.[29] However, the first Bill passed by the current Oireachtas was initiated by the Opposition, the Competition Amendment Act 2017. Secondly, there have been complaints of legislation becoming bogged down in committee.[30] The Dáil no longer applies a guillotine to speed up or close down debate on Bills, meaning that conclusions are often delayed. Debate will only come to an end where there are no further proposed amendments to consider and nobody left who wishes to make a contribution to the debate. Only at that point can the question be put to move the Bill to the next stage. Thirdly, the requirement of Opposition consent for the passage of legislation has made it more difficult to pass controversial legislation. Some commentators have alleged that this has led to few major Bills and no controversial Bills.[31] Fourthly, as we shall see in chapter six, the Government has been accused of employing its particular powers in respect of appropriations legislation in order to stymie legislation more generally. The overall picture is one of a much less efficient legislative process. It is too early to say whether this more lengthy and deliberative approach improves the quality of legislation, whether in terms of clarity or its effectiveness in meeting shared and/or reasonable legislative objectives.

VIII. THE INTERPRETATION OF LEGISLATION BY THE COURTS

The point of legislation is to guide people's behaviour. We therefore cannot understand the legislative component of governance without understanding how legislation is interpreted. Of course, legislation is interpreted in all sorts of circumstances by all sorts of people. However, the judicial method of interpretation holds pre-eminence because court interpretations are final in the case of dispute. Some academic commentators have argued that the constitutional division of legislative and judicial roles mandates a particular form of statutory interpretation, whereby the courts must give effect to the intention of the legislature as revealed by the literal meaning of the legislative text.[32] However, as

---

[29] 'Only one Private Members' Bill in 87 enacted – FG', *The Irish Times* 14 July 2008.

[30] 'The New Politics: 10 Changes it has Brought to the Oireachtas', *The Irish Times* 28 February 2017.

[31] N Whelan, 'New politics means little legislation', *The Irish Times* 27 January 2017.

[32] See, for instance, N Dodd, *Statutory Interpretation in Ireland* (Tottel Publishing, 2008) 117, 281, 282, 288, 289, 292.

Curran has argued, this does not follow.[33] The distinction drawn between law-making and law-interpreting functions tells us nothing about where the dividing line between making and interpreting lies, still less about what the appropriate method of interpretation is.

In assessing how the courts exercise their interpretative role, we must distinguish between – to adopt Curran's useful phrase – the prevailing theory of interpretation and the actuality of interpretation. The prevailing theory emerges from court judgments in which the courts seek to articulate how they interpret statutes, as distinct from cases in which the courts simply go about the task of interpretation. The prevailing theory also finds expression in academic commentary and – to a certain extent – in the Interpretation Act 2005. It holds that the courts are obliged to give effect to the intention of the legislature as revealed by the literal meaning of the legislative text. Where the literal meaning of the text is plain or clear, the judge's job is done. However, where the literal meaning is ambiguous, or where it would be absurd or fail to reflect the plain intention of the Oireachtas, then the court can give an interpretation that would reflect the plain intention of the Oireachtas, as discerned from the Act as a whole.

The difference between the two stages, however, is not so clear-cut. If the courts are not permitted to give effect to an absurd interpretation, they must check every literal interpretation to ensure that it is not absurd. This necessarily involves an element of the purposive approach even at the first stage, in which the courts ask themselves whether it would make sense for the Oireachtas to be trying to achieve what a literal interpretation of the statute would suggest. Purposive interpretation is actually dominant since it is a sense of purpose that circumscribes the domain of literal interpretation, not *vice versa*.

In *Crilly v TJ Farrington Ltd*, the Supreme Court held that it was impermissible for the courts to have regard to debates of the Oireachtas as an aid to the construction of statutes.[34] The Oireachtas legislated as a collective entity; its intent was to be inferred primarily from the words it used, not the expressed subjective intentions of its various members. When the Irish courts engage in purposive interpretation, therefore, they are deliberately not asking a factual question about what intentions were actually held by individual legislators. Instead, they are asking a question

---

[33] C Curran, *Statutory Interpretation and the Rule of Law in Ireland* (PhD Thesis, Trinity College Dublin, 2014) 49.

[34] *Crilly v TJ Farrington Ltd* [2001] 3 IR 267.

about what intentions can rationally be ascribed to the legal entity that is the legislator. The primary evidence to support this ascription is the actual words used by the legislator. However, this ascription is checked by the judges' own sense of what purpose the legislator might rationally have been trying to achieve. *Crilly* has implications for how legislation is debated in the Oireachtas, since there is no incentive for legislators, particularly Government Ministers, to place statements on the record in order to influence the future interpretation of that legislation.

IX. CONCLUSION

The Government implements the legislative dimension of its political programme through its control of the Dáil and the weakness of the Seanad. This is the principal way in which the operation of the Irish constitutional order departs from the tripartite separation of powers announced in Article 6. This concentration of political power in the Government is somewhat checked by the public scrutiny entailed by passage of legislation through the Oireachtas. This is enhanced by the judicial application, however inconsistent, of the non-delegation doctrine. Political constraints on the Government derive from the central dynamic of democratic governance identified in chapter three: TDs who support and form the Government face re-election in highly competitive multi-seat constituencies. Indeed, the concentration of political power in the Government arguably enhances public accountability at election time, since Governments cannot attribute their failures to the need to collaborate with other powerful actors. Once again, we have seen how the current configuration of political parties within the Dáil has disrupted this constitutional order, introducing something more akin to the tripartite separation of powers promised by Article 6. It is too early to say whether this will lead to a more consensual legislative process or a form of political stasis in which it becomes impossible for the electorate to ascertain who has been responsible for the governance of the State.

FURTHER READING

Eoin Carolan, 'Democratic Control or "High-Sounding Hocus-Pocus"? – A Public Choice Analysis of the Non-Delegation Doctrine' (2007) 29 *Dublin University Law Journal* 111

Niall Dodd, *Statutory Interpretation in Ireland* (Tottel Publishing, 2008)

Brian Foley, 'Presuming the Legislature Acts Constitutionally: Legislative Process and Constitutional Decision-Making' (2007) 29 *Dublin University Law Journal* 141

Michael Gallagher, 'The Oireachtas: President and Parliament' in John Coakley and Michael Gallagher (eds), *Politics in the Republic of Ireland*, 6th edn (London, Routledge, 2017)

Muiris MacCarthaigh and Maurice Manning (eds), *The Houses of the Oireachtas: Parliament in Ireland* (Dublin, Institute of Public Administration, 2009)

David Gwynn Morgan, The Separation of Powers in the Irish Constitution (Dublin, Round Hall Sweet & Maxwell, 1997) 222–263

6

Governance and Public Administration

Executive Power – Public Administration – The Operation of Government –
Dynamics Within the Government – Financial Governance – Local
Government

I. INTRODUCTION

IN CHAPTER FIVE, we saw how the Government's typical control of the
legislative process allows it to enact and repeal legislation as necessary to give effect to its political programme, subject to the political
constraint associated with the requirement to pass legislation through
the public processes of the Oireachtas. There are two further elements of
the Government's power: executive and administrative. The Constitution
directly grants executive power to the Government. As important as
executive power, however, is the Government's administrative power. The
Government's control of the legislative process allows it to create new
administrative powers. Through legislation, the Government can assign
those administrative powers to itself or, more typical in recent decades,
to a statutory administrative agency that remains subject to the ultimate
direction of the Government. The governance of the State therefore
occurs through a complex interaction of legislative, executive and
administrative power.

In this chapter, we shall first explore the contours of executive and
administrative power, paying particular attention to the way in which
they interact with legislation. We shall then consider the way in which the
Government exercises its governance function. We shall explore in detail
how the financial governance of the State is effected, taking up the special
procedures for financial legislation left over in chapter five. Finally, we
shall consider a number of more peripheral instances of State governance:
local government, semi-State companies and privatised utilities.

II. EXECUTIVE POWER

Article 6 of the Constitution states that all powers of government, legislative, executive and judicial, must be exercised by organs of government established by the Constitution. Article 28 vests the executive power of the State in the Government. There is very little textual guidance, however, as to what the executive power actually consists of. Articles 28 and 29 do assign specific powers to the Government, implicitly deeming them to be aspects of the executive power. For instance, Article 28.3.2° assigns to the Government the responsibility of protecting the State in a time of invasion. Article 28.4.4° provides that the Government shall prepare estimates of the receipts and estimates of the expenditure of the State for each financial year and present them to the Dáil. Article 29.4.1° provides that the executive power in connection with external relations shall be exercised by or on the authority of the Government. As well as these explicit executive powers, however, the courts have recognised that there can be implicit executive powers, holding that the Government enjoys the 'powers normally exercised by such organs in a sovereign and democratic state'.[1]

Different approaches have been suggested for the identification of such implicit executive powers. James Casey suggested that the executive power is what is left of state power when legislative and judicial powers are subtracted.[2] As we saw in chapter two, although the courts have excised royal prerogatives from Irish law, they have recognised inherent State powers that are broadly analogous to non-royalist prerogatives, such as the power to control immigration or claim historical artefacts. If those powers are neither legislative nor judicial in character, they necessarily – under Casey's suggested approach – fall within the executive power. David Gwynn Morgan has argued for a historical approach whereby functions that have traditionally been exercised by the executive branch of government are deemed to be executive powers.[3] In practice, these two approaches largely overlap. Our sense of what count as inherent state powers is likely to reflect the sorts of powers actually exercised by states in the past.

The Irish courts have given most consideration to this issue in the context of immigration law. In *Re Article 26 and the Illegal Immigrants (Trafficking) Bill 1999*, the Supreme Court characterised immigration control as 'an inherent element of State sovereignty over national

---

[1] *Haughey v Moriarty* [1999] 3 IR 1, 32.

[2] J Casey, *Constitutional Law in Ireland*, 3rd edn (Dublin, Round Hall Sweet & Maxwell, 2000) 230–1.

[3] DG Morgan, *The Separation of Powers in the Irish Constitution* (Dublin, Round Hall Sweet & Maxwell, 1997) 271–2.

territory long recognised in both domestic and international law'.[4] In *Laurentiu v Minister for Justice*, several members of the Supreme Court emphasised that the Government had the constitutional authority to control immigration, irrespective of the lack of any explicit reference in the Constitution to immigration.[5] The presumptive vesting of implicit constitutional powers in the Government reduces the need for the Government publicly to justify its own powers through the legislative process. As we saw in chapter five, a majority of the Supreme Court held in *Laurentiu* that s 5(1)(e) of the Aliens Act 1935 breached Art 15.2 of the Constitution in delegating legislative power to the Minister for Justice. However, a majority of the Supreme Court identified no difficulty with the fact that the Oireachtas had attempted to regulate the exercise of the immigration-control power in the first place. Denham J referred to the legislature having 'grasped the power over aliens from the executive'.[6]

This starkly distinguishes the executive power from the other constitutional powers of government. We saw in chapter five that the Oireachtas is presumptively precluded from delegating its own legislative power. We shall see in chapter eight that the courts zealously protect the judicial power from any legislative interference. The exclusive law-making power of the Oireachtas does not extend to removing judicial matters from the courts. However, the clear implication of *Laurentiu* is that executive power can be taken and controlled by the Oireachtas. In formal terms, this different approach to the executive power may be justified by the constitutional accountability of the Government to the Dáil. However, we know that this formal accountability of the Government to the Dáil is rarely a constitutional reality: typically, the Government controls the Dáil. This constitutional reality, however, also mitigates the significance of the courts' decision that the Oireachras can take over and control the executive power. Given that the Government typically controls the Oireachtas, there is little shift in the constitutional balance of power by allowing the Oireachtas to legislate for aspects of the executive power. The Oireachtas asserting control of the immigration-control power is not a constitutional power-grab. Rather, it reflects a decision on the part of the Government that it would prefer to control immigration through legislation rather than simply through exercises of the executive power. This again emphasises how we should see the executive power and legislative power as different tools that the Government uses in conjunction with each other in order to govern the State.

---

[4] *Re Article 26 and the Illegal Immigrants (Trafficking) Bill 1999* [2000] 2 IR 360.
[5] *Laurentiu v Minister for Justice* [1999] 4 IR 26.
[6] ibid 63.

III. PUBLIC ADMINISTRATION

As we have seen in the previous section, executive power consists either of textually explicit power, such as the Government's power in relation to foreign affairs, or of implicit State powers that necessarily inhere in Ireland and which fall to be exercised by the Government, such as the immigration control power. The Supreme Court has held that Government Ministers, when exercising powers conferred on them by legislation, are not exercising the executive power of the State. They are merely the designated officials for the exercise of statutory power.[7] These powers are best characterised as administrative. Typically, the Oireachtas enacts a new statute that creates new powers to make administrative decisions. This can include legally binding decisions on individuals. In this regard, Article 37.1 of the Constitution authorises the exercise of 'limited functions and powers of a judicial nature' in matters other than criminal matters by persons duly authorised by law to exercise such functions. Administrative powers can also include policy-making powers. A good example of administrative power is provided by the Local Government (Planning and Development) Act 1963, which was the first attempt to regulate the built environment. It granted to local authorities the power (and obligation) to make development plans to guide the development of their local area. Local authorities were also granted the power to grant or refuse planning permission for particular developments.

Administrative powers are sometimes conferred on Government Ministers. Section 26 of the Local Government (Planning and Development) Act 1963, for example, allowed any person to appeal to the Minister for Local Government against a decision of a planning authority to grant or refuse planning permission. Over time, particularly in recent decades, there has been a growing tendency to assign administrative powers to statutory agencies rather than Ministers. There is no formal criterion to judge whether a particular statutory body exercises administrative power. I suggest that it depends on an interaction of four factors: the extent to which the body is controlled by the Government (who appoints and removes its members?); its remit and in particular whether it is under an obligation to have regard to or implement Government policy; whether its powers apply primarily to private bodies or public bodies; whether it has a status protected in EU law or is under an obligation to

---

[7] *Murphy v Dublin Corporation* [1972] IR 215.

apply EU law. These are all indicators of the extent to which the body exercises administrative power as opposed to constraining public power. In chapter seven, I shall return to these factors in identifying statutory bodies that constrain public power. In this chapter, my focus is on statutory bodies that exercise administrative power.

Applying these criteria, An Bord Pleanála (the Planning Board) is a useful example of an administrative agency. Established by the Local Government (Planning and Development) Act 1976, An Bord Pleanála was assigned a number of powers that had previously been exercised by the Minister for Local Government. In particular, the 1976 Act removed the Minister's appellate power in respect of local authority decisions to grant or refuse planning permission. This succeeded in removing very sensitive administrative decisions from direct political control. In the following 40 years, An Bord Pleanála has been given more decision-making powers reflecting both the expansion of planning control and a political preference to vest decisions over individual cases in statutory agencies, rather than Government Ministers.[8] The powers of An Bord Pleanála are primarily exercisable against private bodies, although it has acquired a role in relation to development by the State.

Administrative agencies, such as An Bord Pleanála, develop in-house expertise in their areas of regulation. They are independent of central government in their day-to-day decision-making, thereby insulating elected politicians from decisions that directly affect individuals. As administrative agencies take over this role of individual decision-making, the Government's activities have focused more on policy formation. Nevertheless, the functional independence of statutory agencies should not be overstated. Public disputes between Government and administrative agencies are rare.[9] Administrative agencies are typically subject to policy direction from the Government. For instance, in making planning decisions An Bord Pleanála must have regard to the policy of Government or any Government Minister, where relevant. Moreover, the Government typically retains control of the membership of statutory agencies.

[8] The independence of An Bord Pleanála from the Government is enhanced by the fact that it also now applies EU law and, in some contexts, has a protected status in EU law as an independent appeals tribunal. Nevertheless, for the reasons outlined in the main text, it remains appropriate to characterise it as an administrative agency.

[9] One example is *Sweetman v An Bord Pleanála* [2009] IEHC 599, in which An Bord Pleanála and the Minister for the Environment disagreed on the interpretation to be given to a European Directive and, as a result, whether An Bord Pleanála was correct to authorise the construction of a motorway. The issue was ultimately resolved by a reference to the Court of Justice of the European Union. Case C-285/11 *Sweetman v An Bord Pleanála*.

For instance, the Chairperson of An Bord Pleanála is appointed by the Government from a shortlist of candidates selected by an independent committee. The other members of the Board are appointed by the Government Minister with responsibility for planning. The Government may remove the chairperson for stated misbehaviour or if her removal appears necessary to the Government for the effective performance by the Board of its functions. Administrative agencies depend on statutory appropriations of funds which, as we shall see below, must be approved by the Government (although this is also the case in respect of the accountability institutions that we shall consider in chapter seven).

Administrative power is pervasive in Irish society. It is more directly relevant to citizens' day-to-day lives than the matters of high constitutional politics subject to executive power. The entitlements of citizens are more likely to be determined by an administrator exercising discretionary power, whether a planning official or social welfare officer, than by a judge exercising judicial power. Administrative power cannot be subsumed within the conceptual categories of legislative, judicial or executive power. As such, we need to expand our conception of governance in Ireland beyond the tripartite separation of powers. At the same time, we should not overstate the independence of the agencies that exercise administrative power.[10] Administrative agencies are best viewed as semi-detached organs of government. They are subject to general direction and control by the Government but are largely independent in their day-to-day decision-making, occasionally but rarely leading them into a position of conflict with the Government. Finally, the diversity of administrative agencies means that there is no unitary administration that could compete with the unitary Government or even Oireachtas. For all these reasons, it remains fair to say that the Government leads the public administration while not being in complete control of all its activities. It is through this leadership of public administration alongside its typical control of the legislative process and its constitutionally secure executive power that the Government governs the State.

Before considering how the Government operates, brief reference should be made to the police service, An Garda Síochána. This is a national organisation that also fulfils a security service function. An Garda Síochána is headed by a Commissioner, appointed by the Government and answerable to the Minister for Justice for meeting

---

[10] For a more radical reconception of the State to take account of administrative power, see E Carolan, *The New Separation of Powers: A Theory for the Modern State* (Oxford, Oxford University Press, 2009).

Government priorities and performance targets.[11] In addition to this political accountability, the independent Garda Síochána Ombudsman Commission can investigate complaints of police misconduct while the Garda Síochána Inspectorate seeks to ensure best practice in policing methods. In 2015, following a political controversy, the Oireachtas established the Policing Authority of Ireland to oversee the performance of an Garda Síochána. This proliferation of accountability bodies partially stems from an ongoing political controversy about the treatment of Garda whistleblowers, which has contributed to the resignation of two Garda Commissioners, two Ministers for Justice and one Taoiseach in four years.

IV. THE OPERATION OF GOVERNMENT

As discussed in chapter three, Article 28.4 requires that the Government meet and act as a collective authority and further guarantees the confidentiality of Cabinet discussions, subject to certain narrow exceptions. Beyond this, the Constitution does not specify how the Government should function, in marked contrast to the detailed specification of rules for the passage of legislation. The Government is led by the Taoiseach who exercises a number of formal and informal responsibilities.[12] Having nominated Government Ministers for appointment by the President, the Taoiseach co-ordinates the work of Government, initiates policy development and encourages other Members of the Government to do likewise. Through chairing cabinet meetings, deciding on the objectives and membership of Cabinet sub-committees, holding the power to sack Government Ministers and (almost always) being leader of the political party with greater electoral support than any other component of the Government, the Taoiseach holds powers and influence to ensure that her will is followed. The Department of the Taoiseach supports the Taoiseach in these tasks and more generally in relation to her constitutional functions and international engagement. The Department also provides the Government Secretariat, which is responsible for Cabinet matters. The Department is small compared with other Government Departments with specific remits, but this is

[11] Garda Síochána Act 2005.
[12] See generally E O'Malley, 'The Apex of Government: Cabinet and Taoiseach in Operation' in E O'Malley and M MacCarthaigh (eds), *Governing Ireland: From Cabinet Government to Delegated Governance* (Dublin, Institute of Public Administration, 2012).

usually the case for Prime Ministers' offices. With 179 civil service staff in 2012, it compares reasonably with other similarly sized countries.[13] The Department of the Taoiseach has a number of policy divisions that allow the Taoiseach either to take the lead in some policy areas or at least be properly supported to engage in policy development alongside other Departments.

The Cabinet Handbook provides non-binding guidelines for the operation of Cabinet government.[14] Cabinet meetings are generally held once a week, although there are fewer over holiday periods and more at times of crisis. The Cabinet has a main agenda, finalised the previous Friday, and a supplementary agenda, finalised the evening before the meeting. If a Government Minister wishes for an item to be discussed at a cabinet meeting, she must provide it to the Government Secretariat in advance. Any Minister with a functional interest in an area covered by the Memorandum must be consulted prior to it being brought to Cabinet. If the promoting Minister does not accept the views of the other Minister, she must reference and address them in the Memorandum. Where the proposal relates to a policy issue (as distinct from a Government appointment, for instance), the promoting Minister must consult with the Departments of the Taoiseach and Finance, as well as the Department of any Party Leader in Government. If the proposals involve any substantive constitutional or legal dimension, the Department of the Attorney General must be consulted. However, if legal advice is required, this must be obtained prior to the circulation of the memorandum for observations. The normal time period for other Departments to provide observations is two weeks, but this may be longer for complex issues. To avoid wasting time at Government, there is an obligation on Ministers and Departments with different views to resolve their differences as far as possible before the memo is brought to Government. If differences emerge after the circulation of a memorandum, the Secretary General to the Government must be informed at once with a view to consulting the Taoiseach.

Eamon Gilmore, former Labour Party Leader and Tánaiste from 2011 to 2014, has described how each party would respond to the cabinet agenda, illustrating the dynamics of cabinet government.[15] His political advisers would quickly identify any issues of particular

---

[13] ibid 45.

[14] https://www.taoiseach.gov.ie/eng/Publications/Publications_Archive/Publications_2007/CABINET_HANDBOOK2007.pdf.

[15] E Gilmore, *Inside the Room: the Untold Story of Ireland's Crisis Coalition* (Kildare, Merrion Press, 2016) 262–3.

contention, exploring them over the weekend before the political advisers of both parties met on the Monday. Gilmore would give his steer to his own advisers on how each issue should be addressed; the advisers would then attempt to resolve any disputes with their Fine Gael counterparts before a meeting of the Labour Ministers at 9.30am on Tuesday morning. The Labour Ministers would identify any issues on which they would not agree; Gilmore would then raise these issues with the Taoiseach, Enda Kenny, without any advisers or civil servants present. These informal negotiations between the two political parties were as important as the formal business of Cabinet.

The Taoiseach has discretion to allow matters be brought to Cabinet more urgently. The Handbook provides that sometimes, for reasons of urgency or confidentiality, matters may be required to be raised orally. In these circumstances, Ministers must give prior notice to the Taoiseach, the Tánaiste, any other Party Leader in Government, any other Minister concerned, and the Government Secretariat. This again recognises the special dynamics of coalition government.

One of the most significant powers of Government, as we shall see in chapter eight, is to nominate judges for appointment by the President. The Handbook specifically requires memoranda envisaging Presidential Action or appointments by the President or Government to be brought to Cabinet. Even where a particular Minister (rather than the Government as a whole) is responsible for making an appointment, she should mention the matter at Cabinet at least two weeks in advance in order to allow other Ministers to make recommendations. This latter requirement illustrates two important features of governance. First, even where a Minister is exercising a statutory administrative power (rather than a constitutional executive power), the matter is opened up for consultation with other Ministers. Secondly, as we saw in the previous section, this power of appointment is one of the ways in which the Government controls the public administration. It is unsurprising, therefore, that appointments are specifically mentioned in the Cabinet Handbook.

The Handbook provides detailed guidelines on the format of memoranda brought to Government. They should be related to issues of strategy and policy, clearly indicating the decision that the Government is being requested to make. Any memorandum seeking approval for legislation involving changes to the regulatory framework must be accompanied by a regulatory impact analysis (RIA). If an RIA is not required, every memorandum must indicate the impact of the proposal for North-South (Ireland-Northern Ireland) and East-West (Ireland-UK) relations, employment, gender equality, persons experiencing or at risk of poverty or social exclusion, people with disabilities, industry costs, the cost to the exchequer, and rural communities. These dimensions reflect issues of political sensitivity or perceived importance. O'Malley argues that it is the Taoiseach's role as chairperson of cabinet that allows her to control the Government, by choosing the venue for a decision, its timing and information supplied, as well as the right to determine if a consensus has been established.[16] He cites an example of the Government in 1993 approving a tax amnesty at the instigation of Taoiseach Albert Reynolds, despite the apparent opposition of the Minister for Finance (Bertie Ahern), the Attorney General, the Revenue Commissioners, the junior coalition party (Labour party) and 13 out of 15 Government Ministers. If this assessment of the political opposition to the measure is correct (and O'Malley notes that there are contested accounts), it illustrates the ability of the Taoiseach to secure Government approval for measures that are not widely supported within the Government. Ahern claims that he opposed the measure but that he was not supported by the Labour Party Ministers who remained silent.[17] Reynolds claims that Ahern supported the measure in Cabinet.[18] Neither Ahern nor Reynolds appears concerned to have breached cabinet confidentiality in his memoirs.

Much of the work of Government is addressed through Cabinet Committees, which typically consist of relevant Government Ministers alongside senior Civil Servants and the Heads of Government Agencies. The number of committees varies as different Taoisigh take different views on their appropriate functions, relative to the responsibility of Cabinet itself. Taoiseach Leo Varadkar in 2017 reduced the number of Cabinet Committees to six, addressing the Economy, Social Policy and Public Services, the EU (including Brexit), Infrastructure, Health, and National Security.[19] Following a Government crisis in November 2017, which required the resignation of the Justice Minister (and Tánaiste) over how she handled ongoing complaints from a whistleblower in an Garda Síochána (the police service), the Taoiseach announced that he would establish a further Cabinet Committee on Justice Affairs.[20]

---

[16] O'Malley (n 12) 50.

[17] B Ahern, *The Autobiography* (London, Arrow Books, 2010) 153.

[18] A Reynolds, *My Autobiography* (London, Transworld Ireland, 2009) 227.

[19] https://www.taoiseach.gov.ie/eng/Taoiseach_and_Government/Cabinet_Committees/ Cabinet_Committees_of_the_31st_Government.html. The national security committee is not mentioned on the Government website but Taoiseach Leo Varadkar has, somewhat controversially, tweeted a picture of it meeting: 'Could Leo Varadkar have breached Irish national security by posting this tweet?' *The Sunday Independent*, 12 November 2017.

[20] 'Mini-reshuffle: Simon Coveney appointed Tánaiste, Humphreys moved to business portfolio' *The Irish Independent*, 30 November 2017.

V. DYNAMICS WITHIN THE GOVERNMENT

The reality of Cabinet Government does not conform to the constitutional model of a unitary actor directing the governance of the State. The elected members of the Government may have different priorities from those held by the permanent civil service. The elected members themselves will have different political and personal agendas. This is particularly acute as between different political parties in a coalition government but also applies as between different members of the same political party. The relationship between the leaders of the different political parties is essential for the Government to function at all. Taoiseach Albert Reynolds allowed two coalition governments to collapse. The Fianna Fáil – Progressive Democrats Government of 1989–1992 collapsed one year after Reynolds became leader of Fianna Fáil and Taoiseach. He and the leader of the Progressive Democrats, Dessie O'Malley, traded allegations against each other at the Beef Tribunal, culminating with Reynolds accusing O'Malley of dishonesty in his evidence to the Tribunal.[21] Following the general election, Fianna Fáil formed a coalition with the Labour Party. This coalition collapsed after two years, ostensibly over the appointment of Attorney General Harry Whelehan as President of the High Court, an incident we will explore in chapter eight. However, this was the manifestation of a deeper deterioration in relationships. In his autobiography, Reynolds reports that the Labour Party was looking for the right excuse to leave the Government.[22] In his account of the same events, Bertie Ahern (then Fianna Fáil Minister for Finance) recounts that Reynolds had written a letter to Dick Spring, leader of the Labour Party, largely in block capitals; Ahern acerbically comments that this was not the sign of a relationship that was going to last.[23] In contrast, Ahern proved a more adept manager of coalition relationships, his two coalitions with the Progressive Democrats lasting the full legislative term. The subsequent Fianna Fáil – Green Party coalition collapsed during the financial crisis, but it is questionable whether any Government could have survived those events.

The policy agenda of coalition governments unsurprisingly depends on negotiations between the parties and their respective strengths. The Fine Gael – Labour coalition of 2011–2016 was required to make significant improvements to the public finances. They agreed the savings

---

[21] Reynolds (n 18) 169–71.
[22] ibid 378.
[23] Ahern (n 17) 154.

would be achieved through a 2:1 ratio of spending cuts to tax increases, reflecting the preferences of each party and the fact that Fine Gael had twice as many seats as the Labour Party.[24] A further dynamic of coalition governments is the tendency of the smaller party to do badly out of the arrangement. The Progressive Democrats ceased to exist after their period in Government ended in 2007. The Green Party lost all their seats in 2011. The Labour Party went from 37 seats in 2011 to seven seats in 2016. O'Malley has shown that between 1927 and 2010 large government parties lost on average 5 per cent of their seats at the next general election, whereas small government parties lost on average 19 per cent of their seats.[25] Knowledge of this trend affects the actions of both parties while in Government, leading the smaller party to emphasise what it has achieved for its own base, in turn irritating the other party. One example of this is the way in which Eamon Gilmore, Labour Leader and Minister for Foreign Affairs, announced the closure of Ireland's Embassy to the Vatican in 2012.[26]

Political differences also exist within political parties. The Taoiseach's power to appoint Ministers is a significant source of control, but it also opens the way for political resentment. When Albert Reynolds was elected Taoiseach in 1991, he took 15 minutes to sack eight Government Ministers. When two Ministers queried his decision, he simply told them that it was nothing personal; they had 'just backed the wrong horse'.[27] He knew there would be political fallout. As noted in chapter three, the leader of each party in a coalition government chooses the Ministers of her own party, the Taoiseach performing the formal role of nominating the Minister to the President for appointment. At the formation of the Labour – Fine Gael Government of 2011–2016, members of the Labour Party met the party leader, Eamon Gilmore, and were given 60 seconds to accept the Ministerial position offered before moving into another room to await a meeting with the Taoiseach.[28] Gilmore offered the deputy party leader, Joan Burton, the Ministry for Social Protection, rather than the finance-related ministry that she had shadowed in opposition. She accepted the position but their relationship has been characterised as a constant and personal war. Leahy describes how Burton in 2013 sought

[24] P Leahy, *The Price of Power: Inside Ireland's Crisis Coalition* (Dublin, Penguin Ireland, 2013) 141–2.

[25] E O'Malley, 'Punch bags for heavyweights? Minor parties in Irish government' (2010) 25 *Irish Political Studies* 539.

[26] ibid 161.

[27] Reynolds (n 18) 153.

[28] Leahy (n 24) 103.

to distance herself from the unpopular aspects of government policy without ever going so far as to provoke outright conflict. Gilmore and Burton were in effect political rivals.[29] Gilmore resigned as Labour leader in 2014, following a poor showing in the local and European Parliament elections. He was replaced by Burton, but this did not arrest the slide in public support for the Labour Party.

In these ways, although the Government remains by far the most powerful constitutional actor, its power is diminished by inevitable internal differences and rivalries. The policy preferences of one group are countered by the preferences of another group. The political power of one actor is undermined by the political power of a rival. Although the Government must act as a collective authority, its power is undermined by the simple reality that it is not a unitary actor. The Cabinet remains important as the body that formally makes Government decisions. However, Cabinet members are far from equal. In an era of coalitions, Government is dominated by the leaders of the two political parties and the Department of Finance. These are the key relationships of political and economic power. At different times, the relationship between these actors has been more or less formalised, but it is always the cornerstone of the Government.

VI. FINANCIAL GOVERNANCE

The constitutional pre-eminence of the Government is at its strongest in respect of financial matters. In most other matters, the Government's control of the legislative process depends on the contingent (but highly likely) fact that the Government will hold a majority in the Dáil, combined with the fact that the Seanad has no ultimate power to insist on legislative amendments. However, in the financial context, the Government and Dáil are accorded specific responsibilities. The Government therefore retains control in respect of financial matters that applies even if the Government does not have a majority in the Dáil. Although the Government must secure support for its own financial measures in the Dáil (a potential problem for a minority government), it can block financial measures proposed by Opposition Parties, even if a majority of the Dáil supports those financial measures. This ensures that one entity, the Government, holds responsibility for all the financial

---

[29] ibid 265–71.

commitments of the State. Although the Cabinet acts as a collective authority, the Minister for Finance is generally believed to be the most powerful Government position, apart from that of Taoiseach.[30] It is the only ministerial role to be expressly mentioned in the Constitution, Article 28 specifying that the Minister for Finance must be a member of the Dáil. This again emphasises the importance of the Dáil vis-à-vis the Seanad in financial matters.

The Department of Finance is the most powerful of all Government Departments. For much of the history of the State, it has arguably been more powerful than the Department of the Taoiseach. This power lessened somewhat during the 1990s and 2000s, when there was more money to spend and the Department of the Taoiseach led a system of social partnership in which many fiscal and spending measures were agreed with representatives of trades unions and employers. However, this process withered in the late 2000s, restoring the primacy of Finance.[31] Between 2011 and 2017, the functions of the Department of Finance were split into two, a Department of Public Expenditure and Reform taking on responsibility for the reduction of the public sector wage Bill. This division of responsibility provided ministerial jobs of equal importance for both parties in the 2011–2016 coalition government,[32] although it continued into the minority administration elected after the 2016 general election. Taoiseach Leo Varadkar re-merged the two Departments after his election in June 2017, significantly enhancing the power of the Minister for Finance.

The domination of Cabinet by Finance has been particularly apparent at moments of financial crisis. In 1993, the Minister for Finance, Bertie Ahern, decided that it was necessary to devalue the currency in order to preserve its place in the European Exchange Rate Mechanism and protect against speculative attacks.[33] He consulted with Taoiseach Albert Reynolds and Tánaiste Dick Spring, leader of the Labour Party. They deferred to Ahern's assessment but there was no question of consulting with the rest of the Cabinet. At the depths of the financial crisis in 2010, Minister for Finance Brian Lenihan denied to fellow Ministers that he was negotiating a financial bailout of the State. The rest of the Cabinet only discovered what was underway when the

---

[30] See J Considine and T Reidy, 'The Department of Finance' in O'Malley and MacCarthaigh (eds) (n 12) 88.
[31] Leahy (n 24) 91.
[32] ibid 107–8.
[33] Ahern (n 17) 143.

Governor of the Central Bank confirmed the negotiations in a radio interview.[34] In 2013 Minister for Finance Michael Noonan was involved in lengthy negotiations with the European Central Bank in relation to the promissory notes that Ireland had to repay for the bailout of banks, leading to the Irish Bank Resolution Corporation Bill considered in chapter five. He refused to brief the Cabinet on the negotiations, on the basis that there would then be leaks making it impossible to conclude the negotiations successfully.[35]

This domination by Finance is also apparent in budgetary processes. Spending negotiations are generally conducted on a bilateral basis between Finance and the other Departments. In 2013, again partly as a reaction against leaks during previous budget negotiations, the Cabinet as a whole was only briefed on the full budget less than a week before it was delivered, its role being characterised as a rubber stamp for decisions made by the Economic Management Committee (EMC).[36] The EMC consisted of the two party leaders and the two ministers for finance. This ensured that there was equal representation of both parties in Government, unlike the Cabinet where Fine Gael Ministers outnumbered Labour Ministers by two to one.[37] Its meetings also included relevant government officials, depending on what issues were being addressed. It arguably supplanted the role of Cabinet, thereby becoming resented by the 11 other members of Government who were not on the EMC. Its non-continuation in the Government elected in 2016 does not reflect a reinvigoration of Cabinet but rather that there is only one political party in Government and a number of non-party TDs who have no finance-related responsibility.

Article 11 of the Constitution provides that all revenues of the State from whatever source form one fund, subject to such exception as may be provided by law. A legal basis is required for all appropriations from this fund. Article 28.4.4° requires that the Government prepare estimates of the receipts and expenditure for the State for each financial year, and must present them to the Dáil for consideration – colloquially referred to as the Budget. The Budget is prepared by the Minister for Finance but approved by the Government collectively. Article 17.1.1° of the Constitution provides that the Dáil shall consider the Estimates as soon as possible after their presentation. Article 17.1.2° provides that, unless

[34] Leahy (n 24) 50.
[35] ibid 217–8.
[36] ibid 162, 191, 200.
[37] Gilmore (n 15) 83.

otherwise provided by law, the legislation required to give effect to the Financial Resolutions of each year shall be enacted within that year. This provides constitutional recognition, and implicitly a justification, for a practice authorised by the Provisional Collection of Taxes Act 1927. In order to address the risk that people might take advantage of the notification of a budget measure before it was enacted into law, section 2 of the 1927 Act provides that certain financial resolutions passed by the Dáil shall have statutory effect as if they were contained in an Act of the Oireachtas.[38] The resolutions may introduce a new tax, increase, reduce, vary or abolish an existing permanent tax, or continue a temporary tax. The resolution ceases to have statutory effect if not subsequently contained in a Finance Act.

The financial measures contained in the Budget are activated in different pieces of legislation. The Finance Act gives effect to the taxation measures contained in the Budget. The Appropriations Act gives effect to the expenditure measures contained in the Budget, by allocating a sum of money to Government Departments and other public services. For instance, the Appropriations Act 2016 allows the appropriation of (approximately) €1 million for the Secret Service, €4 million for the salaries and expenses of the Office of the President, €391 million for pensions under the Superannuation Acts 1834–2004, €11 billion for the Department of Social Protection and €13.5 billion for the Department of Health. The Central Fund (Permanent Provisions) Act 1965 allows the Minister for Finance to pay out each year, before the enactment of the Appropriations Act for that year, four fifths of the amount appropriated the previous year. The Oireachtas must enact the annual Appropriations Act within the year, in order to give final legal effect to resolutions appropriating expenditure during the year.

We noted in chapter five that Money Bills are treated to a different legislative process from other Bills. There is no pretence that the Seanad can amend Money Bills. The Seanad has only 21 days to consider the legislation, may not even formally reject the legislation and can propose only 'recommendations' for the consideration of the Dáil. Article 22 provides a broad definition of a Money Bill, covering taxation, debt financing and appropriation. The President, following consultation with the Council of State, may establish a Committee of Privileges chaired by a Supreme Court judge to determine whether a Bill is a Money Bill. This provision has never been exercised. These provisions ensure the primacy

---

[38] Were it not for the reference in Article 17.1.2°, it is arguable that this would amount to an unconstitutional delegation of legislative power to the Dáil. See ch 5.

of the Dáil over the Seanad in financial matters, reflecting both the democratic mandate of the Dáil and the desirability of unitary control of finances. The Dáil's control of public finances is further enhanced by the fact that the President is precluded from referring Money Bills to the Supreme Court under Article 26.

Article 17.2 enhances the unitary control of finances by providing that no public moneys can be appropriated unless the purpose of the appropriation shall have been recommended to the Dáil by a message from the Government signed by the Taoiseach. Where the Government is supported by a majority in the Dáil, this provision plays relatively little role. However, it is an important safeguard of financial control and responsibility where the Government has no majority in the Dáil as is currently the case. Different majorities could coalesce around different spending proposals, without any one politically accountable actor having responsibility for the solvency of the common fund. Article 17.2 does not protect the country from a profligate Government but it does facilitate political accountability for profligacy. At the same time, Article 17.2 provides a convenient mechanism for a minority Government to stymie opposition legislation. The former Clerk of the Dáil claimed that the minority Government formed after the 2016 general election refused to provide this recommendation for Opposition legislation not because of real concerns over financial expenditure but rather to delay legislation, perhaps while the Government prepared its own.[39] Dáil Standing Order 179 implements Article 17.2 but provides no procedure for determining whether a Bill or proposed amendment comes within the scope of Article 17.2 or Standing Order 179.

In May 2012, the people amended the Constitution to allow Ireland ratify and give effect to the Treaty on Stability, Coordination and Governance in the Economic and Monetary Union. The Fiscal Responsibility Act 2012 imposes a weak substantive obligation on the Government to endeavour to secure compliance with European rules on public debt and budgetary deficits. The Act also imposes a strong procedural obligation on the Government to prepare a plan and lay it before the Dáil either where the Government considers that there may be

---

[39] K Coughlan, 'Government relying on little known rule to block Bills' *The Irish Times* 26 June 2017. One campaign group has alleged that the Government delayed a Bill that would protect workers from exploitation on the ground that it would increase the workload of the Workplace Relations Commission, and therefore required an appropriation. See https://dunnesworkers.com/2017/10/06/government-plays-cynical-game-with-dunnes-workers-livelihoods/ (visited 7 October 2017).

a deviation from those rules or where the Government receives a warning from the European Commission. It is highly unusual for the Oireachtas to enact legislation constraining the Government's freedom of action in the financial sphere. As a result, there are few ready precedents to assist in establishing who might be in a position to enforce the obligations under the Act. Based on the courts' existing approach to fiscal matters, it seems unlikely that the courts would allow the judicial enforcement of the substantive obligations in the Act. The courts have insisted that high levels of judicial deference are appropriate in respect of all taxation and spending matters.[40] However, in the unlikely event that the Government failed to respond to a warning from the Commission, the courts might allow judicial enforcement.

VII. LOCAL GOVERNMENT

Local government has marginal constitutional significance. Article 28A was inserted into the Constitution in 1999 in order to provide constitutional recognition for the role of local government 'in providing a forum for the democratic representation of local communities, in exercising and performing at local level powers and functions conferred by law and in promoting by its initiatives the interests of such communities'. There must be directly elected local authorities, with elections being held at least every five years, by a franchise consisting of at least those entitled to vote in elections for the Dáil. Provided these requirements are observed, local government may be regulated in any way by the Oireachtas. Local government essentially consists of 31 administrative agencies, called 'local authorities', created by statute and exercising the powers conferred by statute in limited geographic areas. Local government has a democratic legitimacy not held by other administrative agencies but this should not be overstated. Local authorities consist of both elected members and a non-elected executive branch. The executive branch holds far greater powers and is not meaningfully accountable to the elected members.

The relative unimportance of local government can be perceived in a number of ways. First, turnout at local elections is considerably lower than for general elections to the Dáil. The Oireachtas Library and Research Service estimates the turnout at the 2007 and 2011 general

---

[40] *MhicMhathúna v Ireland* [1995] 1 IR 484.

elections as 72 per cent and 73 per cent of the voting age population.[41] It estimates the turnout for local elections of 2009 and 2014, which coincided with elections to the European Parliament, at 58 per cent and 52 per cent respectively. Local elections function largely as a poll on the popularity of the parties in central Government rather than as an election of a local government. For instance, following the performance of the Labour Party in the local elections of 2014, the leader of the party concluded that he had no option but to resign.[42]

Secondly, the legislative powers of local government, although exercised by the elected members, are severely limited. The Local Government Act 2001 authorises local authorities to make bye-laws for or in relation to the use, operation, protection, regulation or management of any land, services, or any other matter provided by or under the control or management of the local authority, whether within or without its functional area or in relation to any connected matter. This power is exercised by the elected members of the local authority. However, several important limits are imposed on this power. Bye-laws cannot be made for any purpose that is addressed by another statute. The Minister for Local Government may prescribe matters or classes of matters in respect of which local authorities cannot make bye-laws. The Minister for Local Government may revoke or nullify any bye-law that she considers to be objectionable.

Thirdly, local government is heavily dependent on central government for finance. Local authorities used to levy rates on all properties in their functional area, but this power was limited to commercial properties in 1977. During the financial crisis, the Finance (Local Property Tax) Act 2012 was introduced. This establishes a nationwide local property tax, set at a national rate and collected by the national Revenue Commissioners. However, individual local authorities may vary the rate upwards or downwards by 15 per cent. The Minister for Finance pays the money raised into the Local Government Fund, which also consists of money received from motor tax and a general Exchequer contribution. Each local authority effectively retains 80 per cent of the tax raised in its area. However, the Government can redirect the remaining 20 per cent to compensate local authorities with a lower tax base. Because of this and because the rate is set by central Government, the local property tax does not significantly enhance the autonomy of local authorities.

[41] 'Election Turnout in Ireland: measurement, trends and policy implications' available at https://www.oireachtas.ie/parliament/media/housesoftheoireachtas/libraryresearch/lrsnotes/Election_Turnout_FINAL_28_Jan2016_180434.pdf visited 3 February 2018.
[42] Gilmore (n 15) ch 14.

Local authorities also receive other payments from the Local Government Fund, determined by central Government, and in return for the provision of services.

Fourthly, although a wide range of administrative powers, in areas such as planning, fire safety and water pollution, are conferred on local authorities, these are mostly exercised by the executive branch of the local authority rather than the elected members. In the planning context, for example, local authorities are usually the first instance decision-maker on planning applications. In the environmental context, many waste activities that carry a lower risk of environmental pollution are regulated by local authorities. However, a number of powers remain vested in the elected members. One of the most significant functions of the elected members is the power to make a development plan for the local area, designed to guide development decisions over a six-year period.

Ultimately, local government cannot be characterised as a competing focus of government power. Rather, it is another aspect of public administration, exercising day-to-day independence but with limited powers and subject to central Government control. The system of government in Ireland remains highly centralised.

VIII. SEMI-STATE COMPANIES AND PRIVATISATION

Many services in Ireland are provided by what are known as semi-State companies. These can be either corporations established by statute or corporations incorporated in the normal manner under the Companies Acts, but with a Government Minister holding all the shares (or a majority of the shares). Statutory corporations are not directly subject to the general provisions of the Companies Acts, although their parent statutes often reflect those more general provisions. For example, public transport in Ireland is provided by three companies incorporated under the Companies Acts, Dublin Bus, Bus Éireann and Iarnród Éireann (Irish Rail), each of which is a wholly owned subsidiary of Córas Iompair Éireann, a statutory corporation. Semi-State companies generally operate in a commercial or semi-commercial environment. They have greater freedom from Government direction than do statutory agencies, but they are subject to control by the Government, as the ultimate owner.

A number of semi-State companies have been sold into private ownership and required to compete with other private companies. Typically, the Government reserves its policy role, establishes a statutory agency as regulator and then allows private entities to compete. For instance, in the context of electricity, the Electricity Supply Board was a semi-State company that held a monopoly on the generation, distribution and sale of electricity. The Electricity Regulation Act 1999 established the Commission for Energy Regulation as a statutory agency with the power to issue licences for the generation and supply of electricity. The Minister for Communications, Climate Action and the Environment retains policy responsibility for the sector.

IX. CONCLUSION

In this chapter, we have further explored how the Government effects the governance of the State. Although the Government holds important executive powers under the Constitution, much of its power derives from its control of the legislative process and its consequent ability to shape and lead public administration. The result is a sprawling but more-or-less unified governance apparatus, directed and coordinated (to varying degrees) by the Government. At the outermost edges, a number of semi-State companies have been privatised. This moves them beyond direct control although they tend to operate in a heavily regulated environment. The Government exercises slightly attenuated control over statutory administrative agencies, through setting policy objectives, appointing members and controlling budgets. The Government directly controls the civil service that staffs the Government Departments, as considered in chapter three. All of this is given political direction by the Cabinet, which generally acts collectively, not only in its exercise of executive powers but also in its leadership of public administration and its decisions on how to control the legislative process in the Oireachtas.

Of course, the Cabinet cannot control all aspects of the apparatus of governance all the time. Even within a hierarchical organisation such as the core civil service, it would not be possible for a Government Minister to control all activities of officials, nor might this be desirable. When dealing with statutory agencies, the opportunities for divergence from Government preferences increase. Disagreements and rivalries within the Cabinet, particularly in the case of coalition governments, reduces the Government's ability to act as a unitary actor, thereby diminishing its domination of the political scene. Notwithstanding all these caveats, however, it remains the case that the Government exercises considerable control of all aspects of governance.

FURTHER READING

Eoin Carolan, *The New Separation of Powers: A Theory for the Modern State* (Oxford, Oxford University Press, 2009)

Conor Casey, 'Under-explored Corners: Inherent Executive Power in the Irish Constitution' (2017) 40 *Dublin University Law Journal* 1

David Gwynn Morgan, *The Separation of Powers in the Irish Constitution* (Dublin, Round Hall Sweet & Maxwell, 1997)

Eoin O'Malley and Muiris MacCarthaigh, *Governing Ireland: From Cabinet Government to Delegated Governance* (Dublin, Institute of Public Administration, 2012)

7

Political Constraints on the Government

Tribunals of Inquiry and Commissions of Investigation – Oireachtas Committees – Accountability in the Dáil – Financial Accountability – Accountability Institutions

I. INTRODUCTION

THE PREVIOUS CHAPTERS have illustrated the extent to which power is concentrated in the Government. One political grouping or coalition will typically hold executive power, control the legislative process and lead the public administration. Differences within the Government diminish its domination of the constitutional landscape, but it remains by far the most powerful political actor. The Irish constitutional order does not provide for competing centres of power that must collaborate with one another in order to implement political projects. However, there are institutions and processes through which the Government can be held to account and its decisions contested. In this chapter, we shall consider ways in which the Government is subject to political accountability and contestation.

The key dynamic that underpins political constraint is the constitutional requirement of general elections. We saw in chapter three how the electoral system means that there are virtually no safe seats. Backbench TDs and Government Ministers alike hold vulnerable positions and therefore are highly sensitive to political pressure. Accountability mechanisms focus political and public pressure in a way that constrains the power of the Government. In this chapter, we shall consider these political constraints under four headings. First, the fundamental but flawed contribution of tribunals of inquiry and commissions of investigation to political accountability will be discussed. Secondly, an alternative mode of investigation, that carried out by parliamentary committees, is assessed. Heavily constrained by judicial interpretation of the Constitution, these committees are as likely to be used by the Government to target its political opponents as to inquire into the activities of the current Government. Nevertheless, they potentially provide an important forum in which to hold Government and public administration accountable. Thirdly, the other accountability mechanisms of the Oireachtas are considered. Given the Government's typical control of the Dáil, it is highly unlikely that the Dáil will exercise its full constitutional powers to hold the Government to account. However, the very attempt of Opposition TDs to use those formal processes, even if doomed to failure, can focus public attention on a political issue, increasing political pressure on the Government. Fourthly, the constitutional mechanisms for financial accountability, mirroring financial governance as a discrete dimension of governmental activity, are considered. Finally, we shall consider the proliferation of statutory agencies that function as sites of contestation of governmental and administrative power, providing an additional protection against maladministration and breaches of fundamental rights. Most important of these is the Ombudsman, established in 1980, but several other agencies have been established in the past 20 years.

The prevalence of these political constraints has increased over the last 25 years, largely as an attempt to ascertain and respond to perceived corruption and malpractice. Tribunals of inquiry explored extensive political corruption in relation to land zoning and connections between national politicians and big business.[1] It was established that former Taoiseach Charles Haughey had received nearly £10 million in donations from businessmen, suggesting deep-seated political corruption. This context explains the increasingly strict approach to political funding, explored in chapter three, as well as the development of accountability institutions, the enhancement of Dáil procedures, and the exploration of different approaches to public inquiries.

II. TRIBUNALS OF INQUIRY AND COMMISSIONS OF INVESTIGATION

Tribunals of inquiry have emerged in Ireland as one of the principal means of seeking non-legal accountability for alleged public maladministration or wrongdoing. Their legislative basis lies in the Tribunal of Inquiries (Evidence) Act 1921, which was carried over into Irish law after independence. Although tribunals of inquiry have been used to explore

---

[1] EA Byrne, *Political Corruption in Ireland 1922–2010: A Crooked Harp?* (Manchester, Manchester University Press, 2012) chs 4 and 5.

policy issues, their main focus in recent decades has been to explore allegations of public maladministration and political corruption. Since the 1990s, tribunals have investigated the infection of haemophiliacs with HIV and hepatitis C from contaminated blood products provided by the Blood Transfusion Services Board, allegations of corruption in the planning process, allegations of police corruption, and allegations of financial payments by a prominent businessman to leading politicians. Tribunals of inquiry are generally established by the Government pursuant to resolutions passed by the Houses of the Oireachtas. The standard practice has been to appoint judges to chair tribunals of inquiry, although this is not a legal requirement.

In *Goodman International v Hamilton (No 1)*, the Supreme Court upheld the constitutionality of tribunals of inquiry.[2] The Government had appointed Mr Liam Hamilton, then President of the High Court, to chair a tribunal of inquiry into alleged illegal activities, fraud and malpractice in the beef processing industry. Goodman International challenged the constitutionality of the tribunal on the basis that it amounted to an exercise of a judicial function and the trial of a criminal charge without the procedural safeguards guaranteed by Article 38 of the Constitution. The Supreme Court rejected these arguments on the basis that the tribunal was inquisitorial in nature; it did not have the power to make any determination of legal rights or liabilities. Because its findings had no legal effect, they did not amount to the exercise of judicial power, let alone such power in a criminal context. This judgment identifies the compromise at the heart of accountability through tribunals of inquiry. The fact that tribunals of inquiry make no legal determinations allows an inquisitorial approach to the establishment of facts. This makes it easier for tribunals of inquiry to get to the truth of a matter. On the other hand, the absence of legal determination means precisely that: findings of a tribunal are – of themselves – of no force and effect. This diminishes their accountability function: accountability is only in the court of public opinion, albeit now informed by the findings of the tribunal.

Although a witness to a tribunal is not at risk of any legal consequence, there is the potential of damage to her reputation. This might occur in two ways. First, the tribunal's report might reach a negative conclusion about an individual, for instance that she had been engaged in corrupt practices. Secondly, even before the final report, another witness at a tribunal might make an allegation that impugned the individual's reputation or the individual might be questioned in a way that

---

[2] *Goodman International v Hamilton (No 1)* [1992] 2 IR 542.

impugned her reputation. Given that Article 40.3.2° of the Constitution protects citizens' good name rights, the courts have identified a number of procedural protections for those who are witnesses at a tribunal or whose activities are otherwise being considered by a tribunal. These originally emerged in the context of a hearing of the Dáil Public Accounts Committee but have come to apply to public inquiries more generally.

In *re Haughey*, the Supreme Court established that persons appearing before committees of inquiry had certain procedural rights.[3] Arising out of the arms crisis in 1970 (see chapter two), Mr Padraic Haughey was scheduled to appear before the Public Accounts Committee. Ó Dálaigh CJ held that Mr Haughey's position was analogous to a party to legal proceedings rather than a witness. His reputation was directly impugned by other evidence tendered to the Committee. As a result, the Court held that Mr Haughey should be: (a) furnished with a copy of the evidence which reflected on his good name; (b) allowed to cross-examine, by counsel, his accuser or accusers; (c) allowed to give rebutting evidence; and (d) permitted to address, again by counsel, the Committee in his own defence.[4] This approach has subsequently been applied to tribunals of inquiry.

Although the Supreme Court established in *Goodman* that tribunals of inquiry were not courts, tribunals have increasingly looked and acted like courts. Chaired by judges, and with the right to legal representation encouraging the proliferation of lawyers, it is scarcely surprising that tribunals adopted court-like procedures, slowing down their work and rendering them more expensive. Furthermore, this may have contributed to a situation in which litigation about tribunals was commonplace, creating further delays and expense. The courts have generally rejected challenges to the ways in which tribunals have interpreted their terms of reference.[5] However, the courts have added further procedural protections, for instance, holding that tribunals must disclose any reports received in private on which they intend to rely.[6]

Tribunals attract considerable media interest and can focus public attention on political issues in a way that Governments find difficult to

---

[3] *Re Haughey* [1971] IR 217.
[4] ibid 263.
[5] See *Desmond v Moriarty* [2004] 1 IR 334, *O'Brien v Moriarty (No2)* [2006] 2 IR 415. However, in *Fitzwilton Ltd v Mahon* [2008] 1 IR 712, the Tribunal's decision on its terms of reference was quashed.
[6] See, for instance, *O'Brien v Moriarty* [2005] IEHC 457.

control. In 1997, Taoiseach Bertie Ahern decided to establish a tribunal to inquire into planning corruption in Dublin, following the admission of Foreign Affairs Minister Ray Burke that he had received an unsolicited political donation of £30,000. Ahern later wrote that the issue was not going to go away; only 'something like a tribunal would give a degree of clarity on the matter'.[7] Burke resigned as Minister for Foreign Affairs and as a TD. He was subsequently convicted of tax evasion and found by the tribunal to have accepted corrupt payments. However, the allegations considered by the tribunal led to further allegations, with the tribunal ultimately inquiring into whether Ahern himself had accepted corrupt payments. Ahern vigorously denied the allegations, offering increasingly convoluted accounts of how he had managed his finances during the 1990s. Ultimately, Ahern decided – in his words – that the incessant publicity of the tribunal made it impossible for him to continue as Taoiseach; he resigned in 2008.[8] This was not the only occasion on which a tribunal brought down a Taoiseach. As we saw in chapter six, events at the Beef Tribunal in 1992 led to the collapse of the Fianna Fáil – Progressive Democrats Government.

It is clear from the foregoing that tribunals of inquiry can have profound political consequences. Often established as a result of political pressure, they can channel that pressure into a forensic report that almost inevitably leads to political resignations. However, they are also deeply flawed – a lengthy and costly method of establishing what has occurred. The Moriarty Tribunal to inquire into payments by businessman Ben Dunne to Charles Haughey (former Taoiseach) and Michael Lowry (former Government Minister) took over 13 years. The Flood and Mahon Tribunal to inquire into planning matters took over 15 years. Part of the problems with these tribunals may have been the Oireachtas setting overly broad terms of reference. Nevertheless, during the early 2000s perceived deficiencies with the tribunal of inquiry model led to the establishment of a new form of public inquiry, the commission of investigation.

The Commissions of Investigation Act 2004 allows the Government, having secured the approval of both Houses of the Oireachtas, to establish a commission to investigate any matter that the Government deems to be of public concern. Section 11 of the 2004 Act provides that a commission shall ordinarily conduct its investigation in private.

---

[7] B Ahern, *The Autobiography* (London, Arrow Books, 2010) 201.
[8] ibid 329.

This means that a person's reputation is not at risk during the course of the inquiry, rendering irrelevant the *Haughey* rights believed to slow down tribunals and be overly costly: legal representation and the right to cross-examine. The Act does provide for some procedural protections, however, notably the obligation on the commission to notify other witnesses of evidence that might be relevant to them and to send the draft report to any person who is identified in or identifiable from the report. Ultimately, the Minister causes the report to be published but she must apply to the High Court for directions in relation to the publication of the report if it might prejudice any criminal proceedings. Several commissions of investigation have been initiated since the 2004 Act. Some have focused on policy failures. For instance, during the financial crisis the Government appointed Mr Peter Nyberg, a Finnish economist, as the sole member of a Commission of Investigation into the banking sector.[9] Others have focused on allegations of wrongdoing. For instance, the Government appointed Judge Catherine Murphy to investigate the handling by Church and State authorities of a representative sample of allegations and suspicions of child sexual abuse against clerics operating under the aegis of the Archdiocese of Dublin over the period 1975 to 2004.[10]

Commissions of investigation have generally proved faster and more effective ways of inquiring into matters of public controversy. As such, they are significant additions to the institutions and processes that can contest government power. However, they are unsurprisingly used as fixes for political problems. We have seen how alleged ministerial incompetence or wrongdoing can place political pressure on the Government; in particular, the smaller coalition party may experience pressure to withdraw from Government. The establishment of a commission of investigation may succeed in removing an item from the active political agenda, allowing a government to continue. For instance, in 2015, the Government appointed Mr Justice Cregan to investigate 37 transactions of the Irish Banking Resolution Corporation involving loan write-offs of over €10 million. Mr Justice Cregan's interim report stated that, even if the Commission were provided with additional legal powers to deal with

---

[9] Misjudging Risk: Causes of the Systemic Banking Crisis in Ireland. Available at http://www.bankinginquiry.gov.ie/Documents/Misjuding%20Risk%20-%20Causes%20of%20the%20Systemic%20Banking%20Crisis%20in%20Ireland.pdf.

[10] Report by Commission of Investigation into the Catholic Archdiocese of Dublin. Available at http://www.inis.gov.ie/en/JELR/Pages/PB09000504.

confidentiality and privilege concerns, it could still take several years to complete its investigation.[11] Although the concerns that led to the establishment of that commission have not yet been addressed, they no longer feature actively on the political agenda. By the time the commission issues its final report, it is likely that most of the relevant political actors will have left the scene. While commissions of investigation have become more prevalent than tribunals of inquiry, the latter are still seen as providing for fuller public accountability. Where political pressure is greater, therefore, the Government may be forced to concede a tribunal of inquiry. For instance, while the Government initially decided in 2017 to establish a commission of investigation into the treatment of police whistle-blowers, it subsequently conceded the need to establish a tribunal of inquiry.[12]

III. OIREACHTAS COMMITTEES

The dissatisfaction with tribunals as a means of ensuring public accountability also led to pressure in another direction: the reinvigoration of Oireachtas committees of inquiry. We saw in chapter three how much of the work of the Oireachtas occurs through committees. As well as having an important legislative function, these committees provide a means through which the Opposition can seek to hold the Government to account. In a relatively recent innovation, the Standing Orders of the Dáil provide that the chairmanship of committees in the Dáil shall be allocated according to the d'Hondt system, although it remains the case that a member of a Government party cannot chair the Public Accounts Committee. This ensures that a Government cannot use its majority in the Dáil to secure the chairmanship of all committees, as had previously been the practice (again with the exception of the Public Accounts Committee). Nevertheless, if the Government has a majority in the Dáil, it will typically retain a majority on each Dáil committee.

The powers of parliamentary committees are limited by the judgment of the Supreme Court in *Maguire v Ardagh*.[13] In April 2000, a man had been shot and killed by police officers. The Garda Commissioner

---

[11] 'IBRC inquiry could take several years, says judge' *The Irish Times*, 11 November 2015.
[12] Tánaiste Frances Fitzgerald moving the motion in Dáil Éireann to establish the Disclosures Tribunal. Available at http://oireachtasdebates.oireachtas.ie/debates%20 authoring/debateswebpack.nsf/takes/dail2017021600020.
[13] *Maguire v Ardagh* [2002] 1 IR 385.

prepared a report on the incident which was presented to the Minister for Justice who in turn placed it before the Oireachtas. A joint committee of both Houses proposed that a sub-committee would inquire into the incident. The sub-committee issued directions to a number of persons to attend and give evidence. In a challenge by a number of Gardaí who had been called to give evidence to the sub-committee, the Supreme Court addressed both the power of the Oireachtas to hold investigations at all and the limits that might apply to that power. The only point definitively decided in *Maguire v Ardagh* was that the Oireachtas had no inherent power to conduct inquiries for the purposes of ascertaining the truth about past events in a context that has significant potential to affect the reputations of private citizens. This narrow conclusion left open the possibility that the Oireachtas could legislate to grant a public inquiry power to the Houses of the Oireachtas. However, several statements by members of the Court strongly suggested that such legislation would itself be unconstitutional. For Murray J, the potential of such public inquiries to affect the constitutionally protected reputation rights of individuals was so great that the Oireachtas could only possess such a power if it were explicitly or implicitly granted by the Constitution, which in his view it had not been. Other judges were less explicit on this point, although several echoed the concerns of Murray J. Hardiman J, in particular, was sceptical about the appropriateness of making a fact-finding inquiry part of the political process. On balance, the import of the majority judgments was that it would be unconstitutional for the Oireachtas to legislate to grant its Houses a public inquiry power that would allow findings of fact to be made that affected the reputations of private individuals. At the very least, there was a significant risk that any such legislation would be held unconstitutional by the courts.

Underlying the judgment of the Supreme Court in *Maguire v Ardagh* was a view that allegations of individual wrong-doing were not appropriate for resolution by elected politicians. Although the Court emphasised in *Goodman* that tribunals are not courts, there still seems to be a judicial view that these sorts of issues should be resolved in a legalistic way through procedures not all that dissimilar (albeit not quite so onerous) as apply in court proceedings. This can be seen as the flipside of the attitude of strong judicial deference to the policy-making and legislative function of the Oireachtas, which we shall explore in chapter nine. In limiting the scope of the Oireachtas to conduct inquiries and in requiring strong procedural protection at such committees and tribunals of inquiry, the courts arguably limited the scope for public accountability for maladministration and corruption.

Several years after the judgment in *Maguire*, the Houses of the Oireachtas approved a Bill to amend the Constitution. This Bill would have amended Article 15 of the Constitution to grant each House the power to conduct an inquiry into any matter stated by the House concerned to be of general public importance. It would have clarified that the House could inquire into the conduct of any person (whether or not a member of either House) and make findings in respect of the conduct of that person. Finally, it would have provided that it was for each House to determine, with due regard to the principles of fair procedures, the appropriate balance between the rights of persons and the public interest for the purposes of ensuring an effective inquiry. This final provision addressed the concern, considered above, that the courts had afforded overly generous procedural protections to people whose actions were considered by parliamentary committees and other inquiries.

The people rejected the proposed constitutional amendment, by the narrow majority of 53 per cent to 47 per cent. Leahy comments that the Government had intended to use the new provisions for 'a lengthy and detailed embarrassment of Fianna Fáil's stewardship of economic and banking matters'.[14] The people's rejection of the referendum proposal suggests that they were not as concerned as politicians and public commentators at the extent to which the courts had constrained the power of parliamentary inquiry. An academic report conducted after the Referendum suggested that there was general popular support for the Oireachtas to be able to hold inquiries into matters of general public interest, but the proposal failed because some thought it gave politicians too much power and others were not provided with sufficient information to allow them to make a decision.[15] This ultimately prompted the Oireachtas to enact new legislation for inquiries that must operate within the confines of the *Maguire* decision. The Houses of the Oireachtas (Inquiries, Privileges and Procedures) Act 2013 prescribes the sorts of inquiries that may be undertaken by the Houses of the Oireachtas. The Act first allows committees to conduct a 'record-and-report' inquiry, ie an inquiry that makes no findings of fact in relation to disputed matters. This ensures that an Oireachtas inquiry does not cast aspersions on the

---

[14] P Leahy, *The Price of Power: Inside Ireland's Crisis Coalition* (Dublin, Penguin Ireland, 2013) 167.

[15] See M Marsh, J Suiter and T Reidy, 'Report on Reasons behind Voter Behaviour in the Oireachtas Inquiry Referendum 2011' (2012). Available at per.gov.ie/wp-content/uploads/OIReferendum-Report-Final-2003-corrected.pdf (visited 3 January 2018).

reputation of non-members of the Oireachtas. This is the closest to a general public inquiry power, but is clearly limited in nature.

Apart from this, the Act allows committees to conduct inquiries that are related to an explicit constitutional function. The Oireachtas has a function in relation to the removal of other constitutional office holders (the President, judges of the superior courts, and the Comptroller and Auditor General). The Oireachtas exercises an equivalent role under statute in relation to a number of statutory officers, such as the Ombudsman. The Act allows committees to conduct inquiries into the removal or proposed removal of all such office-holders. Each House may conduct an inquiry into the behaviour of a member of the House. This reflects Article 15.10 of the Constitution, which provides that each House shall make its own rules and standing orders, with power to attach penalties for their infringement. The Act allows a Dáil committee to conduct an inquiry into any matter relevant to holding the Government to account under Article 28.4 of the Constitution, or a person who is constitutionally or legally liable to being held to account by the Dáil, such as the Secretary General of a Government Department.

A committee cannot proceed with an inquiry unless the terms of reference for the inquiry have been approved by the House as a whole. The House must specify which type of inquiry is involved and whether the committee will have the power to compel witnesses and documents. Under Dáil Standing Orders, the Committee on Procedures and Privileges considers all requests from other committees to conduct an inquiry and prepares a report for the Dáil, which may include draft terms of reference. Although such committees of inquiry are often presented as a means of enhancing public accountability, this is open to question. The fact that a majority of the relevant House controls the establishment of an inquiry means that, at least under normal political conditions, inquiries will not be established against the wishes of the Government. To date, the only public accountability inquiry established pursuant to the 2013 Act was the Joint Committee of Inquiry into the Banking Crisis. It adopted a 'record-and-report' format. Established in November 2014, this inquiry allowed the then Fine Gael – Labour Government to ensure public scrutiny of one of the most significant failings that occurred under the previous Fianna Fáil-led Government that had lost office in February 2011. The Committee published its report on 27 January 2016, just one week before then Taoiseach Enda Kenny advised the President to dissolve the Dáil, triggering a general election in which Fine Gael's principal competitor was Fianna Fáil. The banking crisis assuredly merited public scrutiny and the committee operated in good faith, producing a worthy report, within the limited parameters of what was permitted by the 2013 Act. Nevertheless, this illustrates that committees of inquiry do not necessarily amount to public contestation and accountability for the Government of the day, but can as easily serve the interests of that Government in undermining its political opponents. They can serve to enhance the power of Government as much as to contest the exercise of that power.

IV. ACCOUNTABILITY IN THE DÁIL

The formal accountability of the Government to the Dáil provides a significant political constraint on government power, even where the Government is supported by a stable majority in the Dáil. It manifests itself principally through two parliamentary procedures: the requirement of the Government to answer questions raised by TDs and the possibility for opposition parties to table motions of no-confidence in the Government or individual Government Ministers. Article 28.10 of the Constitution provides that the Taoiseach shall resign from office upon ceasing to retain the support of a majority in the Dáil unless, on the advice of the Taoiseach, the President dissolves the Dáil and causes a general election. As we saw in chapter four, however, the President retains a discretion to refuse a dissolution to a Taoiseach who has lost the support of a majority in the Dáil. Motions of no confidence allow the Opposition to threaten a situation in which the Taoiseach could be said to have lost the support of a majority in the Dáil, likely precipitating a general election. Where a Government holds a secure majority in the Dáil, a motion of no confidence is unlikely to be successful unless one party leaves a coalition government or the Taoiseach loses the support of her own backbenchers. However, such motions provide an effective means for opposition parties to focus political and public attention on claimed government misconduct or incompetence. This can diminish public confidence in the Government, thereby improving the chances of opposition parties at the next general election.

As well as tabling a motion of no-confidence in the Taoiseach or Government, an opposition party can table a motion of no-confidence in a particular Government Minister. Such a motion again usually serves the purpose of increasing public pressure on the Taoiseach to request the resignation of the Minister concerned. If a motion of no-confidence in an individual Minister is passed, that Minister would have to resign. Given the collective responsibility of the Government, however, this also has implications for the Government as a whole. A Taoiseach would ordinarily pre-empt such an outcome by requesting the resignation of the Government Minister or advising the President to dissolve the Dáil. If the Dáil passes a motion of no-confidence in a particular Minister, the Government would likely be thought to have lost the support of a majority in the Dáil unless the Dáil subsequently passed a motion of confidence in the Government. The dynamics between the parties in a coalition government will affect how no-confidence motions are treated. Generally speaking, each party's Ministers are seen to be that party's problem, at least up to a certain point. For instance in the Fine Gael – Labour coalition of 2011–2016, the Labour Party had no confidence and trust in the Fine Gael Minister for Health, James Reilly. But if they had supported opposition motions of no-confidence in the Minister, they would have brought down the Government. This was a price they were not prepared to pay. For the same reasons, they voted against opposition motions of no-confidence in the Fine Gael Minister for Justice, Alan Shatter.[16] Other political dynamics can serve to protect Ministers from motions of no-confidence. Then Fine Gael Minister for Transport, Leo Varadkar, commented on television that some of Reilly's decisions 'looked like stroke politics'.[17] Leahy observes that Varadkar had good reason, however, not to apply too much pressure: he feared being appointed Minister for Health himself in Reilly's place. (Ultimately Reilly was moved to another position in a cabinet reshuffle in 2014. Varadkar was appointed Minister for Health, a posting that he survived[18]). The opposition motion of no-confidence did serve the purpose, however, of flushing out the Labour Junior Minister for Health, Roisin Shortall. She had serious difficulties with Reilly. Although she voted against the motion of no-confidence, she shortly afterwards resigned as a Junior Minister and from the Labour party itself.[19]

Although such motions are potent weapons for the opposition parties, they can only be used sparingly. There are risks for an opposition party in misjudging the public mood by pushing for the resignation of a Minister or Government in which the public have not lost confidence. Furthermore, as outlined in chapter three, opposition parties have very

---

[16] See generally Leahy (n 14) 272–4. Shatter was ultimately required to resign in 2014.
[17] ibid 186.
[18] Brian Cowen, former Minister for Health and later Taoiseach, is reported to have described the Department of Health as 'Angola', due to the unexploded landmines ready to detonate at any moment. 'Onward from "Angola"', *The Irish Times* 21 March 2002.
[19] Leahy (n 14) 181–8.

limited access to time in the Dáil. They must decide whether it is a good use of that limited time to table a motion of no confidence. Ordinarily, TDs are not permitted to re-open discussion on a question already discussed during the previous six months, reducing the possibility for repeated motions of no confidence.

Parliamentary questions provide a further way in which the Government can be held to account. The Standing Orders of the Dáil allow questions to be asked with a view to an oral or written reply. Recent decades have seen a significant increase in the number of parliamentary questions, from 5,000 per-year in the mid 1970s to 12,000 per year in the mid 1990s and 35,000 per year by the late 2000s.[20] Over the same period, there has (unsurprisingly) been a significant shift in the ratio of oral and written answers. In the mid-1970s, nearly all questions were answered orally. As the number of questions increased, the number of oral answers decreased both as a proportion and in real terms. Although administrative agencies are formally accountable to the Government rather than the Dáil, in practice many administrative agencies will provide information to their Government Minister to allow that Minister answer questions in the Dáil.[21] However, the division of responsibility between Government and administrative agencies can make political accountability more difficult.

All questions are examined by the Ceann Comhairle (Chairperson of the Dáil) to determine if they are in accordance with the Standing Orders.[22] They must relate to public affairs or matters of administration for which the Minister is officially responsible. However, Ministers may transfer the question to another Minister who is more appropriate to answer the question. The Ceann Comhairle has no role in ensuring that questions are answered or the quality of answers, unless the Minister has breached the rules of parliamentary debate in her response.

For many purposes, a written answer is as good as an oral answer. The TD may well have asked the question on behalf of a constituent who simply wanted an answer. Even if the question is of broader political significance, a TD may publicise the contents of a written answer. Answers to written questions may help to put a matter on the political agenda, leading to further political pressure. Nevertheless, given

---

[20] M MacCarthaigh, 'Parliamentary Scrutiny of Departments and Agencies' in M MacCarthaigh and M Manning eds, *The Houses of the Oireachtas: Parliament in Ireland* (Dublin, Institute of Public Administration, 2010) 370.

[21] ibid.

[22] R Caffrey, 'Procedure in the Dáil' in MacCarthaigh and Manning (eds) (n 20) 265–6.

that media attention enhances political accountability, oral replies are more politically desirable for the opposition. However, they also use up the scarce time of the Dáil. Accordingly, the Standing Orders prescribe in considerable detail the method for putting oral questions to the Government. The Taoiseach must be available for leaders' questions two days each week, for a period of no more than 21 minutes. The Ceann Comhairle may, in her discretion, permit a question from each leader of an opposition political party or a technical group within the Dáil. The Standing Order allows for a question, reply, follow-up question and follow-up reply (taking up to seven minutes in total) so it would not be possible, given the current number of parties and technical groups, for each leader to ask a question on each occasion. The innovation of leaders' questions was formalised in 2001 to ensure that opposition parties could press the Government on topical issues, without the need to provide notice in advance.[23]

In addition to these sessions for leaders' questions, there are further opportunities to ask questions of the Taoiseach and all other Government Ministers. Standing Order 36 requires that these must relate to public affairs connected with the Department or to matters of administration for which that Minister is officially responsible. Considerably more time is allocated to questions for the Taoiseach (two periods of up to 45 minutes each week) than to questions for any other member of the Government (three hours and thirty minutes each week allocated on a rota between the 14 other members of the Government – three Ministers each week). This again reflects the importance of the Taoiseach as the public face of the government, as well as the political imperative for opposition parties to be able visibly to hold the Taoiseach to account.

V. FINANCIAL ACCOUNTABILITY

As seen in chapter six, financial governance is where the control of the Government is strongest. The Constitution ensures that there is one entity with clear political responsibility for the State's finances, but it provides no guarantee that the Government must act responsibly. Holding the Government to account for its financial decision-making is a task that falls to a number of institutions and processes. Article 33 of the Constitution establishes a Comptroller and Auditor General 'to control

---

[23] ibid 263–4.

on behalf of the State all disbursements and to audit all accounts of money administered by or under the authority of the Oireachtas.' The Comptroller is appointed by the President on the nomination of Dáil Éireann, reflecting the Dáil's primacy in financial matters and the fact that the Comptroller is to hold the Government to account. The Comptroller reports to the Dáil and may only be removed from office by a resolution of both Houses of the Oireachtas. This form of accountability, the same as that afforded to superior court judges (see chapter eight), emphasises the independence of the position.

The principal Act governing the Comptroller and Auditor General is the Comptroller and Auditor General (Amendment) Act 1993. The Comptroller is required to audit the appropriation accounts for the previous financial year, prepared by all Government Departments. In addition, the Comptroller has an audit function in relation to other public agencies. Section 9 of the 1993 Act allows the Comptroller to carry out targeted examinations to determine whether public resources have been acquired, used or disposed of economically and efficiently. Each year, the Comptroller must prepare a report for the Dáil including details on such matters as she considers appropriate arising from the examinations and audits carried out during the year. The Dáil Committee of Public Accounts, which is always chaired by an opposition TD,[24] considers the report of the Comptroller. Secretaries General of Government Departments, who are the 'accounting officers' for their Departments, are obliged to give evidence to the Committee about the financial affairs of their Departments. However, in giving this evidence, they are precluded from questioning or expressing any opinion on the merits of any policy of the Government or a Government Minister.[25]

Although these procedures ensure some scrutiny of government expenditure, they did not anticipate the complete collapse in State finances that occurred in 2008-2010. An independent peer review report in 2008 was critical of the Comptroller's limited ability to engage in value-for-money audits of public expenditure.[26] Even such audits, however, might not have addressed the broader threat to financial stability. Following the bailout of Ireland in 2010 by the Troika of the European Commission, European Central Bank and International Monetary Fund, the Oireachtas established the Irish Fiscal Advisory Council to

---

[24] Dáil Standing Order 93.
[25] Comptroller and Auditor General (Amendment) Act 1993, s 19(2).
[26] Available at http://www.audgen.gov.ie/viewdoc.asp?DocID=1156&CatID=23&UserLang=EN (visited 3 January 2017).

monitor whether the State was meeting the budgetary rules required by the Fiscal Compact Treaty (see chapter six). If the Government does not accept the Fiscal Council's assessment of these matters, the Minister for Finance must lay before the Dáil within two months a statement of the Government's reasons for not accepting it. The Fiscal Council also has a broader duty to provide an assessment of official forecasts and whether, in relation to each Budget, the fiscal stance is conducive to 'prudent economic and budgetary management'. The Government is under no obligation to respond to these assessments, but they do create a further political constraint on the Government's power.

VI. ACCOUNTABILITY INSTITUTIONS

As seen in chapter six, the Government leads the public administration. We shall see in chapter eight how the courts have developed detailed rules of administrative law to check the powers of administrative agencies. However, there is a further type of statutory agency, which we may characterise as an accountability institution, that does not exercise administrative power but rather constrains administrative power. The distinction between administrative agencies and accountability institutions is not entirely clear cut. There are several dimensions of differentiation, which may cut across one another. The first dimension of differentiation is the manner in which officers are appointed and removed. The solemnity of appointment by the President, even on nomination of the Government, emphasises that an institution is not simply an agent of the Government. Requiring resolutions of the Oireachtas for removal of office protects the independence of the institution. Given that the Houses of the Oireachtas, unlike the Government, do not have unitary policy objectives, it is likely that the officers of these bodies would only be removed for fundamental failures of performance, rather than failure to follow any preferred policy objective. The second dimension is whether the remit is one of rights protection or policy implementation. The third dimension is whether the body is protected by and charged with implementing EU law as distinct from purely domestic law. Bodies with an EU law dimension are much less subject to direction by the Government. The fourth dimension is whether the body primarily controls private actors or public bodies.

The paradigm of an administrative agency is a body whose officers are appointed and removed by the Government, that is charged with implementing Government policy, primarily directed towards private actors and not protected by EU law. The paradigm of an accountability institution has officers appointed by the President on the nomination of the Oireachtas, and removed by resolution of the Oireachtas. Its role is the enforcement of rights, it is protected by EU law, and it is primarily directed against public bodies. Between these two paradigms, the characterisation is more contestable. In this section, we shall consider a number of bodies that approach the paradigm of an accountability institution.

Established in 1980, the role of the Ombudsman is to ensure a level of competence and fairness in public administration. She is appointed by the President upon the nomination of both Houses of the Oireachtas and can only be removed from office by a resolution of both Houses of the Oireachtas. The Ombudsman may institute an investigation of her own initiative or where there has been a complaint. Investigations by the Ombudsman focus on questions such as whether the administrative action was taken as a result of negligence or carelessness or was based on an undesirable administrative practice, as well as issues that could ground a legal complaint, such as lack of proper authority or consideration of relevant grounds.[27] The Ombudsman may, having completed her investigation, recommend to the organisation that the action be reconsidered or that specified measures be taken to remedy, mitigate or alter the adverse effect of the action. She may also make a recommendation in general terms to a class of agencies.[28] If she considers that the measures taken by the organisation were not satisfactory, she may include a special report on the case to be included in her annual report to the Houses of the Oireachtas. Thus, there is ultimately no power of enforcement on the part of the Ombudsman to compel the organisations under her remit to comply with her recommendations. Nevertheless, there would likely be considerable political pressure to comply with the recommendations. The Government itself would suffer adverse political consequences for failing to ensure that an agency under its ultimate control respected the decisions of the Ombudsman.

For many years, the Ombudsman was arguably the sole instance of an accountability institution in the Irish constitutional order. However, since the late 1990s this general model has been applied in other areas. Since 2002, there has been an Ombudsman for Children, who is appointed and removed in the same way as the Ombudsman, responsible generally for

---

[27] Ombudsman (Amendment) Act 2012, s 6.
[28] Ombudsman (Amendment) Act 2012, s 9.

promoting the rights and welfare of children.[29] She exercises an investi-
gatory and oversight power in respect of how State administration treats
children.

There are also several statutory bodies charged with protecting
individual rights. The Irish Human Rights and Equality Commission
(IHREC) has broad responsibilities in relation to protecting human
rights and equality, including functions in relation to enforcement and
compliance as well as policy and culture.[30] This body merges the functions of the Equality Authority, originally established in 1998, and the
Human Rights Commission, originally established in 2000. Members of
the Commission are appointed by the President on the nomination of the
Government, supported by resolutions in both Houses of the Oireachtas.
The Government may remove a member of the Commission only on
specified grounds and following a resolution passed by both Houses
of the Oireachtas. The IHREC has stronger enforcement powers than
the Ombudsman. It may issue Equality and Human Rights Compliance
Notices, including against public bodies. Such notices can be appealed to
the Labour Court (if they concern employment issues) or to the District
Court (if they concern the provision of services). Failure to comply with
such a notice is a criminal offence.

The Freedom of Information Acts 1997–2014, established an
Information Commissioner responsible for deciding on applications
under those Acts. She is appointed and subject to removal in the same
way as the Ombudsman. In practice, the same person has always held the
office of Ombudsman and the office of the Information Commissioner.
The Information Commissioner can direct public bodies subject to
the Acts to make documents available to those who have sought them.
Decisions of the Information Commissioner can be appealed to the
High Court. Although the Information Commissioner does not identify
wrongdoing on the part of public bodies, access to information is an
important step in allowing the contestation of government power. There
are other institutions responsible for the enforcement of important rights
to which Ireland is committed as a matter of international or European
law. For instance, the Data Protection Commissioner is responsible for

[29] See generally the Ombudsman for Children Act 2002. Although the Ombudsman
model has been applied to other topics, not all positions can be treated as accountability
institutions. For instance, the Pensions and Financial Services Ombudsman is appointed
and dismissed by the Minister for Finance and primarily has oversight over private bodies.
[30] Irish Human Rights and Equality Commission Act 2014.

enforcing the data protection legislation. Although she may be removed by the Government and has a remit that applies to private actors as much as public bodies, her role in the enforcement of EU law means that she functions as an accountability institution at least in some respects.

VII. CONCLUSION

In chapters three, five and six, we saw how the constitutional order concentrates significant power in the Government. Once elected, the Government holds the constitutional executive power, typically controls the legislative process and leads the public administration. In this chapter, we have considered several political constraints on the Government's power. These constraints largely depend for their force on the desire of Government TDs to secure re-election. Questions in the Dáil, the findings of tribunals, the decisions of accountability institutions, all focus public attention on allegations of Government incompetence or corruption. The Government will seek to avoid such controversies or to diffuse them, on occasion by the resignation of some of its members. All of this constrains the way in which the Government can exercise its political power. Although significant, these constraints should not be overstated. More fundamental are the legal constraints imposed by the courts, the core of Ireland's bipartite separation of powers.

FURTHER READING

Elaine A Byrne, *Political Corruption in Ireland 1922–2010: A Crooked Harp?* (Manchester, Manchester University Press, 2012)

Richard Caffrey, 'Procedure in the Dáil' in MacCarthaigh and Manning eds, *The Houses of the Oireachtas: Parliament in Ireland* (Dublin, Institute of Public Administration, 2010)

Muiris MacCarthaigh, 'Parliamentary Scrutiny of Departments and Agencies' in Muiris MacCarthaigh and Maurice Manning eds, *The Houses of the Oireachtas: Parliament in Ireland* (Dublin, Institute of Public Administration, 2010) 358

John O'Dowd, 'Knowing how Way Leads on to Way: Some Reflections on the Abbeylara Decision' (2003) 38 *Irish Jurist* 162

8

Courts and the Legal Constraint of the Government

Court Structure – Judicial Control of Legislative, Executive and Administrative Power – Judicial Independence and the Appointments Process – Security of Judicial Tenure – Security of Judicial Remuneration – The Profile of the Judiciary

I. INTRODUCTION

A RECURRING THEME of this book has been how constitutional reality belies the claim of Article 6 to establish a tripartite separation of powers. The Government typically controls the legislative process, exercises executive power and leads the public administration. The desire of the Government to avoid public controversy and be re-elected creates political constraints. Although certain institutions and processes can be used to increase public controversy, these do not amount to a competing organ of constitutional power. The Constitution's fundamental distribution of power is a bipartite one between the Government and the courts, underpinned (as we shall see in chapter ten) by the requirement of a referendum to amend the Constitution. In this chapter, we shall begin by outlining the court structure, with particular attention to the power of the courts to resolve constitutional disputes. We shall then outline the basis of the courts' power to constrain legislative, executive and administrative power. Given the courts' role as the principal constraint on the Government, the level of judicial independence is a crucial consideration. We shall therefore pay particular attention to the institutional features of the court system that allow them to implement these constraints in an independent manner: the appointment process, the removal process, and security of remuneration. Finally, we shall make some observations about the profile of the judiciary, before setting the scene for the detailed consideration of constitutional rights in chapter nine.

II. COURT STRUCTURE

The Constitution provides that justice shall be administered in public in courts established by the law.[1] There is no specialised constitutional court; the ordinary courts deal with constitutional issues. With the exception of Article 26 presidential references,[2] therefore, constitutional issues usually come before the courts at the instigation of individual litigants, either as an incidental issue that arises in the course of another case or in proceedings specifically conceived to challenge the constitutionality of some legislation or administrative decision. Constitutional cases are therefore treated as a subset of all legal cases, rather than something qualitatively different. Three courts have the power to determine constitutional issues: the High Court (a court of first instance), the Supreme Court (the court of final appeal), and an intermediate Court of Appeal, established following a referendum in 2013. Prior to the introduction of the Court of Appeal, there was a general right of appeal from the High Court to the Supreme Court. This could be limited by law although not with respect to constitutional challenges to legislation. As a result, the Supreme Court had a wide and unfocused remit. The introduction of the Court of Appeal may allow the Supreme Court to take a more focused approach to the clarification and development of areas of law, constitutional law in particular. However, it is still too early to judge if this will be the case.

The Constitution also allows for the establishment by legislation of local and limited courts. Detailed legislation distributes cases between the High Court, Circuit Court and District Court, based on their complexity and importance. There is a general right to jury trial, apart from non-minor offences and cases where it may be determined in accordance with such law that the ordinary courts are inadequate to secure the effective administration of justice, and the preservation of public peace and order.[3] Part V of the Offences against the State Act 1939, which can be activated by Government proclamation and annulled by resolution of the Dáil, provides an apparatus for the trial of offences in this Special Criminal Court.[4] The original purpose of the Court was to try subversive offences, but its remit has been extended to organised crime.

---

[1] Art 34.
[2] See ch 4.
[3] Art 38.3.
[4] See generally F Davis, *The Special Criminal Court, 1922–2005* (Dublin, Four Courts Press, 2007).

The number of judges in each Court is determined by law. At present, there are eight members of the Supreme Court, which can sit in divisions of three, five or seven, although at least five judges are required for a presidential reference of a Bill under Article 26 of the Constitution. The Chief Justice decides on the number of judges and assigns judges to cases. The Constitution was amended in 1941 to require that the Court could deliver only one judgment in cases concerning a challenge to the constitutionality of a post-1937 Statute. This requirement was removed by referendum in 2013, except for Article 26 references. The one-judgment rule can sometimes make it more difficult to ascertain the rationale of the Court's decision, an issue we encountered in respect of *Crotty v An Taoiseach* in chapter two.[5] At present, there are 10 Members of the Court of Appeal and 38 High Court judges. Overall, these features of the courts system somewhat reduce the importance of judicial personalities in the development of constitutional law. There is not one panel of judges sparring across an ideological cleavage in case after case. Most judges serve until the retirement age of 70 and therefore cannot time their retirement to coincide with a Government that might appoint a like-minded successor. This helps to depoliticise the appointments process. That said, the ability of the Supreme Court to control its docket and the new possibility for dissenting judgments may see its members take a more self-conscious approach to the shaping of constitutional law.

III. JUDICIAL CONTROL OF LEGISLATIVE, EXECUTIVE AND ADMINISTRATIVE POWER

The Constitution provides that the Oireachtas shall not enact any law that is unconstitutional,[6] and that all laws in force in the Irish Free State in 1937 continued to be of full force and effect unless or until amended by the Oireachtas, subject to the extent to which they were not inconsistent with the Constitution.[7] Separately, the Constitution grants to the courts the power to review the constitutionality of legislation.[8] In *Murphy v Attorney General*, the Supreme Court emphasised that unconstitutional

---

[5] [1987] IR 713.
[6] Art 15.4.
[7] Art 50.
[8] Art 34.3.

laws were ultra vires and void ab initio.[9] The Irish constitutional order therefore functions on the basis of strong-form judicial review, in which courts can displace a legislative judgment, rather than weak-form judicial review, in which the Legislature or Government can reject constitutional rulings by the judiciary.[10]

In the early days of the new Constitution, the courts were required to defend their power of constitutional review against legislative encroachment. As we saw in chapter three, the two largest political parties in the country, Fianna Fáil and Cumann na nGaedhal (later Fine Gael), had both emerged from Sinn Féin in the 1920s; the continuing Sinn Féin was a far smaller party opposed to the constitutional settlement. In 1924, the honorary treasurers of Sinn Féin held a sum of over £8,500 as trustees. Disputes subsequently arose between them as to who was entitled to the money. The plaintiffs, who were members of Sinn Féin, subsequently brought an action against the Attorney General (as representative of the public) seeking a declaration that the money belonged to the Sinn Féin organisation.[11] This was an affront to the other political parties who regarded themselves as the legitimate successors to the Sinn Féin party that had led the struggle for independence and to which the money had been donated. While the action was pending before the High Court, the Oireachtas passed the Sinn Féin Funds Act 1947. Section 10 of that Act provided that all proceedings pending before the High Court in relation to the money should be stayed and that, upon application being made by the Attorney General, the High Court should strike out such proceedings. The Act also provided that the funds should then be distributed in a particular way.

The High Court and the Supreme Court both held the 1947 Act unconstitutional as an interference with the judicial power: the Oireachtas could not intervene to determine the outcome of cases pending before the courts. The Supreme Court also held that the Act was an unconstitutional interference with property rights. Importantly, the Court rejected an argument of the Attorney General that it was exclusively a matter for the Oireachtas to determine whether an interference with property rights was justified. In these two findings, the Court preserved the judicial

---

[9] *Murphy v Attorney General* [1982] IR 237, 309. This statement reflected the constitutional practice up to that point, but required articulation in this case which concerned the retrospective effects of a declaration of unconstitutionality.

[10] For this distinction, see M Tushnet, *Weak Courts, Strong Rights: Judicial Review and Social Welfare Rights in Comparative Constitutional Law* (Princeton, Princeton University Press, 2008) ch 2.

[11] *Buckley v Attorney General* [1950] IR 67.

power and the vitality of the Constitution as a potential check on legislative power. *Buckley* is the foundational case that establishes the bipartite separation of powers: if the courts had not insisted on their authority to determine litigation and to review the constitutionality of legislation, the political power of the Government would not be legally constrained. In chapter nine, we shall consider how the courts have exercised their power to ensure that legislation respects constitutional rights.

The judicial control of executive action has a more complicated basis. The Constitution provides that the executive power of the State shall, subject to the Constitution, be exercised by or on the authority of the Government,[12] suggesting that the Government is constrained by the Constitution in the same way as the Oireachtas. However, unlike legislation, there is no provision granting the courts the power to review the constitutionality of executive action. In *Boland v An Taoiseach*, the Supreme Court addressed this constitutional lacuna. Considering a challenge to a Northern Ireland peace agreement, Fitzgerald CJ observed that the courts had 'no power, either express or implied, to supervise or interfere with the exercise by the Government of its executive functions, unless the circumstances [were] such as to amount to a clear disregard by the Government of the powers and duties conferred on it by the Constitution'.[13] Although this was stated as a negative proposition, it implies that the courts have a power (and perhaps a duty) to intervene where the Government acts in clear disregard of the Constitution, whatever that may mean. The courts have held executive action unconstitutional in a number of cases, although the judicial formula of 'clear disregard' leaves the lingering suspicion that a higher degree of unconstitutionality must be demonstrated in respect of executive action than in respect of legislative action.[14]

As we saw in chapter six, much governance occurs through the exercise of administrative power, led but not fully controlled by the Government. Because administrative powers are created by statute, they are subject to the terms of statute as interpreted by the courts. In addition to requiring that statutory agencies act within the scope of their power (and recall from chapter six that Government Ministers function

---

[12] Art 28.2.

[13] *Boland v An Taoiseach* [1974] IR 338, 362.

[14] In *TD v Minister for Education* [2001] 4 IR 259, the majority of the Supreme Court held that 'clear disregard' implied a conscious and deliberate breach of constitutional rights. This suggestion, however, may simply reflect the general antipathy of the Court to the enforcement of socioeconomic rights rather than to the control of executive power more generally. See discussion in ch 9.

as statutory agencies when exercising statutory powers), the courts hold statutory agencies to a number of mostly procedural standards. They must consider all relevant matters and may not consider any irrelevant matters. Statutory agencies must, within certain limits, respect legitimate expectations. They must not fetter their discretion in advance. They must respect the rules of natural justice, *audi alteram partem* and *nemo iudex in causa sua*. Indeed, the Irish courts have elevated these rules of natural justice to constitutional status, ensuring that legislation cannot interfere with these rights.[15] In addition to these procedural constraints, the courts have also imposed the substantive constraint that administrative decisions cannot be irrational. These legal constraints significantly control the way in which statutory agencies exercise their power, attempting to ensure some basic level of fairness at the point at which State power meets individual lives. Different issues arise when we consider whether statutory agencies must respect constitutional rights. One of the oddities of Irish constitutional law, however, is the way in which the question of constitutional constraints on administrative bodies has largely been approached as an issue of administrative law, rather than constitutional law. We shall explore this curious dynamic towards the end of chapter nine.

IV. JUDICIAL INDEPENDENCE AND THE APPOINTMENTS PROCESS

The ability of the courts to constrain the Government depends on the willingness of judges to act independently. The Constitution provides that all judges shall be independent in the exercise of their judicial functions and subject only to the Constitution and the law.[16] Judges cannot be members of either House of the Oireachtas (a significant change from the House of Lords in the United Kingdom). In this section, we shall consider whether the appointments process facilitates independence. In the following two sections, we will take up two further aspects of judicial independence: security of tenure and security of remuneration.

Judges are appointed by the President, on the nomination of the Government. Such an appointment mechanism could potentially undermine the ability of the courts to act as a check on the Government. However, this has not occurred – for three related reasons. First, the

---

[15] *McDonald v Bord na gCon* [1965] IR 217.
[16] Art 35.2.

Oireachtas has legislated to establish minimum criteria of eligibility for judicial appointment. As a result, all judges have been drawn from the legal profession and may be presumed to have achieved a certain level of legal competence. Secondly, the culture of the legal profession values independence, such that judges could not see themselves as working for the Government. The vast majority of judges would have been engaged in private legal practice (for the most part as self-employed barristers) prior to appointment. Although this in no way guarantees that judges will strongly protect constitutional rights against State power, it does ensure a level of independent mindedness that might not exist if judges had primarily been Government employees prior to appointment. Thirdly, as we saw in chapter three, Governments have all been led by centrist parties. As a result, the ideological stakes of judicial appointments for the Government are (generally) low, diminishing the incentive for Governments to politicise the judiciary. This is reflected in the judgments of the Supreme Court, a study having shown that there is no disagreement on the Supreme Court arising from the fact that judges were nominated by different political parties (Fianna Fáil or Fine Gael).[17] All that said, the system of judicial appointment is far from criticism. It is open to objections of opacity, favouritism and a failure to produce a diverse judiciary.

Only practising lawyers may be appointed as judges. The most significant change over the years has been the gradual extension of eligibility to include solicitors as well as barristers.[18] At present, one must be a practising solicitor or barrister of 10 years standing for appointment to the lower courts, or 12 years standing for appointment to the Superior Courts. Serving judges may be appointed to other courts. These provisions ensure – for good or ill – that the Irish judiciary is composed exclusively of individuals with professional experience in the practice of law. As a result, judges share a common culture with lawyers, particularly senior barristers. A positive aspect of this is a sense of independence from the Government. There are more negative aspects, to which I shall return at the end of this chapter.

The Courts and Courts Officers Act 1995 introduced a Judicial Appointments Advisory Board (JAAB) to suggest judicial nominees to

---

[17] R Elgie, A McAuley and E O'Malley, 'The (not-so-surprising) Non-Partisanship of the Irish Supreme Court' (2018) 33 *Irish Political Studies* 88.

[18] Courts Act 1924, the Courts (Supplemental Provisions) Act 1961, the Courts and Court Officers Act 1995 and the Courts and Court Officers Act 2002. Ireland has a split legal profession: barristers focus on court advocacy; solicitors provide the full range of legal services, but generally do not engage in court advocacy.

the Government. This Act was a response to a political crisis the previous year. A coalition government collapsed when the Fianna Fáil members of the Cabinet nominated the serving Attorney General, Harry Whelehan, for appointment as President of the High Court, against the wishes of the other party in the coalition government, the Labour Party. This reflected a general breakdown in the relationship between the two parties.[19] The JAAB consists of 10 officers, including senior members of the judiciary, legal practitioners and up to three nominees of the Minister for Justice. The JAAB process may have been intended to reduce the level of political involvement in judicial appointments but it has failed to secure that effect for several reasons. First, the JAAB has interpreted its remit to require the recommendation of seven candidates for each judicial position, provided that there are seven qualified candidates. If it were making recommendations in relation to three High Court positions at the same time, therefore, it could recommend up to 21 candidates. While this allows the JAAB to screen out wholly unsuitable candidates, it still leaves the Government with considerable discretion. Secondly, the Government may nominate a practising lawyer outside the JAAB process. Thirdly, the JAAB process does not apply to the promotion of existing judges, which would generally be the case for the most important positions, those on the Supreme Court.

Carroll MacNeill argues as a result that the JAAB process has not meaningfully altered the political approach to judicial appointments.[20] The Government retains significant control. There is no real discussion at Cabinet of proposed nominees; instead, the Cabinet acquiesces in the proposal of the Taoiseach. The most important political actors are the Taoiseach, the Minister for Justice, the Attorney General and, if she is the leader of a second party in a coalition government, the Tánaiste (deputy Prime Minister).[21] As there are no formal processes, the precise balance of influence between these actors seems to depend much on the personalities of those involved, the degree of respect for the Attorney General in question, and the extent to which the Taoiseach of the day takes an interest in court processes and judicial appointments.

In June 2017, the Government published a Judicial Appointments Council Bill that would, if enacted, make significant changes to the

---

[19] R Mac Cormaic, *The Supreme Court* (Dublin, Penguin Ireland, 2016) 302–9.
[20] J Carroll MacNeill, *The Politics of Judicial Selection in Ireland* (Dublin, Round Hall Press, 2016).
[21] ibid 134–7.

appointment process. It extends eligibility for appointment to legal academics who had previously practised as barristers or solicitors. It explicitly makes merit the basis for appointment, but also references the desirable objectives of having equal numbers of male and female judges, as well as a judiciary that reflects the diversity within the population. The 13-member Commission would have a lay majority and chairperson. It would recommend only three names for judicial appointments; the Government would be required to consider the recommended names first; the Government's nomination to the President would indicate whether the nominee was recommended by the Commission.

In a letter to the Government, the Judiciary criticised these proposals on a number of grounds.[22] The main areas of concern for the Judiciary are the lay majority and the low number of judges (in particular the exclusion of the Presidents of the lower courts) on the commission.[23] Judges have previously expressed their view that the principle of merit-based appointment ought not to be qualified with reference to diversity.[24] As has been pointed out by Kenny, however, merit functions as little more than a placeholder for the qualities considered relevant to judging. In Kenny's view, members of the judiciary form an interpretative community whose views about the law are validated as objectively correct when other members of the group reach the same decision. Viewed in this way, limiting judicial appointment to group members erroneously enforces the belief in a meritocracy, since group members effortlessly achieve the standard of knowing what the group already thinks. For Kenny, 'the professional focus in appointments is not a neutral mechanism that objectively selects the best candidates, but a political mechanism that selects those most likely to agree with the prevailing (but contestable and contested) judicial ideology'.[25] At the time of writing,

---

[22] For a detailed account of the judiciary's approach to the proposed legislation, see J Carroll MacNeill, 'Changing the Judicial Selection System in Ireland in 2017' in E Carolan (ed), *Judicial Power in Ireland* (Dublin, Institute of Public Administration, 2018).

[23] 'Senior judges criticise planned reforms to judicial appointments', *The Irish Times* 18 August 2017.

[24] Judicial Appointments Review Committee, Preliminary Submission to to the Department of Justice and Equality's Public Consultation on the Judicial Appointments Process 30 January 2014. Available at <http://www.supremecourt.ie/SupremeCourt/sclibrary3. nsf/(WebFiles)/51E71A71B9961BD680257C70005CCE2D/$FILE/A%20Preliminary%20 Submission%20of%20J.A.R.C.%2030.01.2014.pdf> (visited 26 April 2016).

[25] D Kenny, 'Merit, Diversity and Interpretative Communities: The (Non-Party) Politics of Judicial Appointments and Constitutional Adjudication' in L Cahillane, J Gallen & T Hickey (eds), *Judges, Politics and the Irish Constitution* (Manchester, Manchester University Press, 2017) 141–2.

the Opposition has made many amendments to the Government Bill, leading the Attorney General to comment that the Bill is a 'dog's dinner' and contains many unconstitutional provisions. It remains to be seen whether, and in what form, it will be enacted into law.[26]

Although I argued above that a succession of centrist governments has reduced the ideological stakes of judicial appointments, there is a significant qualification to this. At times, the Government has used its appointments power to influence the direction of the courts. In 1961, the Government nominated Cearbhall Ó Dálaigh as Chief Justice and Brian Walsh as an ordinary member of the Supreme Court. Walsh later stated that Taoiseach Seán Lemass had told both him and Ó Dálaigh that he would like the Irish Supreme Court to become more like the US Supreme Court.[27] If this was Lemass's wish, he had chosen the right men for the job. The following decade was the most activist in the history of the Court, taking a far more interventionist approach to the recognition and enforcement of constitutional rights. In 1972, the Government proposed to nominate Ó Dálaigh as Ireland's first member of the European Court of Justice in Luxembourg. It therefore faced a choice whether to nominate Walsh, by any reckoning the most eminent jurist in the State following Ó Dálaigh's departure, as Chief Justice. In correspondence between the pair, Ó Dálaigh hoped that Walsh would succeed him as Chief Justice but Walsh anticipated (correctly) 'that the administration may also avail of the opportunity so to adjust the leadership and the personnel of the Court to reduce the risk of a continuation of the Court's "initiatives" of the past decade'.[28] The Government instead nominated Billy FitzGerald as Chief Justice. When FitzGerald died a year later, he was replaced by Tom O'Higgins. Neither man, for all his virtues, had the legal stature or adventurist zeal of Walsh. Overlooking Walsh for Chief Justice did not result in an anything like an immediate departure from judicial activism. However, it did confirm the end of the Court's most adventurous period. A more recent watershed moment was 1999–2000, when the Government was able to appoint a Chief Justice and five ordinary members of the Court within a short period. This was followed by a number of cases, analysed in chapter nine, that marked out a much more deferential approach on the part of the Supreme Court.

---

[26] 'Judges Bill is a complete "dog's dinner" claims AG', *The Irish Independent* 24 March 2018.

[27] B Girvin, 'Church, State and Society in Ireland since 1960' (2008) 43 *Éire/Ireland* 74–99.

[28] Mac Cormaic (n 19) 149.

V. SECURITY OF JUDICIAL TENURE

Superior Court judges can only be removed from office for stated misbehaviour or incapacity, upon a resolution passed by both Houses of the Oireachtas.[29] The Taoiseach shall notify the President of such resolutions; the President shall then remove the judge from office. In the history of the State, only two cases of judicial misbehaviour have led to the resignation of judges.[30] The first involved Circuit Court Judge Brian Curtin, who was charged with possession of child pornography. The prosecution case against him collapsed when the trial judge ruled that his computer could not be admitted in evidence, as it had been seized during an unconstitutional search of his dwelling. The Houses of the Oireachtas commenced the process of removing Judge Curtin from office. In *Curtin v Clerk of Dáil Éireann*, the Supreme Court provided some guidance on the process for removing judges from office.[31] Murray CJ held that it was permissible, although not constitutionally required, for the Oireachtas to employ committees to gather evidence. However, the Court did direct that the Oireachtas would have to give separate consideration to the questions of whether there had been misbehaviour and, if so, whether removal from office was appropriate. Judge Curtin resigned after the completion of the court case (and after he had accrued five years' service as a Circuit Court Judge sufficient to earn some pension entitlements).[32]

The other judicial controversy involved alleged misconduct in the judicial role. In 1999, Circuit Court Judge Cyril Kelly directed that a convicted man be released early from prison. It was alleged that Mr Justice O'Flaherty, a Supreme Court judge, had played an improper role in the re-listing of the case and that Judge Kelly had also acted improperly in directing the release. The judges involved denied the allegations. However, Chief Justice Liam Hamilton issued a report that concluded that Judge Kelly's handling of the case had compromised the administration of justice. He also concluded that Mr Justice O'Flaherty had acted in an inappropriate and unwise way, which left his motives and

---

[29] Art 35.4.1°. S 29 of the Courts of Justice Act 1924 extended the same tenure to Circuit Court judges as that enjoyed by Superior Court judges.

[30] We saw above how Harry Whelehan resigned a few days after being appointed President of the High Court in 1994, but this was due to the circumstances of his appointment rather than any issue of judicial misconduct on his part.

[31] [2006] IESC 14.

[32] 'Disgraced judge Curtin will be paid €20,000 pension' *The Irish Independent*, 9 February 2007.

actions open to misinterpretation, and was therefore damaging to the administration of justice. Both judges resigned shortly afterwards, but it is almost certain that the Houses of the Oireachtas would otherwise have taken steps to remove them from office.[33]

The allegations against Judge Curtin, if true, were grossly inconsistent with any judicial position. The concerns raised in respect of Judge Kelly and Mr Justice O'Flaherty were about the reality or impression of special favours within the justice system. Both were appropriate cases in which to consider the removal of a judge from office; neither involved a political sanction against a judge for adopting an unpopular position. The fact that the formal procedure for removal of a judge has only been contemplated in these situations demonstrates that the guaranteed security of tenure is effective. Nevertheless, it is problematic that the only sanction that can be imposed against a judge is the nuclear option of removal from office. There is a real danger that lesser indiscretions will go unaddressed. A committee on judicial conduct and ethics recommended in 2000 that a statutory judicial council be established. In June 2017, the Government introduced a Judicial Council Bill that would establish a Council with lay members but a judicial majority that could consider complaints of judicial misconduct. Ultimately, the Committee could issue advice to the judge concerned, recommend that the judge take a particular course of action, issue an admonishment, or refer the matter to the Minister for Justice to consider removal under Article 35 of the Constitution.

VI. SECURITY OF JUDICIAL REMUNERATION

Apart from security of tenure, the most important guarantee of judicial independence relates to salary security. Judicial concerns over pay have been a running concern since the foundation of the State. In 1932, the Government of the Irish Free State had asked judges to accept a voluntary pay cut. When the judges refused, the Government threatened a constitutional amendment to facilitate a compulsory reduction in pay. This threat was not implemented, however, and Article 35.5 of the new Constitution guaranteed that the salaries of all judges could not be reduced during their period in office. In the early 1950s, Chief Justice Maguire wrote to the Taoiseach to suggest that the judges

[33] Mac Cormaic (n 19) ch 16.

believed that this constitutional provision prohibited income tax being levied on their salaries, even hinting that a judge might take a constitutional case to determine the issue. The Government unsurprisingly rejected the argument. Three years later, the widow of Mr Justice O'Byrne took this case but was ultimately unsuccessful, a 3:2 majority of the Supreme Court (including Maguire) holding against her.[34] The concern over pay resurfaced in the 1960s, with judges pressing for an increase in salaries to take account of inflation. They claimed that the real remuneration of a Supreme Court judge in 1967 was only 53 per cent of what it had been in 1924 due to the limited extent of pay increases granted in the intervening period. It was not until 1971 that the Government agreed to raise judicial salaries in the manner sought by the judiciary.[35]

During the financial crisis that commenced in 2008, a doubt emerged whether a pension levy, which was being imposed on all public sector workers, could also be imposed on judges. Most judges agreed to pay the levy voluntarily. In 2011, however, the Government went further and secured popular approval for an amendment of Article 35.5. Article 35.5 now clarifies that judges are subject to the introduction of taxes, charges and levies that are imposed by law on persons generally or persons belonging to a particular class. More importantly, it also allows for reductions to be made to judicial salaries proportionate to reductions being made to the remuneration of classes of persons also paid out of the public purse. Although it is difficult to contend that judges should have been immune from the general reduction in salaries experienced by public sector workers during the financial crisis, this provision is problematic in that it places reduction of judicial salaries directly within the competence of the Oireachtas.

In November 2011, shortly after the judicial pay referendum, members of the Judiciary established an Association of Judges in Ireland, which they claim represents more than 90 per cent of the members of the judiciary.[36] The Association has a wide range of non-contentious objectives, such as maintaining and promoting the highest standards in the administration of justice and in judicial conduct. The Association also has objectives, however, that open up the potential for conflict with the other organs of government, including a commitment to promote the interests of their members in their professional capacities. In this regard,

---

[34] *O'Byrne v Minister for Finance* [1959] IR 1. See Mac Cormaic (n 19) 364.
[35] Mac Cormaic (n 19) 110.
[36] https://aji.ie/about-us/foundation/ (visited 7 February 2018).

it has made public comment in respect of changes to judicial remuneration. The Association has claimed that the take-home pay of existing judges is 33 per cent less than it was in 2009, while the take-home pay of new judges is 45 per cent less than it was in 2009.[37] This arises from a combination of salary cuts, pension levies, increased pension contributions and increases in general taxation. In a public lecture delivered in February 2016, a Supreme Court judge, Mr Justice Donal O'Donnell, criticised the absence of any body or institution with responsibility for considering the cumulative impact of the changes on the position of the judiciary and the ability to attract motivated and talented candidates for judicial office.[38]

The past decade, therefore, has witnessed a worsening in relationships between the Judiciary and the Government. Political actors have asserted their entitlement to regulate both the appointment process and the terms and conditions of employment as a judge. In particular, the judicial pay referendum demonstrated the political ability of the Government to marshal popular support for proposals that reduce judicial independence. This has destabilised the constitutional balance between the courts and the Government. At the same time, many of the concerns expressed by the Judiciary – particularly on the appointments issue – are overstated and lend support to a caricature of a privileged elite trying to preserve itself.

VII. THE PROFILE OF THE JUDICIARY

The system of judicial appointments unsurprisingly has implications for the profile of the judiciary, limiting it to practising lawyers who are favourable to elected politicians. It seems clear that judges, prior to appointment, are more likely to have political affiliations than the population in general. At the level of the Superior Courts, however, there has been a marked diminution in judges admitting to political affiliations. Comparing a 1969 survey with a 2004 survey, the number of judges denying any political affiliation rose from 12 per cent to 62 per cent; this remains a significantly higher level of political affiliation than in the general population, however.[39] Political connections

---

[37] 'Judges say take home pay has fallen by a third since 2009', *The Irish Times* 17 April 2013.
[38] D O'Donnell, 'Some Reflections on the Independence of the Judiciary in Ireland in 21st Century Europe' (2016) 19 *Trinity College Law Review* 5.
[39] Carroll MacNeill (n 20) 109.

are much more important at the level of the District Court, where local politicians take a strong interest in who is appointed. In terms of Superior Court appointments, personal and professional knowledge of the candidates is considered important; this correlates with political affiliations. Finally, coalition governments tend to make a general arrangement about the distribution of judicial vacancies between supporters of the two parties.[40]

In 2005, 94.6 per cent of judges had been Senior Counsel (the equivalent of Queen's Counsel in the United Kingdom) prior to their first judicial appointment.[41] There has been an increased tendency to promote judges from the Circuit Court to the High Court, although the majority are still appointed to the High Court directly from practice. It is unusual, but not unheard of, for a practitioner to be appointed directly to the Court of Appeal or the Supreme Court. In terms of background, 40 per cent of judges had a lawyer in their family. 79 per cent of judges received their primary degree from University College Dublin. 40 per cent of judges had a primary degree in law; 45 per cent of judges had a primary degree in arts. 72 per cent of judges were first employed as barristers. Most judges were resistant to attempts to identify themselves as belonging to a particular social class or as holding a particular ideological perspective. 30 per cent of judges in the superior courts are now women. As these figures make clear, the Irish judiciary at superior court level is socially homogenous. Whatever about their family background, at the time of appointment, judges are drawn from a small pool of wealthy legal practitioners, most of whom are personally known to one another.

This phenomenon has continuing relevance after appointment. I have argued elsewhere that the Irish judiciary and senior legal practitioners form a close-knit social group in which conventional views about what constitutional law is – often at odds with the explicitly stated law – are seamlessly communicated.[42] Conformity to the beliefs of this group may be taken to be a sensible and practical knowledge of the law. It also provides the context for judicial opposition to diversity as a relevant factor in judicial appointment. This is a key dynamic in the development of Irish constitutional law that will be explored in chapter nine.

---

[40] ibid 137.

[41] J Carroll, 'You Be the Judge, Part I' (2005) 10(5) Bar Review 153; and J Carroll, 'You Be the Judge, Part II' (2005) 10(6) *Bar Review* 182.

[42] O Doyle, 'Conventional Constitutional Law' (2015) 38 *Dublin University Law Journal* 311.

VIII. CONCLUSION

The relationship between the Government and the Judiciary is the fulcrum of the balance of power under the Constitution. The formal constitutional procedures for the appointment and removal of judges could potentially undermine that balance. However, they have (subject to one exception to which I will return below) not been operated in this way. The requirement that judges have considerable experience as practising lawyers reduces the scope for political favouritism. It also arguably allows judges to share an independent-mindedness with the legal profession, itself an important check on Government power. By the same token, the Government has only twice moved towards the removal of judges, both in cases of alleged misconduct which was in no way related to the actions of a judge in holding the Government to account. The issue of judicial remuneration has been a greater source of conflict between the Government and the judiciary. Although it is difficult to argue that judges should not have suffered the same cuts in pay as other public servants during the financial crisis, the judicial pay referendum of 2011 is worrying for two reasons. First, it has left control of judicial pay directly in the hands of the Oireachtas. Secondly, it illustrated the ability of the Government to direct popular opinion and secure constitutional change on an aspect close to the fulcrum of the bipartite separation of powers. This may point to a constitutional fragility of which a future Government could take advantage.

These issues are also relevant to a separate narrative of judicial homogeneity. Considerable advances have been made in increasing the number of women judges. Nevertheless, judges are drawn almost exclusively from a small pool of wealthy former legal practitioners. This creates a culture in which shared understandings and assumptions about the constitutional order, separate from and occasionally in opposition to the constitutional text and the decided case law, can determine the course of constitutional development. We saw three examples of how the Government used its power of appointment to shift this judicial culture: the appointment of Cearbhall Ó Dálaigh as Chief Justice and Brian Walsh to the Supreme Court in the early 1960s; the subsequent non-appointment of Brian Walsh as Chief Justice in the mid-1970s; the appointment of five new Supreme Court judges in 1999–2000. Through these appointments, the Government managed to nudge judicial culture first in a more activist direction and then twice towards a disposition that was less likely to challenge the exercise of Government power. There is nothing improper in this. The Government is a democratically accountable actor that holds the power of judicial appointment for good reason. All judges involved, whether activist or non-activist, exercised their functions in accordance with their understanding of what the Constitution required. Nevertheless, the evolution in constitutional rights, which we shall explore in the next chapter, cannot be understood without attention to these shifts in judicial disposition. Judges' interpretation of constitutional rights and their assessment of interference with those rights, both crucial to the constitutional order, have changed in the past and will likely continue to change in the future.

FURTHER READING

Hilary Biehler, *Judicial Review of Administrative Action: A Comparative Analysis*, 3rd edn (Dublin, Round Hall, 2013)

Jennifer Carroll MacNeill, *The Politics of Judicial Selection in Ireland* (Dublin, Round Hall Press, 2016)

Fergal Davis, *The Special Criminal Court, 1922–2005* (Dublin, Four Courts Press, 2007)

Oran Doyle, 'Conventional Constitutional Law' (2015) 38 *Dublin University Law Journal* 311

Robert Elgie, Adam McAuley and Eoin O'Malley, 'The (not-so-surprising) Non-Partisanship of the Irish Supreme Court' (2018) 33 *Irish Political Studies* 88

Ronan Keane, 'Across the Cherokee Frontier of Irish Constitutional Jurisprudence' in Eoin O'Dell (ed), *Leading Cases of the Twentieth Century* (Dublin, Round Hall Sweet & Maxwell), 2000) 185

David Kenny, 'Merit, Diversity and Interpretative Communities: The (Non-Party) Politics of Judicial Appointments and Constitutional Adjudication' in Laura Cahillane, James Gallen and Tom Hickey (eds), *Judges, Politics and the Irish Constitution* (Manchester, Manchester University Press, 2017)

Ruadhán Mac Cormaic, *The Supreme Court* (Dublin, Penguin Ireland, 2016)

9

Fundamental Rights
and Judicial Power

Competing Intellectual Traditions – Waning of Natural Law
Influences – The Move to Non-intervention – Standards of Review and
Judicial Deference – Administrative Action – Crime – Emergencies and
Exceptions – Influence of the ECHR – Horizontality – Processes of
Rights Litigation

I. INTRODUCTION

A
S WE SAW in chapter eight, the Constitution explicitly empowers
the courts to review the constitutionality of legislation and
has been interpreted to confer a similar power on the courts in
respect of executive action. This establishes the fundamental bipartite
separation of powers between the Government and the courts. The
courts' power to constrain the Government primarily arises as a result of
the fact that they are charged with interpreting the Constitution. While
some constraints derive from structural provisions of the Constitution,
such as the non-delegation doctrine considered in chapter five, the most
important constraints follow from the protection of constitutional
rights. The broad wording of these rights, however, has allowed the
courts to take different approaches at different times, resulting in two
key developments of constitutional law over time.

The first development is an ideological shift. Many (but far from all)
of the fundamental rights provisions in the Constitution reflect religious
influences, specifically Roman Catholic natural law teaching. Through
judicial interpretation, these provisions have largely been reimagined as
generic liberal constitutional rights.[1] The second development is a shift

---

[1] In ch 10, we shall explore how the same ideological shift has manifested itself through
the formal amendment process.

in the constitutional balance of power. The courts effectively determine the scope of their own power through their choices about how to interpret the Constitution. In deciding whether to give restrictive or expansive interpretations to constitutional rights, or whether to be more or less sympathetic to governmental reasons for restricting rights, the courts increase or reduce their own power. While the fundamental separation of powers in the Constitution is a bipartite one between Government and courts, the precise balance of power between the two institutions depends on judicial attitudes to that relationship. These have differed over time and between different subject-areas.

Broadly speaking, the heyday of judicial interventionism occurred between 1965 and 2000. Since 2000, however, the courts have adopted a decidedly non-interventionist attitude to their interpretation and enforcement of constitutional rights. They no longer exercise a power to create new constitutional rights, they have restricted the remedies that exist for breach of constitutional rights, and they exhibit considerable deference when reviewing the acts of legislative, executive and administrative authorities. This has undercut the extent to which the institution of strong form judicial review provides a site of contestation in the Irish constitutional order. This is not to say that the courts never declare legislation unconstitutional. Rather, their interventions and development of constitutional law tend to be more technocratic and incremental, occasionally trammelling the means but rarely proscribing the ends of the elected organs of government. Alongside this chronological story, there is a thematic story. The courts have been interventionist when protecting constitutional rights in the criminal context but wary of socioeconomic rights, even though the latter (such as the right to free primary education) have some textual recognition in the Constitution.

The judicial enforcement of constitutional rights is a significant site of political contestation. It is a domain in which judges – with varying degrees of reference to the constitutional text – compete *both* with the Government *and* among themselves over the standards of justice that Ireland should meet. Unravelling these strands of deference and intervention will form the bulk of this chapter. We shall conclude with a consideration of some miscellaneous issues that touch incidentally on these themes, such as the influence of the European Convention on Human Rights, the courts' attitude to the horizontal applicability of constitutional rights, and the processes that the courts have developed to govern constitutional litigation.

II. CONSTITUTIONAL TEXT: COMPETING
INTELLECTUAL TRADITIONS

The constitutional protection of fundamental rights is principally located in Articles 38 and 40–45 of the Constitution. Article 40 protects broadly liberal democratic rights, such as equality, life, liberty, inviolability of the dwelling as well as freedom of expression, assembly and association. Hogan has argued that 'one would be hard put to find *any* Catholic influences whatever in Article 40'.[2] The constitutional protection of process rights in the criminal context likewise reflects a liberal tradition, although it could not be said to be inconsistent with a natural law tradition either. Article 38 provides that trials shall be in due course of law, as well as a general right to jury trial. Religious freedom and non-discrimination are protected by Article 44 in broadly liberal democratic terms, albeit alongside a statement that the homage of public worship is due to Almighty God.

A natural law ethos, however, is very much to the fore in the constitutional provisions that deal with the family, education and children. These speak of the Family as the natural primary and fundamental unit group of Society' and as 'a moral institution possessing inalienable and imprescriptible rights, antecedent and superior to all positive law'. The State is assigned a subsidiary role, respectful of the decisions made by parents and empowered to intervene in families in narrowly prescribed circumstances. The provisions of Article 41 reflect Pope Pius XI's Encyclical on Christian Marriage, *Casti Connubii* (1930) while the provisions of Article 42 owe more to *Divini Illius Magistri* (1929). Article 43 on the protection of private property also reflects this natural law tradition and rhetoric, specifically the middle-ground between Marxism and laissez-faire economics exemplified in the encyclicals of Pope Leo XIII (*Rerum Novarum*) and Pope Pius XI (*Quadragesimo Anno*). In a similar vein are the non-justiciable 'Directive Principles of Social Policy'. These principles – unlike the equivalent provisions contained in the Indian Constitution – have had little influence on either the courts or the legislature.

Some have sought to emphasise one intellectual tradition. Foster comments that the fundamental rights provisions assumed 'that the nature and identity of the Irish polity was Catholic'.[3] Whyte contended that the rights provisions of the 1937 Constitution, in comparison to

---

[2] G Hogan, 'De Valera, the Constitution, and the Historians' (2005) 40 *Irish Jurist* 293, 303. This overlooks how Article 40.1 guarantees the equality of all citizens 'as human persons', a phrase drawn from Roman Catholic social teaching.

[3] R Foster, *Modern Ireland 1600–1972* (London, Penguin, 1988) 544.

the 1922 Constitution, were 'obviously marked by Catholic thought'.[4] Foster and Whyte both underestimate the significance of rights provisions in the liberal democratic tradition. Hogan argues against the interpretations of Foster and Whyte, drawing attention to the liberal democratic provisions and comparing those provisions arguably influenced by the natural law with cognate provisions in other contemporary constitutions. For instance, Hogan draws attention to Article 6 of the German Basic Law, which provides that marriage and family enjoy the special protection of the State.[5] There is a crucial ideological difference, however. The Irish Constitution's placement of the family almost beyond the reach of positive law has significant effects, as will be seen below. The truth is simply that the fundamental rights provisions of the Irish Constitution reflect two competing intellectual traditions. Some reflect natural law influences, others reflect liberal influences; many reflect both natural law and liberal influences. Hogan's willingness to reconceptualise natural law provisions as liberal provisions, however, reflects similar moves on the part of the courts. It is to this trend that we now turn.

III. WANING OF NATURAL LAW INFLUENCES

Over time, the courts have reconstructed many provisions influenced by natural law into more typical liberal democratic provisions. This can be seen both through explicit judicial dicta and the gradual move of the courts' case law to a set of positions that cohere as effectively with generic liberal democratic ideas as with any natural law ethos. There is also a marked change in judicial language, as judges come to reflect the increasingly post-Catholic character of the society from which they are drawn.[6] The strongest example of this tendency is the courts' treatment of the constitutional protection of private property. Property rights are protected in two different constitutional articles: alongside the rights to life, person and good name in Article 40.3.2° and as the sole focus of Article 43. As noted above, the intellectual lineage of Article 43 unquestionably lies in the natural law tradition: man in virtue of his rational being has the natural right, antecedent to all positive law, to the private ownership of external goods. The bases for restricting property rights

---

[4] JH Whyte, *Church and State in Modern Ireland*, 2nd ed (Dublin, Gill & MacMillan, 1980) 51.
[5] Hogan (n 2) 304–5.
[6] E Daly, *Religion, Law and the Irish State* (Dublin, Clarus Press, 2012) 41–50.

again reflect natural law concerns with social justice and the common good. The courts have not, however, relied on this philosophical tradition in their case law but instead have fashioned a liberal protection of property that is not significantly different, for example, from the doctrines developed by the ECtHR interpreting the First Protocol of the ECHR. The courts have concluded that the Constitution protects both the institution of private property and individuals' rights over the property that they happen to own. Almost all items to which an economic value attaches, including intellectual property,[7] are constitutionally protected.

Interferences with private property rights are tested through standards of review that I will consider in greater detail below. However, some broad trends emerge. The courts disfavour arbitrary and incoherent interferences in property rights. In *Blake v Attorney General*, the Supreme Court declared unconstitutional a rent control scheme that had over time become almost completely detached from commercial reality.[8] The courts grant the legislature a wide discretion in respect of tax policy,[9] although will question badly designed tax measures that impose unnecessary hardships on individuals.[10] By 1997, Hogan could argue that the actual language of Articles 40.3.2° and 43 did not matter. '[E]ven if Article 43 was inspired by Catholic social teaching, the case-law has long since broken loose of that particular inspirational source.'[11] The Supreme Court placed more emphasis on the language of the constitutional provisions in *re Article 26 and the Health (Amendment) (No 2) Bill 2004*, striking down the retrospective abolition of public nursing home residents' right to claim back unlawfully levied charges.[12] Nevertheless, Hogan's assessment remains broadly correct, although it has been argued that the natural law language of 'social justice' and 'common good' has led the courts to be particularly deferential of property rights restrictions.[13]

Judicial wariness about the natural law philosophy of rights antecedent to positive law has intensified. In the mid-1970s, Walsh J commented that Articles 41, 42 and 43 all emphatically rejected the theory that there are no rights without law. 'They indicate that justice is placed above the law and acknowledge that natural rights, or human rights, are not created

---

[7] *Phonographic Performance (Ireland) Ltd v Cody* [1998] 4 IR 504.

[8] *Blake v Attorney General* [1982] IR 117.

[9] *Madigan v Attorney General* [1986] ILRM 136.

[10] *Daly v Revenue Commissioners* [1995] 3 IR 1.

[11] G Hogan, 'The Constitution, Property Rights and Proportionality' (1997) 32 *Irish Jurist* 373, 396.

[12] [2005] IESC 7. See R Walsh, 'The Constitution, Property Rights and Proportionality – A Re-appraisal' (2009) 31 *Dublin University Law Journal* 1.

[13] Walsh (n 12).

by law but that the Constitution confirms their existence and gives them protection.'[14] Walsh J's judgment was steeped in the Thomistic tradition, a philosophy with which he was both comfortable and familiar. However, just 20 years later the courts had become uncomfortable with this sort of language and wary of its implications. Upholding the constitutionality of a referendum that allowed for the provision of information about abortion services lawfully available abroad (arguably in breach of the natural law), the Supreme Court blithely stated that the courts had 'at no stage recognised the provisions of the natural law as superior to the Constitution'.[15]

Further evidence of the courts' move away from a natural law approach can be seen in how they have addressed certain implications of Articles 41 and 42, dealing with family and education. In a series of cases from the 1970s to the 2000s, the courts held that there was a constitutional presumption that the best interests of a child required that she be raised by her married parents. Accordingly, where unmarried parents placed their child for adoption but the adoption process was not completed and the biological parents subsequently married, the child should be returned to the married parents notwithstanding the amount of time spent with the adoptive parents.[16] By the time of *N v HSE* in 2006, however, Hardiman J characterised the constitutional presumption as one in favour of *natural parents*, without explicitly adverting to how this differed from the case law's natural law preference for *marital parents*.[17] Hardiman J's uneasiness with the natural law basis of Articles 41 and 42 can also be seen in the earlier case of *Northwestern Health Board v HW*, in which he commented that the provisions did not uniquely reflect a confessional view: the emphasis on parental autonomy was just as consistent with a Benthamite philosophy.[18] Hardiman J's philosophical exegesis is questionable,[19] but well illustrates the judicial tendency to reconstruct the natural law influenced provisions of the Constitution in more secular terms.

Notwithstanding these expressions of unease, meaningful effect is still given to Articles 41 and 42, consistent with their natural law ethos.

---

[14] *McGee v Attorney General* [1974] IR 245, 310.
[15] *Re Article 26 and the Regulation of Information (Services Outside the State for Termination of Pregnancies) Bill 1995* [1995] 1 IR 1, 43.
[16] See, for instance, *Re JH* [1985] IR 375.
[17] *N v HSE* [2006] IESC 60.
[18] *Northwestern Health Board v HW* [2001] 3 IR 622.
[19] See O Doyle, 'Family Autonomy and Children's Best Interests: Ireland, Bentham and the Natural Law' (2010) 1 *International Journal of the Jurisprudence of the Family* 55.

In *Northwestern Health Board v HW*, the Supreme Court upheld the refusal of parents to submit their child to a PKU test.[20] This minimally intrusive procedure tests for controllable diseases; if undiagnosed, the diseases can all lead to severe mental handicap. The parents objected that taking a pinprick of blood would violate their child's bodily integrity. In the view of the majority of the Court, the parents had not failed in their duty to their child, as required by Article 42.5 before State intervention could be considered. The Court would not impose its own view of the child's best interests against the wishes of these conscientious, if seriously misguided, parents. However, where a child faces an immediate and catastrophic detriment, such as the child of Jehovah's Witnesses who needs a blood transfusion to stay alive,[21] the courts do overrule the preferences of parents. Article 42.5 has been repealed by referendum and replaced with Article 42A. However, it is unlikely that the new constitutional provision would make any difference to the approach taken in *Northwestern Health Board*.

IV. THE MOVE TO NON-INTERVENTION

The early years of the Constitution saw relatively little judicial engagement with the constitutional text, generally attributed to a judiciary schooled in the British tradition of parliamentary sovereignty.[22] This may be overstating things: the High Court and Supreme Court delivered several seminal constitutional judgments in the 1940s and 1950s, such as *Buckley v Attorney General*.[23] The real era of judicial activism, however, began in the 1960s with the appointment of a new generation of judges to the Supreme Court, particularly the appointment of Cearbhall Ó Dálaigh as Chief Justice and Brian Walsh as an ordinary judge of the court. As we saw in chapter eight, Taoiseach Seán Lemass told both Walsh and Ó Dálaigh that he would like the Irish Supreme Court to become more like the US Supreme Court. In this section, I will trace how that period of activism gave way slowly at first but then quite precipitously to the current era of judicial non-intervention. Several decisions illustrate the initial judicial activism. For instance, in *People*

[20] *Northwestern Health Board v HW* [2001] 3 IR 622.
[21] *Temple Street Hospital v D* [2011] IEHC 1.
[22] For this general point, see J Kelly, *The Irish Constitution* (Dublin, Jurist Publishing, 1980), preface.
[23] *Buckley v Attorney General* [1950] IR 67. See ch 8.

(Attorney General) v O'Callaghan, the Supreme Court established a presumptive entitlement to bail, based on the presumption of innocence and the constitution's protection of personal liberty.[24] In *People (Attorney General) v O'Brien*, as we shall see below, the Supreme Court took the first steps towards an exclusionary rule for unconstitutionally obtained evidence.[25] The rise and fall of judicial activism can most clearly be seen, however, through the unenumerated rights doctrine.

In *Ryan v Attorney General*, considering a challenge to the fluoridation of the public water supply, the High Court held that the courts had the power to identify and protect constitutional rights that were not stated in the Constitution.[26] This followed, in the Court's view, from that fact that Article 40.3.1° referred to 'the personal rights of the citizen' while Article 40.3.2° referred 'in particular' to a number of specific rights (life, property, person and good name). This doctrine was accepted and applied by the Supreme Court in subsequent cases. The courts took several different approaches to the recognition of new rights under this doctrine. In some cases, the courts held that the Constitution protected whatever rights flowed from the Christian and democratic nature of the State. Walsh J relied on Thomistic natural law, on the basis that the Constitution recognised this form of natural law as superior to all positive law. Henchy J, the other pre-eminent jurist of this period, held that the Constitution protected whatever rights inhered in a citizen by virtue of her human personality. Finally, the courts sometimes used Article 40.3.1° more prosaically as a repository for rights textually implicit in other provisions of the constitution. These diverse approaches led to the recognition of, among other rights, a right to bodily integrity, a right to travel, a right to privacy, a right to marital privacy, and a right of an unmarried mother to raise her children.

The unenumerated rights doctrine effectively established the courts as an alternative site of State power. It freed the courts from the constraint of interpreting what was in the Constitution, instead allowing them to develop their own vision of a just Irish State, albeit that they could only do so in the context of cases brought before them. In *Ryan*, Kenny J had relied on a papal encyclical to identify the right to bodily integrity.

---

[24] *People (Attorney General) v O'Callaghan* [1966] IR 501. 30 years later this led to a constitutional amendment to allow bail to be refused where a person was accused of committing a serious offence where 'it is reasonably considered necessary to prevent the commission of a serious offence by that person'.

[25] *People (Attorney General) v O'Brien* [1965] IR 142.

[26] *Ryan v Attorney General* [1965] IR 294.

In *McGee v Attorney General*, Walsh J relied on Thomistic natural law to identify a right to marital privacy that allowed married couples access to contraception – a conclusion not favoured by many Thomists and in particular not by the Pope in his then recent encyclical, *Humanae Vitae.*[27] In *Norris v Attorney General*, rival versions of Christianity featured in the majority judgment of O'Higgins CJ, reasoning that all Christian denominations condemned homosexuality, and the minority judgment of McCarthy J, who preferred to focus on the great doctrine of charity preached by Christ.[28] Henchy J's approach of focusing on the rights inherent in human personality provided little further guidance. The unenumerated rights doctrine functioned to confer an almost unlimited discretion on judges to recognise new constitutional rights. Democratically enacted legislation was struck down where it failed to accord with the worldview of judges. This posed the most significant challenge to the dominance of the Government in the history of the State.

Over time, academics and then judges became unsettled at the amount of power that this doctrine provided to judges. This change in attitude may partly be attributed to the decision of the Government to shift the direction of the Supreme Court in the mid-1970s by overlooking Mr Justice Walsh for the position of Chief Justice, as discussed in chapter eight. However, legal, academic and judicial concern had been growing in any event. Over time, the rate of recognition for new rights slowed down; judicial doubts were openly expressed. In 1997, a majority of the Supreme Court recognised, in the context of adoption, a new right to know the identity of one's parents but held that this must be balanced with the privacy rights of parents.[29] Keane J, however, strongly dissented, doubting the point of recognising new rights that would be balanced away against existing rights and questioning the whole basis of the unenumerated rights doctrine. Three years later, Mr Justice Keane was promoted to Chief Justice and several new judges were appointed to the Supreme Court. The unenumerated rights doctrine appears to have withered at this point; its only meaningful consideration subsequently was in *TD v Minister for Education*, in which Keane CJ and Murphy J held *obiter* that it would be inappropriate *ever* to recognise an unenumerated right with socioeconomic implications.[30]

---

[27] *McGee v Attorney General* [1974] IR 284.
[28] *Norris v Attorney General* [1984] IR 36.
[29] *O'T v B* [1998] 2 IR 32.
[30] *TD v Minister for Education* [2001] 4 IR 259.

The move from judicial activism to non-intervention can also be seen in the general approach to the enforcement of socioeconomic rights. In *TD*, the State conceded – for the purposes of an appeal – that Article 42.5 imposed an obligation on the State to care for children whose parents had failed them.[31] In *TD*, however, a majority of the Supreme Court accepted the State's argument that this constitutional obligation could be enforced only by way of court declaration; the Court should not issue a mandatory injunction compelling the Minister to build a particular facility. Hardiman and Murray JJ reasoned that mandatory orders would lead to the courts straying into the domain of policy, reserved by the Constitution to the electorally accountable organs of government. In Hardiman J's view, such an order 'could only be made as an absolutely final resort in circumstances of great crisis and for the protection of the constitutional order itself'.[32] Murray J held that such an order could only be granted if there were 'a conscious and deliberate decision by the organ of State to act in breach of its constitutional obligation to other parties, accompanied by bad faith or recklessness'.[33]

The majority judgments in *TD* can be and have been criticised.[34] For present purposes, however, they further illustrate the move of the courts away from activism to non-intervention. They are consistent with the approach of the Supreme Court in a claim by an autistic man to be provided with free primary education.[35] The Court held that although the constitutional guarantee of 'free primary education' was not limited to scholastic education, it did not apply to people over the age of 18. Hardiman J also held that the constitutional obligation could not be enforced by way of mandatory injunction. This is particularly telling, since *Sinnott* involved the textually explicit constitutional obligation on the State to provide for free primary education. The reluctance of the courts to enforce a textually explicit socio-economic right sits uneasily with the courts' willingness to enforce non-explicit rights in the criminal process, as we shall see below.

The move towards non-intervention can also be seen in the courts' approach to the content of constitutional guarantees. In *Fleming v Ireland*, the plaintiff, who was in the later stages of multiple

---

[31] The High Court had come to this conclusion in *FN v Minister for Education* [1995] 1 IR 409.

[32] *TD v Minister for Education* [2001] 4 IR 259, 372.

[33] ibid 337.

[34] See, for instance, G Whyte, 'The Role of the Supreme Court in our Democracy: A Reply to Mr Justice Hardiman' (2006) 28 *Dublin University Law Journal* 1.

[35] *Sinnott v Minister for Education* [2001] 2 IR 545.

sclerosis, challenged the constitutionality of section 2 of the Criminal Law (Suicide) Act 1993, which decriminalised suicide but made assisting suicide a discrete criminal offence.[36] Ms Fleming wished to end her own life but could not do so as she had lost the use of her arms. Her partner would assist her to take her life but only if it was lawful to do so. The Supreme Court held that, in order to succeed in her claim, Ms Fleming had to establish that there was within the Constitution a 'right to commit suicide, a right to determine the time and method of death, and to have assistance with the exercise of that right'. Having framed the issue with such specificity, the Court rejected the argument that the right to die a natural death, recognised in the earlier case of *In re a Ward (Withholding Medical Treatment)*,[37] extended to a right to take one's own life.

It is easy to imagine how the Supreme Court could have taken a different approach. Indeed, the Supreme Court of Canada shortly afterwards reached precisely the opposite conclusion in *Carter v Canada* against the backdrop of reasonably similar constitutional provisions.[38] But the Irish Supreme Court eschewed an expansive approach, with the result that it was not required even to scrutinise the possible reasons for the legislative approach. The Court has similarly stepped away from a role in resolving moral issues in the context of assisted human reproduction. In *Roche v Roche*, considering whether a woman could insist on the transplant of frozen embryos into her womb contrary to the wishes of her husband (whose sperm had fertilised the embryos prior to a breakdown in their relationship), the Supreme Court held that the unborn outside the womb did not benefit from the protection of the right to life of the unborn in Article 40.3.3° of the constitution.[39] Murray CJ commented that the onus was on the Oireachtas to make the initial policy determination and define by law when the life of the unborn acquires protection. In *MR v DR*, the Supreme Court did not employ the Constitution to reconsider the statutory position that only the birth mother – and not the genetic mother – could be registered as the mother of a child.[40]

---

[36] *Fleming v Ireland* [2013] IESC 19.
[37] *In re a Ward (Withholding Medical Treatment)* [1996] 2 IR 79.
[38] *Carter v Canada* 2015 SCC 5. For a comparison of the Irish and Canadian approaches, see D Kenny, 'A Tale of Two Cases: Rights, Assisted Suicide, and Lessons for Comparative Constitutional Law from Canada and Ireland' paper presented to International Society of Public Law Conference, New York, 2 July 2015. Available at https://tcd.academia.edu/DavidKenny.
[39] *Roche v Roche* [2009] IESC 82.
[40] *MR v DR* [2014] IESC 60.

Denham CJ commented that the lacuna in the law should be addressed by the legislature, not the courts.

The point here is to observe rather than criticise the change in judicial attitude. It is difficult to imagine that, if such issues had arisen for consideration 30 years previously, Walsh J or Henchy J would have concluded that the Constitution was irrelevant. This is not simply because of Walsh J's commitment to the Thomistic philosophy that, in his view, underpinned the constitution. More generally, judges of that generation assumed that the Constitution always spoke. They were not slow to extend constitutional principles into contentious moral domains that had previously been beyond constitutional purview. The current approach reduces the interpretative role of the courts, marking a significant change in the balance of power between the Government and the courts. Irrespective of whether one approves of this change, it creates a real risk that elected representatives, assuming the courts still play the role they did in the 1970s, may fail to ensure that the justice implications of legislation are properly considered during the legislative process. Conversely, it may also be that the Government has not fully appreciated the legislative freedom of action now afforded to it by the courts. Eoin Daly criticises the general way in which judicially enforced rights constitutionalise political decision-making, but draws specific attention to a number of cases in which the Oireachtas has appeared to believe the constitutional constraints greater than was actually the case.[41]

A further example of changing judicial attitudes is the courts' current treatment of the equality guarantee. Article 40.1 guarantees that all citizens shall, as human persons, be held equal before the law. This is qualified to allow enactments have due regard to differences of social function and of physical and moral capacity. This long remained a Cinderella provision, seldom successfully invoked even during the heyday of judicial activism.[42] In 1998 and 2000, however, two judgments of the Supreme Court suggested a far greater role for Article 40.1. In *re Article 26 and the Employment Equality Bill 1997*, the Supreme Court held that classifications based on sex, race, language, religious or political opinions were all presumptively proscribed.[43] Two years later, in *An Blascaod Mór*

---

[41] E Daly, 'Reappraising Judicial Supremacy' in L Cahillane, J Gallen and T Hickey, *Judges, Politics and the Irish Constitution* (Manchester, Manchester University Press, 2017) 36–45.

[42] For a general account of this provision, see O Doyle, *Constitutional Equality Law* (Dublin: Round Hall Thomson, 2004).

[43] *re Article 26 and the Employment Equality Bill 1997* [1997] 2 IR 321, 347.

Teoranta v Commissioners of Public Works, the Supreme Court held unconstitutional a pedigree-based exemption from compulsory purchase legislation.[44] In the view of the Court, the preference for those whose ancestors had owned land on the Great Blasket Island was based on a principle of pedigree that – outside the law of succession – had no place in a democratic society committed to the principle of equality.

The Supreme Court has not implemented this more exacting approach to the equality guarantee in subsequent cases. The most telling example is *D v Ireland*.[45] The Criminal Law (Sexual Offences) Act 2006 established a new set of criminal offences proscribing sexual conduct with people under the age of 17. Under the Act, a female under the age of 17 who has sexual intercourse with a male under the age of 17 is not guilty of a criminal offence; the male is guilty of a criminal offence. Where a male and female both under the age of 17 engage in a range of sexual acts other than sexual intercourse, both commit a criminal offence. Mr D, charged with having sexual intercourse with a girl under the age of 17 while himself under the age of 17, challenged the constitutionality of this sex discrimination. The Supreme Court did not refer to any of its previous case law on Article 40.1. Far from treating the sex discrimination as presumptively proscribed, the Court held that decisions on 'matters of such social sensitivity and difficulty' were in essence a matter for the legislature. 'Courts should be deferential to the legislative view on such matters of social policy.'[46] This lack of scrutiny arguably led the court to overlook the fact that the legislation may have encouraged teenage girls to engage in sexual intercourse, at least in preference to the other sorts of sexual conduct that left them open to criminal sanction.[47] Article 40.1 has become almost a dead-letter. It has been employed in largely technocratic cases such as remission rules for young offenders,[48] and an anomaly in rules about fitness to plead in a criminal trial.[49] However, when faced with a clear legislative policy choice, the Supreme Court simply deferred to that choice rather than articulate any sense of what the constitutional equality guarantee might require.[50]

---

[44] *An Blascaod Mór Teoranta v Commissioners of Public Works* [2000] 1 IR 6.

[45] *D v Ireland* [2012] IESC 10.

[46] ibid para 50.

[47] See O Doyle, 'Judicial Scrutiny of Legislative Classification' (2012) 47(1) *The Irish Jurist* 175.

[48] *Byrne v Director of Oberstown School* [2013] IEHC 562.

[49] *BG v Judge Murphy* 2 [2011] IEHC 445.

[50] Hogan, Kenny and Walsh show that declarations of unconstitutionality have been granted 16 times on the basis of Article 40.1, although they are also of the view that this

One final illustration of the move from activism is the judicial approach to the resolution of competing constitutional rights. In *Quinn's Supermarket v Attorney General*, the Supreme Court considered the conflict between Article 44.2.3°, which prohibits religious discrimination, and Article 44.2.1°, which protects freedom of religious conscience.[51] The discrimination in question facilitated members of the Jewish faith to purchase meat after sundown on the Sabbath, by exempting Kosher butcher shops from a prohibition on evening opening. Walsh J commented that any generally applicable law that restricted the free profession or practice of religion would be unconstitutional. This would have *required* freedom of conscience exemptions for all laws of general application. 25 years later, however, the Supreme Court subtly moderated this position, holding that it was constitutionally permissible (but not required) for the Oireachtas to discriminate on grounds of religious profession belief or status insofar as this might be necessary to give life and reality to the guarantee of the free profession and practice of religion.[52]

Across a range of contexts, therefore, the courts interpreted constitutional rights in ways that expanded the scope for the Government to determine public policy: the elimination of the unenumerated rights doctrine, the eschewal of mandatory orders, the narrow reading of constitutional rights, and the resolution of competing constitutional rights. Each move, although itself an exercise of judicial power, renders the Constitution less determinative of public policy, removing a constraint on Government action and reducing judicial power for the future. In some areas, such as socioeconomic rights, the courts have come close to a doctrine of non-justiciability removing all constraints from the Government. In other areas, the courts have left open the scope for a largely technocratic review of legislative means but one that does not challenge legislative objectives.

These observations are borne out by Hogan, Kenny and Walsh's anthology of declarations of unconstitutionality, although this dataset is both narrower (in its exclusive focus on declarations of unconstitutionality) and wider (in its application beyond constitutional rights). On their count, there have been 93 declarations of unconstitutionality in total: three in the 1950s, eight in the 1960s, 17 in the 1970s, 20 in the 1980s,

---

statistical frequency is not reflected in substantive impact. G Hogan, D Kenny and R Walsh, 'An Anthology of Declarations of Unconstitutionality' (2015) 54(2) *The Irish Jurist* 1, 24.

[51] [1972] IR 1.

[52] *Re Article 26 and the Employment Equality Bill 1996* [1997] 2 IR 321, 358. The provision in question allowed religious employers to discriminate in order to maintain their religious ethos.

15 in the 1990s, 14 in the 2000s, and 11 in the first half of the 2010s.[53] This downward trend is exacerbated by three features. First, one would have expected the declarations of unconstitutionality in the 1970s and 1980s to set precedents that might ground further declarations in the future. Secondly, there are currently 56 superior court judges, empowered to grant declarations of unconstitutionality, compared to 14 in 1975. This provides a very rough guide to the volume of litigation and, by extension, the prevalence of declarations of unconstitutionality as a feature of judicial work. Thirdly, Hogan, Kenny and Walsh note that a 'striking feature of the declarations of unconstitutionality issued by the courts from the year 2000 to date on the basis of the rights provisions of the Constitution is the extent to which they are generally concerned with procedural matters, rather than with the substantive protection of the relevant rights'.[54] This again supports the narrative of judges reducing the extent to which the courts control the Government.

Writing extra-judicially, Hogan has commented that the period from the late 1970s has been one of missed judicial opportunities, the courts frequently upholding legislation on questionable bases. He attributes this to judiciary's 'hidden love of the common law', preferring an 'incremental, step by step, fact specific, result orientated approach of the common law in favour of an entire re-alignment of a corpus of the law by reference to general abstract principles contained in a few paragraphs in the Constitution'.[55] Although this argument is plausible, it fails to explain why the preference for a common law method of reasoning has become more entrenched the longer the Constitution has been in existence.

V. STANDARDS OF REVIEW AND JUDICIAL DEFERENCE

Within two years of the passage of the constitution, a High Court judge commented that it must be accepted as an axiom 'that a law passed by the Oireachtas, the elected representatives of the people, is presumed to be constitutional unless and until the contrary is clearly established'.[56] In its narrowest terms, this is merely an indication that the plaintiff bears

---

[53] Hogan, Kenny and Walsh (n 50) 3.
[54] ibid 27.
[55] G Hogan, 'Harkening to the Tristan Chords: the Constitution at 80' (2018) 42 *Dublin University Law Journal* (forthcoming).
[56] *Pigs Marketing Board v Donnelly* [1939] IR 413, 417. See generally, Brian Foley, *Deference and the Presumption of Constitutionality* (Dublin, Institute of Public Administration, 2008).

the onus of proof in a constitutional case. However, the presumption evinces a stronger and more substantive attitude of deference to the decisions of democratically accountable representatives. This is most clearly visible in those cases where the courts review whether a *prima facie* legislative interference with a constitutional right is justified.

The constitutional text generally makes clear that rights are not absolutely protected.[57] The personal rights in Article 40.3 are protected only against *unjust* attack. Article 43 allows property rights to be delimited in the *interests of the common good*. The courts have not placed much emphasis on the different language used by different constitutional provisions to authorise legislative restriction of constitutional rights. This issue attracted little judicial attention until the 1990s, when the courts began to elaborate more structured approaches to test the legitimacy of legislative restrictions on constitutional rights. In *Heaney v Ireland*,[58] considering a legislative interference with the right to silence, the High Court adopted the Canadian proportionality test *verbatim* from the case of *Chaulk v R*.[59] This test essentially imposes four requirements. First, there must be an important objective for the legislative measure. Secondly, the means must be rationally connected to that objective. Thirdly, the means must impair the right as little as possible. Fourthly, the effect on rights must be proportional to the objective. The middle two questions are essentially technocratic: is this measure necessary to achieve this objective? In contrast, the first and particularly the last question open up the scope for contestation between courts and legislature: is the legislative objective *sufficiently important* to justify this interference with constitutional rights? In their application of the proportionality test, however, the Irish courts have focused almost exclusively on the first two limbs. Indeed, because the Irish courts have held that they cannot have regard to legislative history and must infer the purposes of a legislative measure from the measure itself,[60] the first two limbs necessarily fold into each other: is this measure rationally connected to an important objective? There are only two cases in which the courts have declared legislation unconstitutional for breaching the final limb of the proportionality test.[61]

---

[57] The only exception is the absolute prohibition on the enactment of any law to provide for the death penalty. This was inserted by referendum in 2001.

[58] *Heaney v Ireland* [1994] 3 IR 593.

[59] *Chaulk v R* [1990] 3 SCR 1303.

[60] *In re Article 26 and the Illegal Immigrants Bill 1999* [2000] 2 IR 360, 392; *Crilly v Farrington* [2001] 3 IR 267, 280-4; *Controller of Patents v Ireland* [2001] 4 IR 229, 246.

[61] *Daly v Revenue Commissioners* [1995] 3 IR 1, striking down a provision that effectively imposed double taxation and *King v Minister for Environment* [2006] IESC 61 that

Rather confusingly, around the same time as *Heaney*, the Supreme Court in *Tuohy v Courtney* articulated a different standard of review to be applied when legislation attempted to balance two competing constitutional rights.[62] The Court held that its role in such cases was 'to determine from an objective stance whether the balance contained in the impugned legislation is so contrary to reason and fairness as to constitute an unjust attack on some individual's constitutional rights'. The plaintiff challenged a six-year limitation period, in circumstances in which he only became aware of his legal claim after the six-year period. The Supreme Court held that the legislation represented a reasonable balance between the plaintiff's right to litigate and the defendant's right to be protected from unjust or burdensome claims, and it was not for the Court to intervene. The Supreme Court has indicated that it is alert to the international debate about standards of review and the malleability of the proportionality test.[63] It is thus possible that a more exacting approach will be taken to the constitutional review of legislation in the future. Conversely, it is possible that the courts may resile from the generically cosmopolitan language of the proportionality test and rely more on the explicit constitutional language to guide the legitimacy of legislative interference with constitutional rights.[64]

VI. ADMINISTRATIVE ACTION

Up to this point, our focus has been on the constitutional review of legislative action. However, as we saw in chapter six, citizens often experience state power directly through the actions of administrative agencies. This is particularly relevant to the context of fundamental rights. Legislation seldom infringes the rights of an individual without the intervention of some other agent, whether it be a police officer choosing to exercise a power of arrest or an administrative agency choosing to exercise a statutory discretion. The Irish case law on this issue has developed in an unusual fashion due to a historic doctrinal division between constitutional law and administrative law.

---

imposed onerous requirements for the nomination of election candidates. Even in these cases, the problem lay with the way in which the Oireachtas had chosen to achieve its objective rather than disproportionality *per se*.

[62] *Tuohy v Courtney* [1994] 3 IR 1.

[63] *Nottinghamshire County Council v KB* [2011] IESC 48 and *Fleming v Ireland* [2013] IESC 19.

[64] Walsh has observed this approach in the context of property rights. Walsh (n 12).

On the one hand, the courts have emphasised the obligation on administrative agencies to act consistently with the Constitution. In *East Donegal Co-operative Livestock Market Ltd v Attorney General*, Walsh J held that it was presumed that the Oireachtas intended that powers granted under an Act would be exercised constitutionally.[65] There are several examples of the courts directly applying constitutional provisions to non-legislative acts. For instance, in *Holland v Governor of Portlaoise Prison*, the High Court held that the prison governor's blanket ban on prisoners communicating with the media was an unconstitutional interference with Mr Holland's right to communicate.[66]

On the other hand, the courts have taken a very different approach in cases that they perceive to involve administrative law. The general rule here is that the courts, when reviewing administrative decisions, should confine themselves to an assessment of the procedures followed rather than the substantive merits of the decision. However, the courts do engage in limited merits-review by assessing whether a decision was reasonable, in a sense broadly analogous to *Wednesbury* reasonableness in UK administrative law. In *State (Keegan) v Stardust Compensation Tribunal*, the Supreme Court held that an administrative decision could be declared invalid where 'it plainly and unambiguously flies in the face of reason and common sense'.[67] In *O'Keeffe v An Bord Pleanála*, the Supreme Court raised the threshold of irrationality by holding, in the context of a challenge to a planning decision, that a decision could only be struck down if there were no relevant material that could support the decision reached.[68] These cases did not involve interference with constitutional rights. However, for reasons that are difficult to fathom, it was sometimes taken to determine the approach that the courts should take to administrative decisions that affected constitutional rights. To address this problem, administrative lawyers sometimes argued that the Irish courts should adopt an approach akin to that taken in the United Kingdom of anxious scrutiny for administrative decisions where human rights were threatened.[69] This was a strange argumentative move. The United Kingdom – at the time – had no explicit protection for human rights. A more cogent argument would simply have invoked the obligation on all public authorities to

---

[65] *East Donegal Co-operative Livestock Market Ltd v Attorney General* [1970] IR 317.
[66] *Holland v Governor of Portlaoise Prison* [2004] 2 IR 573.
[67] *State (Keegan) v Stardust Compensation Tribunal* [1986] IR 642, 658.
[68] *O'Keeffe v An Bord Pleanála* [1993] 1 IR 39, 72.
[69] See, for instance, *Bailey v Flood* [2006] IEHC 169.

act consistently with the Constitution. Nevertheless, this administrative law mindset took hold and set the frame for all further consideration of this issue.

In *Meadows v Minister for Justice, Equality and Law Reform*, a narrowly divided Supreme Court, in the context of a challenge to a deportation decision, held that a requirement of proportionality applied to administrative decisions that infringed fundamental rights.[70] *Keegan* is once again the standard rationality test for administrative decisions, with the *O'Keeffe* 'no evidence' rule applying where the decision-maker has special expertise – quintessentially planning decisions. However, where the decision affects fundamental rights, *Keegan* is now held to import a separate requirement of proportionality, in the sense of proportionality between the effect on rights and the objective of the measure. Hardiman J strongly dissented from the majority approach, focusing on its implications for deportation decisions. In his view, it represented 'a major transfer of power from the executive to the judicial arm of government by conferring on the latter a general supervisory role over the exercise of a function conferred by law on a member of the government'.[71]

The decision in *Meadows* has been considered in many subsequent High Court cases in the deportation context, with different judges taking radically different interpretations. Some judges have held that *Meadows* only requires the courts to review, on a *Keegan* basis, whether the decision-maker has applied a proportionality approach.[72] Other judges have held that the court itself must apply the proportionality requirement, often with little deference to the non-expert decision-makers.[73] The conflicting approaches reflect, I suggest, confusion over the character of the right at stake in deportation decisions. In *Dimbo v Minister for Justice, Equality and Law Reform*, the Supreme Court held that the Minister – before making a deportation decision – must consider the impact of that decision on relevant constitutional and ECHR rights, typically family rights and children's rights.[74] In the deportation context, the *Meadows* proportionality requirement structures the type of consideration that the Minister must give to these rights. This is essentially the

---

[70] *Meadows v Minister for Justice, Equality and Law Reform* [2010] 2 IR 701.

[71] ibid [183].

[72] See, for instance, the judgment of Cooke J in *ISOF v Minister for Justice, Equality and Law Reform* [2010] IEHC 386.

[73] See, for instance, the judgments of Hogan J in *Efe v Minister for Justice Equality and Law Reform* [2011] IEHC 214 and *O'Leary v Minister for Justice, Equality and Law Reform* [2011] IEHC 256.

[74] *Dimbo v Minister for Justice, Equality and Law Reform* [2008] IESC 26.

approach taken by the Supreme Court in the one case that substantively considered the proportionality requirement laid down in *Meadows*. In *AMS v Minister for Justice and Equality*, Clarke J, with whom the other members of the court agreed, held that the court should afford a reasonable margin of appreciation to the decision-maker but intervene 'where an applicant discharges the burden of demonstrating that the proportionality judgment of the decision maker was unreasonable'.[75] Outside the deportation context, however, where the rights do impose substantive constraints, this approach would – I suggest – be inappropriate and amount to a judicial abdication of the courts' responsibility to enforce the Constitution.

VII. CRIME

The courts' application of the Constitution to criminal procedures and the criminal law does not straightforwardly fit within the narratives traced thus far in this chapter. Criminal process rights are equally consistent with natural law and liberal democratic thinking; the move from activism has been far less pronounced than in all other areas of constitutional law. The approach of the courts generally reflects a belief that the courts are the primary guardians of a fair criminal process. Where there is no legislation, the courts are activist in their design of constitutional safeguards to control other actors (including trial courts) in the criminal process. However, where there is legislation, the courts remain quite deferential to the judgment of the Oireachtas. In *People (DPP) v Quilligan (No 3)*, the Supreme Court upheld the constitutionality of section 30 of the Offences Against the State Act 1939.[76] This provision allows the police to arrest a person on suspicion of committing an offence scheduled under that Act and then detain that person for an initial period of 24 hours which can be extended by a further 24 hours. The Supreme Court did not explore the need for this lengthy detention period, but rather upheld it largely due to the procedural protections, such as the right of legal assistance, afforded to a person arrested pursuant to section 30.

In *Heaney v Ireland*, the Supreme Court upheld the constitutionality of section 52 of the Offences Against the State Act 1939,[77] which allows a police officer to require an arrested person to give, inter alia,

---

[75] *AMS v Minister for Justice and Equality* [2014] IESC 65.
[76] *People (DPP) v Quilligan (No 3)* [1993] 2 IR 305.
[77] *Heaney v Ireland* [1996] 1 IR 580.

'a full account of his movements and actions during any specified period'. Failure to do so was a criminal offence. Although holding that the right to silence was constitutionally protected, O'Flaherty J noted that innocent people would have nothing to fear from the section. The rights of the State to defend itself from people with something to hide had to take precedence over the rights of people who might wish to take a stand 'on grounds of principle'. This weak protection of the right to silence continued in *Rock v Ireland*, in which the Supreme Court upheld provisions of the Criminal Justice Act 1984 that allowed a trial court to draw inferences from the failure of an accused person to explain certain facts while being questioned.[78] Apparently in response to developments in the ECtHR, the Supreme Court strengthened its protection of the right to silence in *Re National Irish Bank*, holding that the non-voluntary confession of an accused person could not be introduced into evidence at trial.[79] This points to the responsiveness of Irish constitutional law to developments in the law of the ECHR, an issue to which I will return in the next section.

This attitude of judicial deference is not absolute. In *Damache v Director of Public Prosecutions*, the Supreme Court declared unconstitutional a statutory provision that allowed a senior police officer to authorise a search of a suspect's dwelling.[80] In this case, the search had been authorised by the senior police officer involved in the investigation itself. The Court held that the constitutional protection of the dwelling in Article 40.5 required that searches be authorised by an independent person. This was a significant judgment but can again fairly be characterised as a judicial constraint on legislative means, rather than a judicial challenge to a legislative objective.

This technical checking of legislative power can also be seen in the judicially created rule that criminal offences cannot be overly vague. In *Douglas v Director of Public Prosecutions*, the High Court struck down the offence of doing an act in a public place in such a way as to 'offend modesty or cause scandal or injure the morals of the community'.[81] Hogan J emphasised that it would be open to the Oireachtas to enact an offence that captured the rather objectionable behaviour in which Mr Douglas had allegedly engaged; the problem was the vagueness of the standard employed in the legislation. In one significant case, however,

---

[78] *Rock v Ireland* [1997] 3 IR 484.
[79] *Re National Irish Bank* [1999] 3 IR 145.
[80] *Damache v Director of Public Prosecutions* [2012] IESC 11.
[81] *Douglas v Director of Public Prosecutions* [2013] IEHC 343.

the Supreme Court did overturn a substantive policy judgment of the Oireachtas. In *C v Ireland (No 2)*, the Court declared section 1(1) of the Criminal Law (Amendment) Act 1935 unconstitutional on the grounds that it did not allow an accused person to plead a reasonable mistake as to age as a defence to a charge of unlawful carnal knowledge of a girl under the age of 15 years.[82] Hardiman J held that to criminalise a person who was mentally innocent was to inflict a grave injury on his dignity and self-worth, and to treat him as little more than a means to an end. This was a highly controversial judgment, provoking a number of calls for constitutional amendment, ultimately not pursued. This is a rare example, at least in recent decades, of the courts directly challenging a policy choice of the Oireachtas on a sensitive social issue. It is particularly stark when set beside the reluctance of the courts to enforce textually protected socioeconomic rights. It suggests that judges' own sense of what is important, rather than what is stated in the master-text constitution, is the most significant factor in determining levels of judicial activism.

The aftermath of *C* illustrates an interesting feature of the Irish constitutional order. A few days later, the High Court ordered the release of Mr A, who had raped the 12 year-old friend of his daughter, on the ground that the offence of which he was convicted no longer existed. The Supreme Court subsequently modified its position on the consequences of a declaration of unconstitutionality and ordered the re-arrest of Mr A.[83] In the intervening seven days, however, the High Court judgment raised the prospect of a series of child rapists being released from prison. Understandably, this caused considerable political and public disquiet. There were calls for constitutional amendments. But there was little or no public or political suggestion that the Supreme Court had got it wrong. Public debate directed criticism at the Government for failing to anticipate and respond to the Supreme Court decision,[84] rather than at the Supreme Court for its questionable adventure in constitutional law-making.[85] Underlying all this are two phenomena. First, a sense that constitutional adjudication is a highly professionalised activity for the courts – there is little public ownership of the Constitution's meaning or public interest in the process for determining that meaning. Secondly, a sense among politicians that it is simply inappropriate for

---

[82] *C v Ireland (No 2)* [2006] IESC 33.

[83] *A v Governor of Arbour Hill Prison* [2006] IESC 45, discussed further below.

[84] 'Government out of touch' *The Irish Times*, 1 June 2006.

[85] D Prendergast, 'The Constitutionality of Strict Liability Offences' (2011) 33 *Dublin University Law Journal* 285.

politicians – particularly members of the Government – to criticise the courts. The deference of the courts to legislative decision-making is repaid by a political and public deference to judicial decision-making. This ensures that the basis for judicial decisions, which often determine matters of fundamental political importance, are rarely subjected to detailed public scrutiny, a regrettable failure of public reason.

The courts have been markedly more interventionist in their constraint of other actors and the courts themselves in the criminal process. Relying on the general guarantee in Article 38.1 of a right to trial in due course of law, the courts have implied rules to protect an accused person against unfair pretrial publicity and undue pre-trial delay.[86] The courts have also implied an obligation on the police to seek out and preserve evidence.[87] The courts have constitutionalised the right to free legal aid, holding the legislative scheme inadequate in some respects and prohibiting trials where the legislation did not allow for an appropriate level of legal representation.[88] Although the Oireachtas had provided for a scheme of legal aid in criminal cases, the constitutional support for that scheme provides a significant additional protection for the rights of the accused, ensuring that gaps in provision cannot be ignored. The courts have also used the Constitution to stipulate rules on the access of a person to her solicitor while in police custody, a point to which I shall return below.

The most significant intervention of the courts in this domain concerns unconstitutionally obtained evidence. In the early 1960s, a minority of the Supreme Court articulated a new constitutional principle that any evidence obtained in conscious and deliberate breach of a person's constitutional rights must be excluded unless there are extraordinary excusing circumstances.[89] This principle was subsequently accepted by a majority of the Supreme Court. Article 40.4 provides that personal liberty can only be deprived in accordance with law; Article 40.5 provides that the dwelling is inviolable save in accordance with law. As a result, any unlawful detention and any unlawful search of a dwelling is unconstitutional. In *O'Brien*, the search warrant – due to an oversight – misstated the address of the property to be searched. The search was therefore considered, even by the minority, not to be in 'conscious and deliberate' breach of Mr O'Brien's constitutional rights. 25 years later, however, the Supreme Court adopted

---

[86] See *D v DPP* [1994] 2 IR 564 and *SH v DPP* [2006] 3 IR 575 respectively.

[87] *Dunne v DPP* [2002] 2 IR 3.

[88] See *The State (Healy) v Donoghue* [1976] IR 325 and *Carmody v Minister for Justice, Equality and Law Reform* [2009] IESC 71.

[89] *People (AG) v O'Brien* [1965] IR 142. Extraordinary excusing circumstances have been held to include where a victim is in peril or evidence might be destroyed.

a much stricter approach: an infringement of constitutional rights was conscious or deliberate where the act itself was deliberate, irrespective of whether the police officers *knew* that they were acting unlawfully. In *People (DPP) v Kenny*, the Supreme Court characterised this as an absolute protection rule.[90] Evidence obtained from Mr Kenny's premises was excluded, even though the procedure for authorising the search warrant had only been declared unlawful after the search took place, meaning that the police officers could not have known that they were breaching Mr Kenny's constitutional rights when they carried out the search.

A judicial unease with the implications of *Kenny* was almost immediately apparent.[91] This judicial unease reflected a broader public concern. In 2006, a Balance in the Criminal Law Review Group, appointed by the Minister for Justice, concluded (by a majority) that the exclusionary rule was too strictly calibrated and recommended that a court have discretion whether to admit the evidence or not, having regard to the totality of the circumstances and in particular the rights of the victim.[92] The Minister welcomed the report as 'fair and balanced' and as providing 'a sound basis for taking forward proposals for reform'.[93] However, there was no easy way to allow the Supreme Court revisit its decision in *Kenny*. The general legal position was that acquittals could never be appealed. Accordingly, the application of an exclusionary rule in favour of an accused person could not become the subject of an appeal. The Oireachtas enacted section 23 of the Criminal Procedure Act 2010 to allow the DPP appeal an acquittal on a 'with-prejudice' basis where the trial judge 'erroneously excluded compelling evidence'.

In *DPP v JC*, the dwelling of the accused had been searched in accordance with a warrant issued under the procedure subsequently declared unconstitutional in *People (DPP) v Damache*, considered above. The accused was arrested in his dwelling and taken to a police station where he made several inculpatory statements. The trial judge held that the inculpatory statements should be excluded because the arrest was unlawful as it followed from an unconstitutional search of the dwelling. As a result, the accused was acquitted. The DPP appealed to the Supreme Court under the new section 23 procedure.[94]

---

[90] *People (DPP) v Kenny* [1990] 2 IR 110, 133.

[91] *People (DPP) v Balfe* [1998] 4 IR 50.

[92] Report of the Balance in the Criminal Law Review Group (2007) 161.

[93] http://www.justice.ie/en/JELR/Pages/Balance-in-Criminal-Law-report-published visited 13 July 2015.

[94] [2015] IESC 31.

The majority held that *Kenny* had been wrongly decided. They conceptualised the issue in a starkly different way from the majority in *Kenny*. For the *JC* majority, it was a question of balance. The Constitution committed the courts both to the administration of justice and the protection of individual rights. The 'remorseless logic' of *Kenny* took no account of the detriment to the administration of justice that occurred if relevant and reliable evidence were to be excluded. In contrast, for the *JC* minority, the question was straightforwardly about the protection of constitutional rights. The administration of justice and the rights of victims were secondary concerns that could not justify interference with constitutional rights. The majority laid down a very elaborate test to determine when evidence obtained in breach of constitutional rights might be admitted. It essentially reverted to the *O'Brien* understanding of 'conscious and deliberate breach' but introduced a number of safeguards to ensure that wilful inadvertence or a culture of blame-shifting could not lead to the admission of evidence.

The decision in *JC* is relevant in two ways to the themes of this chapter. In terms of the development of the law, it marks a further shift away from a strong protection of constitutional rights to a less interventionist attitude on the part of the courts. In terms of process, it reflects an unusual form of constitutional dialogue between the courts and the Government, alongside broader civil society. The majority judges unquestionably were of the view that *Kenny* was wrongly decided. Nevertheless, legislative intervention was required to allow the courts revisit the issue and they ultimately did so in a context where the views of the Government at least had been clearly expressed, even though neither the Government nor the Oireachtas was represented before the Court.

VIII. EMERGENCIES AND EXCEPTIONS

Article 28.3 provides a procedure through which the Oireachtas can immunise legislation from constitutional review in times of war or armed rebellion. The legislation must simply express that it is 'for the purpose of securing the public safety and the preservation of the State in time of war or armed rebellion'.[95] Article 28.3 was amended in September 1939 to stipulate that 'time of war' included 'a time when

---

[95] The 2001 amendment to prohibit the death penalty also amended Article 28.3 to ensure that the prohibition on the death penalty would still apply notwithstanding any legislative invocation of Article 28.3.

there is taking place an armed conflict in which the State is not a participant but in respect of which each of the Houses of the Oireachtas shall
have resolved that, arising out of such armed conflict, a national emergency exists affecting the vital interests of the State'. The Oireachtas
immediately made that resolution in respect of World War II, in which
Ireland remained neutral, and enacted the Emergency Powers Act 1939,
granting far reaching powers to the Government. This Act was repealed
after the end of World War II but the Oireachtas did not resolve that
the underlying state of emergency had ended until 1976. It then immediately resolved that a new emergency existed, 'arising out of the
armed conflict now taking place in Northern Ireland'. The Oireachtas
enacted the Emergency Powers Bill 1976, which granted police officers significant powers for warrantless arrests and searches. As we saw
in chapter four, President Cearbhall Ó Dálaigh doubted whether the
constitutional prerequisites for a state of emergency pertained and
referred the Bill to the Supreme Court pursuant to Article 26. The
Supreme Court held that the President was entitled to refer the Bill but
that the Court could only review whether the Oireachtas was entitled
to enact emergency legislation, not the content of the legislation. In
this regard, the Court held that there was a presumption that the facts
stated by the Oireachtas were correct and that presumption had not
been displaced.[96] This state of emergency continued until 1995. Davis
and Thornhill argue that the lengthy emergencies engendered a crime
control culture that affected the courts' attitude to criminal legislation
in general.[97] This may partly explain the judicial deference traced in the
previous section.

IX. INFLUENCE OF THE EUROPEAN CONVENTION
ON HUMAN RIGHTS

Ireland was an original signatory to the ECHR in 1953. However, because
of the dualist approach to international law,[98] the ECHR had no direct

---

[96] *Re Article 26 and the Emergency Powers Bill 1976* [1976] IR 159. See generally
A Greene, 'The Historical Evolution of Article 28.3.3° of the Irish Constitution' (2012) 48
The Irish Jurist 117. As discussed in ch 4, this episode led to the resignation of President
Ó Dálaigh.

[97] F Davis and C Thornhill, 'Article 28.3.3°: Terrorism, Democracy, Supra-Legality and
the 'State of Emergency' in the Irish Constitution' in E Carolan (ed), *The Constitution of
Ireland: Perspectives and Prospects* (Dublin, Bloomsbury, 2012) 355–72.

[98] See ch 2.

relevance for the Irish courts. The European Convention on Human Rights Act 2003, however, indirectly incorporates the Convention at sub-constitutional level. Obligations are imposed on various public actors to act consistently with Ireland's obligations under the Convention, in a manner not dissimilar from that adopted in the UK by the Human Rights Act 1998. Section 3 obliges public authorities to carry out their functions in accordance with Ireland's obligations under the Convention. Section 2 obliges the courts to interpret legislation in accordance with the Convention, subject to the existing canons of construction. Section 5 provides a procedure for establishing inconsistency between legislation and the Convention, leading to a declaration of incompatibility. However, this does not affect the continued operation of the statute. The remedies provided by the 2003 Act, in some cases by design and in other cases as a result of judicial interpretation, remain notably inferior to the remedies available under the Constitution.[99] As a result, constitutional claims must be considered in litigation before claims based on the ECHR, reducing the scope for Convention principles to play a significant role in Irish human rights law.[100]

The ECHR is also relevant, however, through the differentiated effect that the jurisprudence of the Strasbourg Court has on the judicial understanding of rights protected by the Irish Constitution. The Strasbourg Court unsurprisingly has the greatest influence where the values of the Convention broadly cohere with those of the Constitution. Thus in *People (DPP) v Gormley*, the Supreme Court significantly altered the parameters of the right of an accused person of reasonable access to a solicitor.[101] The courts had previously held that this right was not necessarily breached where the police questioned a suspect before she had the opportunity to consult with her solicitor.[102] In reversing this position, the Supreme Court placed considerable reliance on the case law of the Strasbourg Court, particularly its decision in *Salduz v Turkey* that the guarantee of a fair trial ordinarily required that an accused person have access to her solicitor before being questioned.[103] The unanimous Supreme Court judgment altered Irish constitutional law to bring it in line with what was required under the Convention.

---

[99] See O Doyle and D Ryan, 'Judicial Interpretation of the European Convention on Human Rights' (2011) 33 *Dublin University Law Journal* 369.

[100] *Carmody v Minister for Justice, Equality and Law Reform* [2009] IESC 71.

[101] *People (DPP) v Gormley* [2014] IESC 17.

[102] *People (Director of Public Prosecutions) v Buck* [2002] 2 IR 268.

[103] *Salduz v Turkey* (2009) 49 EHRR 19.

Where the Constitution and the Convention reflect different values, however, the jurisprudence of the ECtHR has little influence on the Irish courts' understanding of the Constitution. This is most obviously the case in respect of family rights. As noted above, Article 41 of the Constitution protects the family based on marriage, as a pre-civil entity. In contrast, Article 8 of the Convention protects an individual right to family life. In *McD v L*, the Supreme Court rejected any suggestion that a lesbian couple and their child, conceived through a sperm donor, could be a constitutionally protected family.[104] The Court refused to follow the jurisprudence of the Strasbourg Court to accept a notion of a *de facto* family.

The final way in which the ECHR has exerted an influence on Irish law has been through the bringing of cases to the European Court of Human Rights in Strasbourg. In some contexts, litigants have managed to secure a benefit in Strasbourg that was denied to them in Ireland. We have already seen examples of this phenomenon in this chapter. David Norris lost his constitutional challenge to Ireland's criminalisation of same-sex activity between men, but was successful before the European Court of Human Rights. The European Court has also taken a more expansive approach to civil legal aid in family law cases, the clarity of procedures for accessing services for the termination of pregnancy, and the right to silence in criminal cases, among other issues.

The courts' approach to the ECHR reflects a more general sense that the interpretation of the Irish Constitution is a self-contained activity. The courts see themselves as giving effect to the Irish Constitution's distinctive (albeit universalistic) understanding of human rights, rather than a transnational elaboration of common human rights standards. This disposition is consistent with the common law tradition and is perhaps also prompted by the fact that the Irish Constitution predates the post-war human rights movement and, of course, the ECHR itself. This militates against any suggestion that the interpretations of the ECtHR are directly relevant to what the Irish Constitution means. That said, the Irish courts are not hostile to the citation of foreign authority, as we have already seen at several points in this chapter. But they view foreign case law as illustrating judicial solutions to similar problems rather than as part of a shared process of human rights elaboration.

---

[104] *McD v L* [2010] IEHC 123, para 87.

X. HORIZONTALITY

A fundamental question about constitutions is whether their rights apply only vertically, as between individuals and the State, or also horizontally, as between citizens themselves. In a number of trade union cases in the 1960s and 1970s, the courts held that the Constitution's guarantee of freedom of association was horizontally applicable, effectively protecting workers who did not wish to join unions.[105] More recently, the Court of Appeal has held that a trade union breached the implicit right to work of a blocklayer by excluding him from membership of the union.[106] Somewhat curiously, the horizontal applicability of constitutional rights gained little traction outside the trade union context. In *Hanrahan v Merck Sharpe and Dohme Ltd*, the Supreme Court held that a cause of action in tort would have to be basically ineffective before the courts could intervene to reshape it in light of constitutional principles.[107]

The *Hanrahan* decision may have impeded the development of horizontally applicable constitutional rights. However, in two discrete areas the courts have more recently revived the doctrine of horizontality. In *Herrity v Associated Newspapers (Ireland) Ltd*, the High Court awarded damages against the defendant for breaching the plaintiff's implied constitutional right to privacy.[108] In *Sullivan v Boylan*, the High Court held that exceptionally unpleasant debt collection tactics by a building contractor unconstitutionally violated the dwelling.[109] It remains to be seen whether the Supreme Court will approve this reinvigoration of horizontality.

XI. PROCESSES OF RIGHTS LITIGATION

The courts have developed a set of procedural rules that limit the circumstances in which they are required to adjudicate on constitutional issues. The courts will avoid such questions unless absolutely necessary to resolve the dispute before them. This is consistent with what was described in *Buckley v Attorney General* as the 'respect which one great organ of State owes to another'. In *Cahill v Sutton*, the Supreme Court

---

[105] *Educational Company of Ireland v Fitzpatrick* [1961] IR 345.
[106] *O'Connell v Building and Allied Trade Union* [2016] IECA 338.
[107] *Hanrahan v Merck Sharpe and Dohme Ltd* [1988] ILRM 629.
[108] *Herrity v Associated Newspapers (Ireland) Ltd* [2008] IEHC 249.
[109] *Sullivan v Boylan* [2012] IEHC 389 and [2013] IEHC 104.

established the basic standing rule that only people personally affected by the impugned measure have standing to challenge the constitutionality of that measure.[110] *Cahill* also stands for the proposition that a litigant cannot invoke a *ius tertii*, an argument that is more properly the argument of another party. However, both of these are subject to exceptions. In *Norris v Attorney General*, the plaintiff was allowed (ultimately unsuccessfully) to challenge the constitutionality of legislation criminalising same-sex activity between men.[111] Although he had never been prosecuted for the offences and there was a de facto policy of non-enforcement, the continued existence of the offence was itself sufficient to confer standing. In *Crotty v An Taoiseach*, the Supreme Court held that citizens have standing to challenge the constitutionality of measures that affect everyone in general but no-one in particular, in this case Ireland's ratification of the Single European Act.[112] In *Society for the Protection of the Unborn Child v Coogan*,[113] the plaintiff was allowed to assert the constitutional rights of unborn children on the basis that it had a bona fide interest in the issue and no foetus could ever be a plaintiff. The generous approach of the courts to standing has enhanced their own power. In particular, a citizen's ability to challenge general Government decisions (as in *Crotty*) makes the courts a significant player in high constitutional politics.

Where legislation is declared unconstitutional, it is theoretically deemed void either *ab initio*, or since 1937 if it was enacted prior to the Constitution coming into force. However, in *A v Governor of Arbour Hill Prison*, the Supreme Court held that any official action taken on foot of legislation prior to a declaration of unconstitutionality would continue to have effect after the declaration of unconstitutionality.[114] In that case, as noted above, the Court ordered the continued imprisonment of a child rapist who had been convicted of an offence subsequently declared unconstitutional in a case raising very different issues.[115] The prospective effect of a declaration of unconstitutionality, however, is *erga omnes*.

The courts have a preference for negative remedies, such as the declaration of unconstitutionality. In *Somjee v Minister for Justice*, the High Court held that there could be no remedy against a legislative measure

---

[110] *Cahill v Sutton* [1980] IR 269.
[111] *Norris v Attorney General* [1984] IR 36.
[112] *Crotty v An Taoiseach* [1987] IR 713. See discussion in ch 2.
[113] *Society for the Protection of the Unborn Child v Coogan* [1989] IR 734.
[114] *A v Governor of Arbour Hill Prison* [2006] IESC 45.
[115] *C v Ireland (No 2)* [2006] IESC 33.

that conferred a benefit unequally on one group of people since striking the measure down would bring no advantage to the aggrieved
plaintiff.[116] The courts have not identified any clear jurisdiction to issue
suspended declarations in a manner similar to the Canadian Supreme
Court. However, in a number of recent cases, the Supreme Court has
taken something akin to this approach.[117] In recent years the courts have
displayed a little more imagination in fashioning remedies. For instance,
in *Carmody v Director of Public Prosecutions*, the Supreme Court held
unconstitutional the categorical non-availability of criminal legal aid
to cover the fees of a barrister (as well as a solicitor) in District Court
proceedings.[118] As a remedy, the Court prohibited the further trial of
Mr Carmody unless or until a legislative scheme was put in place to allow
him apply for such criminal legal aid. The courts' aversion to positive
remedies is seen most clearly in the case of *TD v Minister for Education*,
discussed above, drastically narrowing the circumstances in which the
courts could issue a mandatory order to enforce constitutional rights.[119]

The courts' power to reinterpret legislation to ensure its compat-
ibility with the Constitution is as significant as their power to declare
legislation unconstitutional. In *McDonald v Bord na gCon*, the Supreme
Court considered a challenge to the constitutionality of certain provisions of the Greyhound Industry Act 1958.[120] On its face, the legislation
did not provide the constitutionally required fair procedures before
Bord na gCon, the Greyhound Board, made decisions such as excluding a person from attending at any public sale of greyhounds. Walsh J
held that where two constructions of a statute were reasonably open, it
must be presumed that the Oireachtas intended only the constitutional
construction. Walsh J therefore read in provisions to the effect that a
proper investigation with natural justice would be carried out before
an exclusion order was made. This illustrates the interpretative extent
to which the courts will go to uphold legislation. However, the courts
will not override express and clear provisions in order to render legislation constitutional; the only remedy in that instance is a declaration of
unconstitutionality.[121]

---

[116] *Somjee v Minister for Justice* [1981] ILRM 324.

[117] *NVH v Minister for Justice and Equality* [2017] IESC 35; *PC v Minister for Social Welfare* [2017] IESC 63. More recently, the Court of Appeal has suspended declarations of unconstitutionality: *AB v The Clinical Director of St Loman's Hospital* [2018] IECA 123.

[118] *Carmody v Minister for Justice, Equality and Law Reform* [2009] IESC 71.

[119] *TD v Minister for Education* [2001] 2 IR 259.

[120] *McDonald v Bord na gCon* [1965] IR 217.

[121] See *Kelly v Minister for the Environment* [2002] 4 IR 191.

XII. CONCLUSION

In chapter one, I noted that Ireland is highly rated internationally both for the quality of its democracy and for its protection of political and civil rights. These are not the only standards against which a constitutional order can or should be judged. Nevertheless, they provide a context for assessing the overall contribution of the courts to the interpretation of fundamental rights. When one steps back from the specifics, the broad picture is one of a reasonably well-balanced scheme of human rights protection. Within that picture, we have identified a number of broad trends. The changing approach of the courts to the interpretation of these provisions has deprived the Constitution of one of its most distinctive features, namely its natural law orientation. Through a series of small changes, the courts have largely reconstructed those provisions most influenced by the natural law into provisions that would be typical of any liberal democratic constitution.

The attitude of the courts to judicial intervention is a more complicated story, with very different approaches taken at different times and in respect of different issues. One could sympathetically construct a rationale for these differences of approach. In the 1960s, Ireland was a sclerotic and conservative society that required liberalisation. The courts took on an atypical role that could no longer be justified after the necessary liberalisation occurred. Now that Ireland is sufficiently liberal democratic, the courts should resume a more passive posture. They should continue to protect individuals from an overbearing State, but should not become involved in the reallocation of resources. It is equally possible, of course, to construct a more critical account. The courts usurped democratic governance by taking such an expansive approach to the Constitution. But if they were going to take this approach, they should not have limited themselves to protecting the rights that were of relevance to upper middle-class liberals, being the social group from which members of the judiciary are almost universally drawn (chapter eight). They should also have protected socioeconomic rights.

There is truth and exaggeration in both of these accounts. Both the activist and the non-activist phases of judicial decision-making fall within the boundaries of what is constitutionally appropriate. The more important point, I suggest, is to recognise the current phase for what it is. Electoral politics must take account of the fact that the courts do not circumscribe the Government to the same extent as in the 1960s and 1970s. This is a double-edged observation. On the one hand, Governments may be freer to implement social change than they realise. The threat of an activist judiciary should not be used to explain governmental inaction. On the other hand, those wary of Government overreach or hoping for social change cannot rely on the courts to protect them or bring this about. Finally, once we historically situate the current judicial approach to the Constitution in this way, we see that it may not continue. The development of Irish constitutional law was driven by a largely Catholic and activist judiciary from the 1960s to the 1990s, and by a largely post-Catholic and non-activist judiciary from the 2000s to date. We cannot predict when this current phase will end, but end it will.

FURTHER READING

Hilary Biehler and Catherine Donnelly 'Proportionality in the Irish Courts: the Need for Guidance' (2014) 3 *European Human Rights Law Review* 272

Eoin Daly, *Religion, Law and the Irish State* (Dublin, Clarus Press, 2012)

Oran Doyle, 'Legal Positivism, Natural Law and the Constitution' (2009) 31 *Dublin University Law Journal* 206

Oran Doyle, *Constitutional Equality Law* (Dublin, Round Hall Thomson, 2004)

Oran Doyle, 'Conventional Constitutional Law' (2015) 38 *DULJ* 206

Brian Foley, *Deference and the Presumption of Constitutionality* (Dublin, Institute of Public Administration, 2008)

Gerard Hogan, 'Unenumerated Personal Rights: Ryan's Case Re-evaluated' (1990–1992) 25–27 *Irish Jurist* 95

Gerard Hogan, 'The Constitution, Property Rights and Proportionality' (1997) 32 *Irish Jurist* 373

Gerard Hogan, David Kenny and Rachael Walsh, 'An Anthology of Declarations of Unconstitutionality' (2015) 54(2) *The Irish Jurist* 24

Gerard Hogan and Gerry Whyte, *Kelly: The Irish Constitution* 4th edn (Dublin, LexisNexis Butterworths, 2003), 1039–2086

Richard Humphreys, 'Interpreting Natural Rights' (1993–1995) *Irish Jurist* 221

Aileen Kavanagh, 'The Irish Constitution at 75 Years: Natural Law, Christian Values and the Idea of Justice' (2012) 47 (2) *Irish Jurist* 71

David Kenny, 'Proportionality and the Inevitability of the Local: a Comparative Localist Analysis of Canada and Ireland (2018) 66 *American Journal of Comparative Law* (forthcoming)

David Gwynn Morgan, 'Judicial-o-centric Separation of Powers on the Wane?' (2004) 34 *Irish Jurist* 142

Colm O'Cinneide, 'The Missing Social Dimension to the Irish Constitutional Order: Time to Think Again about the Legal Protection of Socio-Economic Rights' (2014) 37 *Dublin University Law Journal* 173

David Prendergast, 'The Constitutionality of Strict Liability in Criminal Law' (2011) 33 *Dublin University Law Journal* 285

Rachael Walsh, 'The Constitution, Property Rights and Proportionality – A Re-appraisal' (2009) 31 *Dublin University Law Journal* 1

Rachael Walsh, 'Private Property Rights in the Drafting of the Irish Constitution: A Communitarian Compromise' (2011) 33 *Dublin University Law Journal* 86

Gerry Whyte, 'The Role of the Supreme Court in our Democracy: A Reply to Mr Justice Hardiman' (2006) 28 *Dublin University Law Journal* 1

Gerry Whyte, 'Education and the Constitution: A Convergence of Paradigm and Praxis' (1992) 25–27 *Irish Jurist* 69

10

Constitutional Change

Informal Constitutional Change – Forms and Limits of Constitutional Amendment – Pattern of Constitutional Amendment – Dilution of Nationalistic and Catholic Characteristics – Social Change and Political Responsibility – Constitutional Change and the Balance of Power

I. INTRODUCTION

THE HISTORY OF constitutional change is a history of the relationship between a constitution and the political community it regulates, shedding light on fundamental societal forces and attitudes. In the preceding chapters, we have traced how the balance of constitutional power has shifted in Ireland since 1937. However, it has been the subject of very little deliberate change through the formal amendment process. This may partly result from the amendment processes but it also bespeaks a general stability in the fundamental governance structures of the State. Formal amendment has played a far greater role in relation to the removal of the distinctive features of the Constitution reflecting a Gaelic national identity and a social teaching rooted in (but not exclusive to) scholastic natural law theory.

A study of constitutional change is of more than historical interest, however. The mechanisms for constitutional change are highly relevant to an assessment of where power lies within the constitutional order. In the Irish context, the mechanisms of constitutional change complicate the picture of Government dominance painted in the previous chapters. Although the Government has, assuming it holds a majority in the Dáil, the sole right to initiate constitutional change, it must secure the approval of the people voting in a referendum. The people thus function as a further legal check on the power of the Government.[1]

---

[1] Although the courts have developed a doctrine of popular sovereignty (see ch 2), the inability of the people to initiate a constitutional change significantly undermines this characterisation. It is better to see the people as an important constraint in the amendment

The potential of a popular veto likely inhibits the sort of amendment proposals that Governments are prepared even to contemplate. This in turn enhances the power of the courts, whose interpretations of the Constitution become more difficult to overturn. It also means that constitutional change is subject to more deliberation and debate than ordinary laws, although not always to a terribly high standard. This has opened up space for the involvement of civic society and interest groups in constitutional politics and, more recently, a turn towards forums of deliberative democracy.

In this chapter, I shall first explain how constitutional change is not limited to formal amendment of the master-text constitution, but also includes informal constitutional change. I shall then examine the processes and limits of formal constitutional amendment, observing how the Irish courts have eschewed any substantive review of amendment proposals while ensuring that fair processes of constitutional amendment are followed. I shall identify the trends of formal constitutional amendment over the past 80 years, highlighting the areas in which the people have been more or less willing to accept constitutional change. I shall then explore in detail how the Constitution has changed, both formally and informally, in relation to hot-button moral issues, such as marriage and abortion, leading to a more generic liberal-democratic Constitution. This leads into a discussion of the roles played by various actors in the promotion of constitutional change.

II. INFORMAL CONSTITUTIONAL CHANGE

As explained in chapter one, we tend to operate with two understandings of the word 'constitution'. On the one hand, there is the master-text constitution, in Ireland's case the document enacted by plebiscite in 1937. On the other hand, there is the set of laws and practices that constitute the governance function of the State. In this book, I have examined the master-text constitution in the context of a broader set of constitutional laws and practices. Broadly speaking, the master-text constitution is changed through formal amendment; the informal constitution is changed through amendments to its laws or development of its practices. Many constitutional theorists, however, have drawn attention to a

process rather than as exercising meaningful control of the Constitution. See E Daly and T Hickey, *The Political Theory of the Irish Constitution: Republicanism and the Basic Law* (Manchester, Manchester University Press, 2015) ch 1.

phenomenon whereby the master-text constitution is changed other than through its own formal amendment mechanism.[2]

I have argued elsewhere that this phenomenon is best characterised as informal constitutional change: without amending the master-text constitution in any way, there is an alteration to the way in which the norms in the master-text constitution operate.[3] A set of posited norms will, if followed, produce a norm-driven pattern of behaviour. When there is an informal constitutional change, that pattern of behaviour departs from what is prescribed by the master-text constitution. This can happen in a number of different ways. Political practices can emerge and settle into constitutional conventions, constraining political actors from exercising their constitutional powers. In chapter three, I identified the constitutional conventions of not extending the term of the Oireachtas beyond five years and implementing the recommendations of independent boundary commissions for Dáil constituencies. A second way in which informal constitutional change occurs is through constitutional statutes, by which I mean statutes that closely relate to the constitution of the governance function of the State. These may regulate issues that in other countries appear in the master-text constitution.[4] Examples of this are the Republic of Ireland Act 1948, which changed the designation of the State and assigned to the President formal powers in relation to foreign affairs that had previously been assigned to the King of England.[5]

A third way in which informal constitutional change occurs is through desuetude. Sometimes, constitutional provisions simply fall out of use, a point we shall explore below. A fourth way in which informal constitutional change can occur is through judicial decision-making. Judicial decisions that go beyond the bounds of legitimate constitutional interpretation cause informal constitutional change, unless or until they are overruled. Because legitimate constitutional interpretation is contested, the boundaries of informal constitutional change by judicial decision will be similarly contested. In Ireland, the unenumerated

---

[2] For a useful recent account of the debate over informal constitutional amendments, see C Martin, 'The Legitimacy of Informal Constitutional Amendment and the "Reinterpretation" of Japan's War Powers' (2017) 40 *Fordham Int'l LJ* 427.

[3] See O Doyle, 'Informal Constitutional Change' (2017) 65 *Buff L Rev* 739.

[4] For an account of constitutional statutes in the United Kingdom, see F Ahmed and A Perry, 'Constitutional Statutes' (2017) 37 *OJLS* 461. For an account of quasi-constitutional statutes in Canada, see V MacDonnell, 'A Theory of Quasi-Constitutional Legislation' (2016) 53 *Osgoode Hall LJ* 508.

[5] See discussion in ch 2.

rights doctrine – established in *Ryan v Attorney General*[6] but with its most compelling appearance in *McGee v Attorney General*[7] – amounts to informal constitutional change.[8] Through these two decisions, the courts first created a power to identify new constitutional rights and then used that power to introduce a radically new type of constitutional right (privacy), leading to the strike-down of a law (the ban on the sale and importation of contraceptives) that was unquestionably considered constitutional by those who had framed and enacted the Constitution in 1937. The Supreme Court decision in *Boland v An Taoiseach*, creating a power on the part of the courts to review the constitutionality of executive action, is arguably a further example of informal constitutional change through judicial decision-making.[9]

III. THE FORMS AND LIMITS
OF CONSTITUTIONAL AMENDMENT

We saw in chapter one how the easy amendability of the Irish Free State Constitution played a significant role in its downfall. An initial eight-year period during which amendments could be made by ordinary legislation was itself extended for a further eight years. The 1937 Constitution determinedly avoids the same mistakes. Article 46 provides that amendment is only possible by way of referendum. Article 51 of the Constitution allowed amendments to be made to any provision of the Constitution by the Oireachtas within a period of three years of the first President coming into office. The President could preclude use of the Article 51 amendment process if, after consultation with the Council of State, she signified her opinion that the proposal was 'of such character and importance that the will of the people thereon ought to be ascertained by referendum'.[10] Article 51 also provided that this amendment process could not be used to amend either Article 46 or Article 51 itself, thereby preventing the unravelling that had occurred under the 1922 Constitution. Amendments were twice passed under the Article 51

[6] *Ryan v Attorney General* [1965] IR 294. See discussion in ch 9.
[7] *McGee v Attorney General* [1974] IR 284.
[8] Indeed, this is one of the bases on which some academic commentators objected to the unenumerated rights doctrine: it amounted to constitutional amendment rather than constitutional interpretation. See for instance G Hogan, 'Unenumerated Personal Rights: Ryan's Case Re-evaluated' (1990–1992) 25–27 *Irish Jurist* 95. See generally ch 9.
[9] *Boland v An Taoiseach* [1974] IR 338. See discussion in ch 8.
[10] This is a further example of the suspensive veto role of the President, argued for by Coffey. See discussion in ch 4.

procedure: one to correct a series of mostly minor errors, the other to amend the emergency provisions of the Constitution upon the outbreak of World War II. These will be considered further below.

Article 46 grants a broad power of constitutional amendment, allowing any provision of the Constitution to be amended, whether by way of variation, addition, or repeal. Every proposal to amend the Constitution must be submitted as a Bill to the Dáil before being passed by both Houses of the Oireachtas. It is then submitted to a referendum where a simple majority of those voting is required to pass. All citizens who are entitled to vote in elections for the Dáil are entitled to vote. The President must sign the Bill into law if she is satisfied that these procedural requirements have been complied with.

The courts have consistently rejected all claims that there are substantive limits on the content of referendum proposals. The most prominent of these cases is *Re Article 26 and the Regulation of Information (Services Outside the State for Termination of Pregnancies) Bill 1995*.[11] In 1983, the people amended the Constitution to insert a new Article 40.3.3°, protecting the right to life of the unborn child. In 1992, the people approved a further amendment stating that the pro-life provision did not limit the freedom to obtain or make available in Ireland information relating to abortion services lawfully available in other States. In order to give legislative effect to this constitutional amendment, the Oireachtas passed a Bill that was referred to the Supreme Court by the President under Article 26 of the Constitution. It was argued that the Bill was unconstitutional because the underlying constitutional amendment was itself unconstitutional. This argument was supported with reference to constitutional provisions and judicial *dicta* that appeared to recognise the natural law as superior to all positive law, by implication including the Constitution. Assuming abortion to be contrary to natural law, it was claimed that any constitutional amendment facilitating access to abortion could not be constitutional. The Supreme Court held, not very convincingly, that there had been no recognition of 'the provisions of natural law as superior to the Constitution.' It followed that the people were entitled to enact the Amendment, which was 'the fundamental and supreme law of the State representing as it does the will of the People'.[12]

---

[11] [1995] 1 IR 1. For discussion, see O Doyle, 'Legal Validity: Reflections on the Irish Constitution' (2003) 25 *Dublin University Law Journal* 56 and A Kavanagh, 'Unconstitutional Constitutional Amendments from Irish Free State to Irish Republic' in E Carolan (ed), *The Constitution of Ireland: Perspectives and Prospects* (Dublin, Bloomsbury Professional, 2012) 331.

[12] *Re Article 26 and the Regulation of Information (Services Outside the State for Termination of Pregnancies) Bill 1995* [1995] 1 IR 1, 43.

In subsequent cases, the Supreme Court has repeatedly emphasised that it will not review the content of constitutional amendments. In *Riordan v An Taoiseach (No 2)*, the Supreme Court rejected a challenge to the constitutionality of the amendments to give effect to the Northern Ireland Peace Settlement.[13] As discussed in chapter two, part of the settlement involved the amendment of the Irish Constitution to remove the territorial claim to Northern Ireland, until then contained in Articles 2 and 3. However, as the settlement involved a complex set of interlocking obligations, there was a concern on the Irish side that the Irish Constitution could be amended without the parallel referendum in Northern Ireland being carried, or without the Northern Ireland parties subsequently meeting their obligations to operate the new institutions in Northern Ireland. For this reason, the Referendum Bill made the proposed revocation of Articles 2 and 3 conditional on a Government declaration that the State had become obliged, pursuant to the Agreement, to give effect to those amendments. Mr Riordan argued that the people had impermissibly delegated the power of constitutional amendment to the Government. The Court rejected this characterisation of the amendment. However, Barrington J also stated concisely the courts' general position:

> Provided the appropriate procedures are complied with there are no circumstances in which this Court could purport to sit in judgment on an authentic expression of the people's will or an amendment of the Constitution made in accordance with the provisions of Article 46.[14]

Although the courts refuse to review the content of amendment proposals, they are prepared to intervene to ensure that correct procedures are followed. Some of these procedures are stipulated in the text of the Constitution, such as the requirement that an Act to Amend the Constitution cannot contain any other proposal.[15]

Beyond the explicit procedural requirements of Article 46, however, the courts have also implied an obligation of fairness in respect of referendum campaigns. In *McKenna v An Taoiseach (No 2)*, the Supreme Court held that it was unconstitutional for the State to spend money supporting only one side of a referendum campaign.[16] There was no clear textual basis for this decision, but it can be defended as a reasonable

---

[13] *Riordan v An Taoiseach (No 2)* [1999] 4 IR 343.
[14] ibid 358–9.
[15] *Morris v Minister for the Environment* [2002] 1 IR 326.
[16] *McKenna v An Taoiseach (No 2)* [1995] 2 IR 10.

judicial intervention to ensure fairness in a fundamental constitutional process. Following this decision, the Government ceased to fund either side of a referendum campaign. Legislation now provides for the creation of an impartial Referendum Commission, chaired by a Judge, tasked with explaining the referendum proposal and encouraging people to vote.[17]

There has been political concern, whenever referendum proposals were rejected, that the Government's role in promoting referendum proposals was unduly restricted by the *McKenna* decision, engendering a lack of public awareness, leading to proposals being rejected by the people on a precautionary basis.[18] For the children's rights referendum in 2012, the Government therefore decided that it would provide its own 'public information campaign', in addition to that provided by the impartial Referendum Commission. In *McCrystal v Minister for Children and Youth Affairs*, the Supreme Court unanimously held that this campaign breached the *McKenna* principles.[19] The Court rejected the Government's claim that the 'public information campaign' was neutral and balanced, pointing to several aspects of the material that appeared calculated to suggest a 'yes' vote. Although the Government had sought to argue that its information campaign was consistent with the *McKenna* principles (rather than challenge the basis for *McKenna* itself), the strength of the Court's judgment likely means that the *McKenna* principles remain secure in Irish constitutional law, despite the unease frequently expressed by political actors. The *McKenna* principles may appear technical but they play a significant role in limiting the ability of the Government to secure constitutional change. Given its dominance within the constitutional order, this helps to prevent unchecked executive dominance. In January 2018, a Citizens' Assembly was tasked by the Oireachtas with considering the manner in which referendums are held. The Assembly recommended (87 per cent vote) to retain the current prohibition on the Government spending money on one side of a referendum campaign, although a slightly smaller majority supported the recommendation that the Government fund both sides equally. This suggests that there is popular, if not political, support

---

[17] Referendum Act 1998, as amended.

[18] G Barrett, 'Building a Swiss Chalet in an Irish Legal Landscape? Referendums on European Union Treaties in Ireland & the Impact of Supreme Court Jurisprudence' (2009) 5 *Eur Const L Rev* 32; B Ruane, 'The Doherty Case and Issues Regarding the Provision of Information and Funding for Constitutional Referenda' in Carolan (ed) (n 11).

[19] *McCrystal v Minister for Children and Youth Affairs* [2012] IESC 53.

for the way in which the *McKenna* principles enhance the constraint of popular approval during referendum campaigns.

Despite their willingness to scrutinise the procedures of constitutional amendment, the courts have only ever granted declaratory relief in respect of breaches of the *McKenna* principles. A week after the Supreme Court judgment in *McKenna*, the amendment proposal was carried by a margin of just 0.6 per cent. The Supreme Court subsequently rejected a challenge to the referendum result, applying the statutory standard that it was necessary for the petitioner to show that the constitutional wrongdoing 'materially affected the result of the referendum as a whole'.[20] This was a virtually impossible standard to meet, given scepticism over opinion poll evidence and a constitutional bar on any citizen being required to give evidence of how she voted. A similar challenge failed in respect of the children's rights referendum in 2012, which had been approved by the much larger margin of 58 per cent to 42 per cent after the Government's unconstitutional information campaign.[21] The Supreme Court appeared to soften its earlier approach, holding that the 'material effect on the outcome of the referendum' test involved establishing that 'it is reasonably possible that the irregularity or interference identified affected the result'. Its purpose was 'to identify the point at which it can be said that a reasonable person would be in doubt about, and no longer trust, the provisional outcome of the election or referendum'. One suspects that this test might have produced a different outcome in the earlier challenge to the divorce referendum. Nevertheless, the test continues to reflect a real concern on the part of the courts not to overturn the sovereign voice of the people, once they have spoken.

IV. PATTERN OF CONSTITUTIONAL AMENDMENT

41 amendment proposals have been approved by the Oireachtas. Two of these were made under the three-year rule and therefore did not require popular approval by referendum. Of the remaining 39, 28 were approved by the people and 11 were rejected. With the exception of the compendious second amendment, largely correcting typographical

---

[20] *Hanafin v Minister for the Environment* [1996] 2 IR 321. This standard was laid down in s 43 of the Referendum Act 1994. Given the constitutional significance of a referendum, however, the Supreme Court could have moulded the standard to produce a less onerous requirement on the petitioner. The Court's decision, therefore, can be taken as its understanding of what the Constitution, not simply the statute, required.

[21] *Jordan v Minister for Children and Youth Affairs* [2015] IESC 33.

errors in the constitutional text, each amendment can fairly be characterised as a discrete constitutional change or set of constitutional
changes. The first 25 years saw two amendments. The second 25 years
saw eight amendments. The last 31 years have seen 20 amendments. This
suggests that the Constitution is not very difficult to amend, although
the actual amendment rate is of course also a product of social and
political forces.[22]

The Constitution makes it relatively easy for political actors to
propose a constitutional amendment. In the ordinary course of politics,
the Government should be able to secure the approval of an amendment proposal so that it can be put to the people. We might therefore
wonder why only 39 amendments have been put to the people. The
simplest explanation would be that political actors have generally seen
little reason to amend the Constitution. Although there is some truth to
this explanation, it is not the full story. As noted above, the people have
rejected 11 of the 39 amendment proposals put before them, an attrition rate of over 25 per cent. The people have come close to rejection
of proposals that had near unanimous support in the Oireachtas, such
as the divorce referendum in 1995 which was supported by all political
parties but approved at referendum by a margin of less than 1 per cent.
Moreover, the people have been particularly sceptical of the more significant changes suggested to core constitutional structures, such as altering
the electoral system for Dáil elections, granting a power of inquiry to
Oireachtas committees, and abolishing the Seanad. This suggests a
conservatism on the part of the people when it comes to constitutional
amendment, or at least a wariness of simply accepting whatever the
political classes recommend. Because the promotion of a referendum
proposal requires significant political capital, the risk of defeat incen-
tivises the Government not to suggest a constitutional amendment in the
first place. In this way, the people function as a real check on the political power of the Government even when not exercising their legal power
to veto referendum proposals.

This power of the people has knock-on implications for other
constitutional actors. Most notably, it empowers the courts, whose interpretations of the Constitution become more difficult to change. Judicial
review is a meaningful power because judicial decisions cannot be easily
circumvented. What results is a balance between the Government,

---

[22] Lutz estimated that the Irish Constitution was the 11th most difficult to amend in
a dataset of 32 constitutions. D Lutz, *Principles of Constitutional Design* (New York,
Cambridge University Press, 2006) 171.

courts and people. The Government holds the greatest autonomy, since it can secure the enactment of new legislation and take new actions to test constitutional standards, as well as holding the power to initiate constitutional change. The courts hold greater power, in the sense that their interpretation of the Constitution is final. However, the courts can only decide cases that are litigated, notwithstanding that they can give some signals as to the sorts of cases that might be successful. The people have no autonomy (they can only vote on referendum proposals approved by the Government) but they hold the ultimate veto power. This assuredly affects the behaviour of the Government and may also affect the courts.

We can see these dynamics play out in a number of ways. Many constitutional amendments can be characterised as directly reactive to court judgments. For example, all the international organisation amendments (with the exception of original accession to the EEC), were thought necessary because of the Supreme Court's decision in *Crotty v An Taoiseach*,[23] requiring an amendment to allow Ireland sign up to the Single European Act. Several amendment proposals have been attempts to overturn the effect of Supreme Court interpretations of the Constitution. Four amendment proposals on abortion were prompted by the *X case*.[24] Without counting the referendums in relation to European and other international treaties, 13 referendum proposals have involved fairly direct responses to judicial interpretations of the Constitution. Amendments have been passed in order to alter the effect of judicial decisions in relation to citizenship, the franchise for Dáil elections, eligibility for bail, cabinet confidentiality, and children's rights. All of these reversed the constitutional law based on judicial decisions as to the meaning of the Constitution. Amendments of this type have been rejected in respect of abortion and the public inquiry power of the Oireachtas.

Some have argued that this capacity for constitutional change is relevant to the way in which the courts should exercise their power of constitutional review.[25] The courts should be less concerned about overturning the democratic will as expressed through the Oireachtas, since it is relatively easy for the Oireachtas to ask the people to return the Constitution back to its meaning prior to the judicial intervention.

---

[23] *Crotty v An Taoiseach* [1987] IR 713. See ch 2.

[24] *Attorney General v X* [1992] 1 IR 1.

[25] G Whyte, 'The role of the Supreme Court in our Democracy: A Response to Mr. Justice Hardiman' (2006) 28 *Dublin University Law Journal* 1.

However, this dialogue is not without its problems. Judge-made constitutional law involves a mixture of broad principles and very specific conclusions. It is difficult to draft laws that can reliably change these conclusions. It is even more difficult to explain those laws to ordinary people during a referendum campaign. The Children's Rights Amendment of 2012 represented the nadir of this approach to constitutional law-making, a vacuous amendment proposal justified by an incoherent account of existing constitutional law.[26]

The relationship between political actors and people is highlighted by the fact that on five occasions, the people have been asked to vote again on a proposal similar to one they had previously rejected. In 1959 and 1968, the people rejected proposals to change the voting system for Dáil elections from PR-STV. In 1986, the people rejected a proposal to amend the constitution to allow for divorce. They subsequently approved a proposal in 1995, although subject to more limitations. In 1992 and 2002, the people rejected referendum proposals designed to overturn the decision of the Supreme Court in the X *case* that allowed for a termination of pregnancy where there was a threat to the woman's life from suicide.[27] During the 2000s, the people twice initially rejected a referendum to allow EU Treaty change (Nice Treaty in 2001; Lisbon Treaty in 2008) before approving a slightly revised proposal roughly 18 months later. In both cases, turnout significantly increased for the second vote, supporting the view that the earlier failure was at least in part attributable to a lacklustre campaign on the part of the Government. Although a feature of the second Nice and Lisbon campaigns was accusations that it was undemocratic to ask the people to vote again, this contention is unsustainable. The people are entitled to change their minds.

Thematically, we can divide referendums into three different types. Twelve amendments relate to what might be termed hot-button social and moral issues. As we saw in chapter one, de Valera described the Constitution as not merely providing a structure of government but also as being a fundamental charter for the Irish people. Issues that in many other countries are now dealt with at legislative level, in Ireland find a home in the Constitution. These dynamics most prominently play out in respect of sex, family, children and abortion. I shall explore

---

[26] O Doyle and D Kenny, 'Constitutional Change and Interest Group Politics' in R Albert, X Contiades and A Fotiadou, *The Foundations and Traditions of Constitutional Amendment* (Oxford, Hart Publishing, 2017).

[27] *Attorney General v X* [1992] 1 IR 1.

these dynamics further in the next section. Eight amendments relate to Ireland's participation in international organisations and are attributable to a cautious interpretation of the judgment of the Supreme Court in *Crotty v An Taoiseach*, which required a constitutional referendum for Ireland to sign up to the common foreign policy elements of the Single European Act.[28]

Ten of the amendments relate to the powers of government. However, these have not significantly altered the structure of government in the State. They address states of emergency (1939), formal judgment requirements for the Supreme Court (1941 and 2013), voting entitlements (1973, 1979 and 1983), cabinet confidentiality (1997), local government (1999), judicial pay (2011) and the establishment of a Court of Appeal (2013). These amendments were not unimportant but none involved significant change to the structure of governance in the State. This becomes even clearer when we consider the proposals rejected by the people. As noted above, the people twice rejected proposals to change the Dáil voting system from PR-STV to first past the post (1959 and 1968). In 2011, the people rejected a proposal to grant a general power of public inquiry to the Houses of the Oireachtas. In 2013, the people rejected a proposal to abolish the Seanad. What these rejected proposals had in common was the further empowerment of the Government, through the diminution of checks and balances in the constitutional system. There may have been good reasons to expand political power in these ways but the popular rejection suggests that the people are reasonably content with constitutional structures, or at least sceptical of granting more powers to political actors. An interesting feature of these rejected proposals is that they were all opposed by the principal opposition party. This further emphasises the importance of the people as a check on the rebalancing of constitutional power to suit a temporary political majority.

Complicating this account, however, are the amendments passed to allow Ireland join the European Communities in 1973 and authorise subsequent amendments to the European treaties. These amendments authorised constitutional changes of great significance: essentially the creation of a new legislature, court and executive with greater powers than the existing constitutional organs in many areas. The people's reluctance to amend the domestic structures of government therefore coexists with an authorisation of significant constitutional change to enable membership of a supranational organisation. Although constitutional concerns motivated many to vote against various European

---

[28] *Crotty v An Taoiseach* [1987] IR 713. See ch 2.

Treaties, it seems reasonable to surmise that voters who supported these amendments did so not because of the constitutional changes per se but rather on the basis of an assessment that Ireland needed to be part of this supranational entity. The debate was over whether constitutional change was a permissible price to pay, not whether the constitutional change was itself desirable. In this regard, continued involvement in European integration may have provided a positive reason to vote for the amendment that was lacking for other proposals to change the structure of governance. As we saw in chapter two, the Irish people are the most positive in Europe about European integration. In short, significant constitutional change has been made to enable Ireland's continued membership of the European Union but this exists alongside a general reluctance to approve significant changes to the domestic constitutional structures.

V. CONSTITUTIONAL CHANGE: DILUTION OF NATIONALISTIC AND CATHOLIC CHARACTERISTICS

Over time, the Irish Constitution has become more like other constitutions. While the nationalistic and religious sentiments were not particularly distinctive in 1937, they became so as interwar constitutions were largely replaced following World War II and the later collapse of dictatorships in Spain and Portugal. We have already seen in chapter two how the nationalistic elements of the Constitution have changed over time. A series of judicial decisions ensured that the Government could effectively recognise Northern Ireland as part of the United Kingdom without constitutional objection.[29] This was formalised with the constitutional amendments in 1998 to give effect to the Northern Ireland peace settlement.

A similar but more convoluted story can be told in respect of the religious features of the Irish Constitution, which came under increasing strain as Irish society gradually became less religious. We have already seen in chapter nine how judicial interpretation of the Constitution has oriented it away from its natural law origins towards a more generic liberal democratic bent. Constitutional change has taken a similar path. Political scientists have identified a 'potentially powerful religious-conservative versus secular-liberal cleavage' underlying politics

---

[29] *Boland v An Taoiseach* [1974] IR 338; *McGimpsey v Ireland* [1990] 1 IR 110. See ch 2.

in Ireland.[30] The notion of a political cleavage is somewhat simplistic and fails to do justice to the reasons for which individuals hold their moral positions. Nevertheless, it does provide some insight into shifting attitudes. Both sides of the political cleavage have employed strategies of formal amendment and informal change to advance their own position. In recent years, the liberal side of the political cleavage has been in the ascendancy, resulting in a more typically liberal-democratic constitution, but this has not been a story of linear development.

The period in the mid-1970s saw some successes for the liberal side of the political cleavage. In 1972, the people approved by a large majority an amendment proposal to remove the reference in Article 44.1 to the special position of the Catholic Church. This was partly an attempt to deconfessionalise the Irish State, albeit one that did not convince one of its target audiences, Northern unionists.[31] The unenumerated rights doctrine, itself an instance of informal constitutional change, provided a route for the recognition of more liberal constitutional rights, most significantly in *McGee v Attorney General*, in which the Supreme Court declared unconstitutional a ban on the importation and sale of contraceptives.[32] Following these initial successes, the more conservative side of the political cleavage came to dominate. Notwithstanding the privacy success in relation to contraception, the litigation strategy to decriminalise same-sex activity between men failed in 1983 in *Norris v Attorney General*.[33] Six months later, the pro-life movement secured the adoption of the Eighth Amendment to the Constitution providing explicit protection to the right to life of the unborn. In 1986, the people rejected a referendum proposal to remove the constitutional prohibition on divorce. However, in the early to mid-1990s, the tide began to flow in the opposite direction. In *Attorney General v X*, the Supreme Court held that the Eighth Amendment allowed a suicidal teenager to access a termination of pregnancy in Ireland.[34] Subsequent to *X*, the people approved two constitutional amendments to allow for the distribution of information about abortion services and a freedom to travel for an abortion, while rejecting an amendment proposal to remove suicide as a ground for a termination

---

[30] R Sinnott, 'Cleavages, parties and referendums: Relationships between representative and direct democracy in the Republic of Ireland' (2002) 41 *Eur J Pol Research* 811, 815.

[31] Milhench, 'Ulster Unionists and the Irish Constitution 1970–1985' in L Cahillane, J Gallen, and E Hickey (eds), *Judges, Politics and the Irish Constitution* (Manchester, Manchester University Press, 2017) 200.

[32] *McGee v Attorney General* [1974] IR 248.

[33] *Norris v Attorney General* [1984] IR 36.

[34] *Attorney General v X* [1992] 1 IR 1.

of pregnancy. (In 2002, a further proposal to remove the suicide ground was also rejected.) In 1995, the people narrowly approved a referendum to remove the prohibition on divorce from the Constitution.

Following the model of the pro-life campaign in the 1980s, liberal interest groups have successfully campaigned for constitutional amendment. In 2012, the people approved a Children's Rights Amendment that made little, if any, change to the constitutional law but which can probably be best understood as a symbolic victory for the liberal side of the political cleavage.[35] In 2015, the people approved a referendum proposal to allow same-sex couples marry. In 2018, the people voted to remove A40.3.3 from the Constitution (dealing with the right to life of the unborn) and specifically authorise the Oireachtas to legislate in relation to the provision of services for the termination of pregnancy.

Constitutional change has also occurred through desuetude. One of the more surprising features of the Irish Constitution is that there has been no amendment of Article 41.2, which equates women with mothers and refers to their life and duties within the home. If any constitutional provision is inconsistent with contemporary social mores, this is it. Its non-amendment is explained largely by its obsolescence. Although the courts used to cite Article 41.2 to justify legislative sex discrimination,[36] it is no longer deployed to this end.[37] The courts have also resisted efforts to find a new role for Article 41.2, sensitive to changed social circumstances.[38] It is a fair conclusion that Article 41.2, while formally unamended, is in a state of desuetude. Desuetude also explains the current status of the unenumerated rights doctrine. I have argued above that this was an informal constitutional change, effected by judicial decision. Its non-use since 2000, described in chapter nine, is a further constitutional change.

When we explore the history of formal and informal constitutional change, therefore, we see a general picture of gradual liberalisation, achieved both through formal amendment and litigation strategies. The special position of the Catholic Church, the ban on divorce, the implicit prohibition on same-sex marriage and the explicit prohibition on abortion have all been removed by constitutional amendment. This trend may well continue, given the Government's commitment to hold

---

[35] Doyle and Kenny (n 26).

[36] See O'Higgins CJ in *de Búrca v Attorney General* [1976] IR 38 (in dissent) upholding the presumptive exclusion of women from jury service.

[37] In *Lowth v Minister for Social Welfare* [1998] 4 IR 321, the Supreme Court, considering a preference for women in the social welfare code, treated Article 41.2 as evidence of a social order in which women had not worked outside the home, rather than as a direct normative justification for the sex discrimination.

[38] *L v L* [1992] 2 IR 77 and *Sinnott v Minister for Education* [2001] 2 IR 545.

referendums in relation to women's role within the home (Article 41.2) and the constitutional offence of blasphemy (Article 40.6) following the recommendations of a Constitutional Convention. At the same time, the courts effected an informal constitutional change to give themselves the power to create new constitutional rights, generally reflective of a liberal position – most notably the privacy right in *McGee*. The courts have subsequently allowed the unenumerated rights doctrine to wither, as part of a general turn to non-intervention traced in chapter nine. The constitutional treatment of abortion now confirms this position. Although there are strong arguments that the right to life of the unborn was implicitly constitutionally protected,[39] the people chose to amend the Constitution to make that protection explicit. This protection was somewhat eroded by subsequent amendments, and arguably by the judgment of the Supreme Court in *Attorney General v X*. Nevertheless, the treatment of abortion remained a distinctive feature of the Irish Constitution, even as the Constitution generally converged on a more generic liberal democratic model. In March 2018, the two Houses of the Oireachtas approved a referendum to repeal Article 40.3.3°, which deals with abortion, and to provide explicitly a power for the Oireachtas to legislate to regulate the provision of terminations of pregnancy. This referendum was passed by a wide margin in May 2018, confirming the broader trend of a liberalising constitution.

VI. THE CONSTITUTIONALISATION OF SOCIAL CHANGE: AN ABDICATION OF POLITICAL RESPONSIBILITY?

In the preceding section, we explored the way in which constitutional change, whether through formal amendment or informal change, has occurred in respect of hot-button moral issues. This analysis potentially feeds a narrative that political actors have abdicated their responsibility to respond to social change. In order to avoid contentious issues surrounding the liberal-conservative cleavage, the argument goes, political actors were content for the courts to grapple with issues such as contraception and more recently have promoted unnecessary

---

[39] In *Re Article 26 and the Regulation of Information (Services outside the State for Termination of Pregnancies) Bill, 1995* [1995] 1 IR 1, 28, the Supreme Court stated, 'The right to life of the unborn was clearly recognised by the courts as one of the unenumerated personal rights which the State guaranteed in its laws to respect, and, as far as practicable, by its laws to defend and vindicate.' The Supreme Court has recently reappraised this area of law in *M v Minister for Justice and Equality* [2018] IESC 14.

constitutional amendments rather than legislate for social change. There is some substance to this charge. In the X *Case*, one member of the Supreme Court trenchantly criticised the Oireachtas for its failure to legislate to elaborate on the meaning of Article 40.3.3 of the Constitution, describing it as inexcusable.[40] It is also the case that where the people have the final say on an issue through a referendum, political parties need not be quite so definitive in their own positions.[41] If the Attorney General advises that legislation would be unconstitutional, the Government will not introduce it and there is no need for a political party to indicate whether it would support the legislation. If the issue is then pushed towards constitutional amendment, it is possible for individual legislators to sidestep responsibility for amendment proposals. Although Article 46 requires that referendum proposals first be approved by both the Dáil and Seanad, it is politically plausible for individual legislators to claim that they support the Bill not because they agree with its substance but rather because they believe that the people should be allowed to express their view. A number of Labour Party TDs and Senators voted in favour of the Referendum Bill to abolish the Seanad in 2013, while indicating their opposition to the proposal. In the view of their party leader, party discipline requirements were satisfied once they voted to approve a Bill to which they were publicly opposed.[42]

The narrative of political abdication, however, is sometimes overstated. A particular case in point is the process that led to the Marriage Referendum of 2015. O'Mahony and Tobin have separately argued that no constitutional change was required to allow for same-sex marriage.[43] They offer differing explanations for why an unnecessary referendum was held. O'Mahony argues that religious-moral controversies have been constitutionalised in Ireland, transcending ordinary politics, such that referendums have become the default way of settling these disputes. Tobin argues that a referendum was chosen because of a lack of determination to tackle the issue in the Oireachtas and a politically opportune recourse to participative democracy, the Government only supporting a

---

[40] *Attorney General v X* [1992] 1 IR 1, 82.

[41] Sinnott (n 30).

[42] See 'Seanad Abolition is no Power Grab, says Gilmore', *The Irish Times*, 12 September 2013.

[43] C O'Mahony, 'Principled Expediency: How the Irish Courts can Compromise on Same-Sex Marriage' (2012) 35 *Dublin University Law Journal* 199; C O'Mahony, 'Marriage Equality in the United States and Ireland: How History Shaped the Future' (2017) *University of Illinois Law Review* 682; B Tobin, 'Marriage Equality in Ireland: The Politico-Legal Context' (2016) 30 *International Journal of Law, Policy and the Family* 115.

referendum after a constitutional convention had voted in favour of it. However, the doctrinal analysis underlying these claims is questionable. Both O'Mahony and Tobin heavily rely on the High Court judgment in *Zappone v Revenue Commissioners*, holding that the constitutional right to marry could not extend to a lesbian couple for several reasons.[44] Having held that it would be impermissible for the courts to update the constitutional meaning of marriage, Dunne J had regard to a then recent statutory definition of 'marriage' to conclude that the contemporary meaning of marriage did not in any event extend to same-sex couples. O'Mahony and Tobin both draw from this obiter dictum the conclusion that the courts would have deferred to any legislative attempt to redefine marriage. But this is an insecure basis for such a bold conclusion. It relies on an unusual obiter dictum from a High Court judge; it would overturn several Supreme Court decisions that defined the constitutional concept of marriage in opposite-sex terms;[45] it would be radically inconsistent with the clearly scholastic natural law ethos of Article 41, recognising opposite-sex marriage as a relationship primarily oriented to reproduction and the raising of children.

Even if O'Mahony and Tobin were correct about the ability of the Oireachtas to legislate for same-sex marriage, there were highly plausible counter-arguments. There is considerable evidence that significant constitutional actors believed the counter-arguments.[46] It seems clear that the Attorney General formed the view that a referendum would be required to allow for same-sex marriage.[47] The simplest explanation for why a referendum was held therefore is that the relevant constitutional actors believed (reasonably, even if mistakenly) that a referendum was legally required.[48] The narratives of political abdication and political cowardice are not convincing, particularly when we consider other social changes that the Oireachtas has passed. In 2010, the Oireachtas introduced Civil Partnership for same-sex couples, at the time almost as controversial as marriage would be five years later. Shortly before the marriage referendum, the Oireachtas made extensive changes to

---

[44] [2006] IEHC 404.

[45] The full Court in *Murphy v Attorney General* [1982] IR 241, 286 and Murray J in *CT v DT* [2003] 1 ILRM 321, 374.

[46] O'Mahony, 'Marriage Equality in the United States and Ireland' (n 43) 691.

[47] Tobin (n 43) 121; O'Mahony, 'Principled Expediency' (n 43) 205–6.

[48] For these reasons, the Irish referendum on same-sex marriage was entirely different from the plebiscite subsequently held in Australia on the same topic. Conversely, international criticism of Ireland for putting minority rights to a popular vote was largely misplaced. See for instance OG Encarnación, 'There's Something about Marriage: Why the Vote in Ireland was Bad for Same-Sex Rights', *Foreign Affairs* 31 May 2015.

family law to allow for IVF and surrogacy in certain circumstances, as well as extending fostering and adoption rights to unmarried couples. Issues relating to children were among the most controversial in the marriage referendum campaign. The willingness of the Oireachtas to address these issues through legislation, albeit after long delays in some instances, undermines the claim of political cowardice or a default preference for referendums.

As noted above, the constitutionalisation of political-moral issues has granted an unusually prominent role to the courts and referendums. This should not be overstated, however. Moreover, the general dynamic in Irish constitutional law is towards the regulation of fewer and fewer of these issues at a constitutional level. Overall, there is little evidence to support the claim that political actors choose to put social and moral issues to referendum votes, despite believing that a referendum is not required. Nevertheless, the requirement for popular approval to some social changes does alter the political dynamics. As noted above, it is politically plausible for a politician to vote in favour of a referendum Bill on the basis that she believes the people should be allowed to have their say, thereby distancing herself from the change proposal. The emergence of deliberative democracy further facilitates this political move. The Labour Party fought the General Election of 2011 with a manifesto commitment to hold a referendum to allow for same-sex marriage. The Fine Gael – Labour Government of 2011–2016 did not agree to hold a referendum but rather assigned the question of marriage equality, along with seven others, to a Constitutional Convention. Ultimately, a strong majority of the Convention favoured an amendment of the Constitution to provide directive or mandatory wording requiring the introduction of same-sex marriage. The Government then committed to hold a referendum to give effect to this recommendation. By the time of the referendum campaign, Taoiseach Enda Kenny, the leader of Fine Gael, had become a supporter of and leading campaigner for same-sex marriage. The referendum was held because relevant constitutional actors honestly and correctly believed that it was legally required. However, it is fair to say that the deferral to the constitutional convention and the ambiguity around supporting a referendum allowed popular support for the proposal to build before all those constitutional actors fully committed themselves to supporting it.

A similar process of political distancing occurred with respect to abortion. Following the General Election of 2016, the Oireachtas established a Citizens Assembly to consider the 8th Amendment to the Constitution and to make such recommendations as it saw fit.

The Assembly was similar in structure to the previous Constitutional Convention but consisted of 99 randomly selected members of the public (no politicians), as well as an independent chair. Having considered legal, medical and ethical issues relating to the 8th Amendment, as well as hearing personal testimony and submissions from expert groups, the Assembly voted on a series of recommendations. The Assembly's core recommendation was that the Constitution should be amended to provide that issues to do with termination of pregnancy would be within the exclusive jurisdiction of the Oireachtas. The citizens then voted on a series of recommendations for new legislation, which would – if accepted by the Oireachtas – represent a significant liberalisation of Irish abortion law. These included the availability of terminations of pregnancy without restriction as to grounds, during the first 12 weeks of pregnancy. As noted above, the people have approved a referendum to remove the constitutional provisions dealing with abortion and specifically provide that the Oireachtas may regulate the provision of terminations of pregnancy. The Government will propose legislation to allow for terminations of pregnancy on request within the first 12 weeks and thereafter on more limited grounds.

VII. CONSTITUTIONAL CHANGE
AND THE BALANCE OF POWER

The dynamics of constitutional change are a crucial feature in assessing the balance of constitutional power. As I have argued throughout this book, the Constitution vests significant power in the Government, exercised through the executive power but also through its typical control of the legislative process and its leadership of public administration. This power is legally checked by the courts but also subject to a number of political constraints. If the Constitution were as easily amendable as the Irish Free State Constitution, the power of the Government would be far greater since it could change the fundamental rules of the constitutional order to suit its own purposes. However, this is not the case. We cannot know whether the people are generally happy with the current balance of power, but they have repeatedly rejected proposals to enhance the power of dominant political actors: PR-STV twice, abolition of the Seanad, and granting a general public inquiry power to the Oireachtas.[49]

---

[49] I explained in ch 7 how such a power, dependent on a majority in the Dáil to be exercised, is as likely to be used to target the Government's political opponents as public maladministration.

For these reasons, we can characterise the people as a further checking actor in the Irish constitutional order. Their legal power to reject referendum proposals, exercised on several occasions, has a wider political effect. It discourages the Government of the day from considering constitutional change. This is reinforced by the *McKenna* principles, which prevent the Government funding the yes campaign. This empowerment of the people also empowers the courts. The difficulty of constitutional amendment makes the courts' constitutional interpretations far more significant.

Interest groups have also been empowered by this amendment process, combined with the fact that many social and moral issues are regulated by the constitution. Litigation strategies can be used to advance social change from which political actors have shied. *McGee* provides the clearest example of this, although this phenomenon has become less prevalent as judges have become less activist in their constitutional interpretations. The greatest security for an interest group, however, is a constitutional amendment that locks in place its proponents' preferred moral position, thereby constraining the Government in the future. The Eighth Amendment to protect the right to life of the unborn is the clearest example of this, but the Children's Rights Amendment of 2012 and the Marriage Amendment of 2015 are arguably further examples. In all cases, interest groups were to the fore in securing commitments to constitutional change, influencing the chosen wording, and campaigning for the amendment. Interest groups again led the campaign for an amendment to remove the provisions of the Constitution dealing with abortion in 2018.

Could all of this revive the argument that political actors have opportunistically relied on the constitution to cede their own responsibility for social change? Again, no. What drives this political dynamic is the simple fact that the Constitution does, both expressly and through its amenability to judicial interpretation, address a wide range of contentious moral and social issues. Given the rules of the amendment process, this relatively disempowers the Government, while relatively empowering the people, the courts and interest groups. Forums of deliberative democracy, such as the Constitutional Convention and Citizens' Assembly, provide a civic space in which constitutional change can be discussed without direct involvement of political actors. But constitutional amendment must be initiated by a political decision of the Government. Moreover, the active political leadership of the Government, in compliance with the *McKenna* rules, is probably necessary to secure the passage of a referendum, as evidenced by the failed Nice and Lisbon Treaty referendums.

VIII. CONCLUSION

The study of constitutional change is relevant for two purposes. First, it provides a lens through which we can assess the position that a constitution holds in its broader political community. Apart from the transfer of significant powers to the European Union, the core governance structures of the Irish Constitution have remained largely untouched by formal amendment, although they have informally evolved in certain ways. This suggests broad satisfaction with how those structures have evolved, or at least a conservative attitude to change. At the same time, however, various processes of constitutional change, both formal and informal, have significantly diluted the nationalistic and Catholic features of the constitution. Secondly, a study of constitutional change is necessary to understand the current constitutional balance of power. The Irish Constitution creates a very strong Government that exercises State power through its own executive power, through its typical control of the legislative process and through its leadership of public administration. This is subject to significant legal checks by the courts and to political checks by opposition parties in the Oireachtas, as well as a number of accountability institutions, such as the Ombudsman. The power of those checking institutions, both legal and political, is enhanced by the need to secure popular approval for any formal amendment to the Constitution. The people have demonstrated their willingness to veto proposals that accord more power to the Government. The Government is therefore constrained by the fact that it cannot unilaterally secure the amendment of the Constitution but must instead build a broad civic and political consensus in support of constitutional change. The constitutional convention and citizens' assembly can best be understood as exercises that assist the Government in this process.

FURTHER READING

Gavin Barrett, 'The Use of Referendums in Ireland: An Analysis' (2017) 23 *Journal of Legislative Studies* 71

Eoin Daly and Tom Hickey, *The Political Theory of the Irish Constitution: Republicanism and the Basic Law* (Manchester, Manchester University Press, 2015) ch 1

Oran Doyle, 'Legal Validity: Reflections on the Irish Constitution' (2003) 25 *Dublin University Law Journal* 56

Aileen Kavanagh, 'Unconstitutional Constitutional Amendments from Irish Free State to Irish Republic' in Eoin Carolan (ed), *The Constitution of Ireland: Perspectives and Prospects* (Dublin, Bloomsbury Professional, 2012) 331

Conor O'Mahony, 'Principled Expediency: How the Irish Courts can Compromise on Same-Sex Marriage' (2012) 35 *Dublin University Law Journal* 199

Conor O'Mahony, 'Marriage Equality in the United States and Ireland: How History Shaped the Future' (2017) *University of Illinois Law Review* 682

Brian Tobin, 'Marriage Equality in Ireland: The Politico-Legal Context' (2016) 30 *International Journal of Law, Policy and the Family* 115.

11

Conclusion

Changing Balance of Constitutional Power – Ideological Change –
Future Directions

THE MOST FUNDAMENTAL feature of the Irish Constitution is the
bipartite separation of powers between the Government and the
courts. Despite the tripartite separation of powers referenced
in Article 6, the system of political parties means that one political
grouping (whether a single party or coalition) will nearly always control
the Dáil. On the one hand, the political power to act is vested in the
Government, through its typical control of the legislative process, its
exercise of the executive power, and its leadership of public administration. The power of the Government is somewhat diminished by internal
divisions within the Government (particularly coalition governments)
and its lesser day-to-day control over the activities of administrative
agencies. Nevertheless, the Government remains by far the most important political actor. On the other hand, the legal power to constrain is
vested in the courts through their interpretation of the Constitution
and their application of administrative law to the public administration. Ireland's membership of the European Union, authorised by a
series of referendums since 1972, was a significant alteration to this
constitutional structure – arguably greater than that caused by the 1937
Constitution. However, membership of the EU has had little impact on
the internal constitutional balance of power.

The fulcrum of the bipartite separation of powers is the relationship between the Government and the judiciary, institutionalised in the
ability of the Government to nominate, remove and control the pay of
judges. We saw in chapter eight that successive Governments have generally exercised these powers in a way that respects the constitutional role
of an independent judiciary constraining the Government. The appointment process may have led to a socially and intellectually homogenous
judiciary. But it is also a judiciary that acts genuinely independently of
the Government and provides a meaningful constraint on Government

power. In the past decade, judges have been highly critical of changes to their pay and conditions. Although the specific complaints of the judiciary seem overstated, the judicial pay referendum of 2011 demonstrates the ease with which the Government can direct popular opinion against the judiciary in order to secure constitutional change. This identifies a worrying fragility in the constitutionally pivotal relationship between Government and judiciary. The requirement of popular approval for constitutional changes, as we saw in chapter ten, has enhanced the importance of the courts and kept executive dominance in check. Ultimately, however, preservation of the constitutional balance of power largely depends on a culture of elected politicians accepting the entitlement of the judiciary to impose constitutional constraints. This culture needs to be nurtured by politicians and judges alike.

We saw in chapter nine how the courts have changed their approach to the interpretation of constitutional rights, significantly affecting the balance of power between the Government and the courts. These changes have been partly prompted by Government choices about whom to appoint to the Supreme Court. The appointments of Mr Justice Walsh and Chief Justice Ó Dálaigh in 1961, the non-appointment of Mr Justice Walsh as Chief Justice in 1974, and the appointment of five Supreme Court judges in 1999–2000 all correlate with significant changes in direction on the part of the Supreme Court. The historical record in respect of 1961 and 1974 suggests that the Government knew and intended their appointments to have this effect. Nevertheless, this is not a simple tale of causation. The changes in judicial attitude also reflected a general mood for change in 1961 and a subsequent unease at the extent to which the Supreme Court had become a significant political actor. The Government's appointments should be seen as harnessing and providing further impetus for immanent changes in judicial attitude. There is nothing improper in this. Democratic control of judicial appointments is important; nominations should reflect democratically expressed preferences. The judges involved, whether activist or non-interventionist, interpreted the Constitution in the manner they thought was constitutionally required. Nevertheless, recognition of these dynamics is critical for any understanding of the Constitution.

In the early days of the Constitution, the courts adopted a largely but not exclusively non-interventionist posture. The 1960s saw a period of judicial activism that had reached its zenith by the mid-1970s and then slowly tapered off over the following 20–25 years. The unenumerated rights doctrine led to decisions such as *McGee v Ireland*, overturning the ban on contraception, a hugely contentious decision. At the same time, the courts considerably expanded protection for accused people in criminal processes. Since 2000, the courts have constricted the range of the Constitution and therefore their own power in several ways: the demise of the unenumerated rights doctrine, the eschewal of mandatory orders, narrow readings of constitutional rights, and a minimalist application of standards of review, such as the proportionality test. As a result of all this, the courts constrain the Government significantly less today than was the case in the mid-1970s. It is questionable, however, whether this governmental freedom of action has been fully internalised by either the Government or civil society. In many ways, there is a casual assumption that the Constitution implements the same balance of power as in the 1970s. This is very far from the case.

At the same time as this reduction in legal constraint, there has been an increase in political constraints on the Government. All Governments since 1989 (with the exception of the minority Government formed in 2016) have been coalitions. This has increased policy and personal disagreement within Government, somewhat reducing its power vis-à-vis other branches. The ability of each party to collapse the Government provides an important internal check on the actions of the other party. However, there has also been an increase in political constraints imposed by other constitutional actors. Since the election of Mary Robinson in 1990, the Presidency has become an institution with considerable rhetorical power, allowing Presidents to question social attitudes while generally avoiding issues of party-political controversy. The Government has increasingly adopted a legislative approach that vests administrative powers in statutory agencies rather than Government Ministers. As public administration has expanded, Government control has lessened. Nevertheless, as I argue in chapter six, the administration in Ireland cannot be viewed as a competing organ of government. Perhaps related to this expansion of public administration, there has been an increase in accountability institutions, such as the Ombudsman. Tribunals of inquiry and commissions of investigation have been used to explore allegations of incompetence and corruption. Changes in Dáil processes, most notably new rules for the election of the Ceann Comhairle of the Dáil and the appointment of Oireachtas committee chairs, have somewhat enhanced the ability of opposition parties at least to draw public attention to alleged maladministration. This is an important source of political constraint. The electoral system of PR-STV in multi-seat constituencies means that there are no safe seats, with members of the Government all at risk of losing their seats at the following general election. As a result, Government Ministers and backbench TDs have strong incentives (possibly too strong) to avoid and quell political controversy.

The inability of any political grouping after the 2016 general election to form a political coalition with the support of a majority in the Dáil has transformed the constitutional order, for the time being, into one operating a tripartite separation of powers. The Government no longer controls the legislative process and is meaningfully accountable to the Dáil. As we saw in chapter seven, the opposition was able in November 2017 to secure the resignation of the Tánaiste (Deputy Prime Minister) as the price for the continuation of the Government in office. On the other hand, the Government's primacy in financial matters has arguably been used to delay and prevent the passage of legislation with which the Government disagrees. It is too early to gauge the success of this experiment in contested government.

Subject to these exceptions, the constitutional order is dominated by the Government. There is always a risk that such Government dominance could lead to democratic decay, the Government using its power to preserve its position for the future through alteration of the rules. This risk has not materialised for several reasons, some political and some legal. We saw in chapter three how two constitutional conventions are observed that reduce the scope for Government dominance: the convention that the maximum Oireachtas term of five years is not extended, and the convention that the Oireachtas implements the recommendations of an independent constituency commission when drawing boundaries for legislative districts. These conventions foreclose some opportunities for temporary majorities to take advantage of their position. Finally, and most important, the requirement of a referendum to amend the Constitution ensures that the Government cannot amend the Constitution to secure its own position without securing broad support from other constitutional actors. The people have rejected several measures that would have further concentrated political power, such as changing the voting system to First Past the Post, giving a power of public inquiry to Oireachtas committees, and abolishing the Seanad. The judicial pay referendum, mentioned above, raises a caveat; however, in broad terms it is the referendum requirement for constitutional change that has secured the stability of the constitutional order.

If the people underpin the constitutional order, it is the constitutional identification of the people that is one of the most significant ideological choices made by the Constitution. We saw in chapter two how there was a mismatch between the dignified and efficient parts of the Constitution. The dignified Constitution summoned an all-island, Gaelic and (implicitly) Catholic people as the locus of constitutional authority and focus of constitutional concern. The real effect of Articles 2 and 3, however, was to secure the removal of Northern Ireland from the constitutional consciousness, establishing a new 26-county State. The constitutional text only caught up with this constitutional reality following the Northern Ireland peace settlement in 1998 and consequent amendments to Articles 2 and 3. National reunification can now only occur with the separate consent of the people in both Northern Ireland and Ireland. In the process, the Constitution has abandoned a core aspect of constitutional identity, its claim to be a Constitution for all the people on the entire island.

The other significant ideological change has been the diminution of Roman Catholic and natural law influences on the Constitution. This has occurred in a number of ways. Formal amendment has altered the text of the Constitution, such as the removal of the special position of the Catholic Church as well as the introduction of divorce, same-sex marriage and (most recently) allowance for the introduction of abortion. Judicial interpretation has created liberal entitlements, such as the right to privacy, and re-characterised rights derived from natural law as liberal guarantees, such as property rights and family rights. Ideological change has also occurred through desuetude, as with the non-utilisation of Article 41.2 (the role of women in the home). In this way, the Constitution has become much more generically liberal than was the case in 1937.

The Constitution has therefore become less ideologically prescriptive. It has created a space in which different understandings of Irishness can evolve free from constitutional dictation. In terms of social legislation, Governments are less constitutionally committed to a particular social vision, whether religiously motivated or otherwise. These ideological changes are reinforced by the general attitude of non-intervention on the part of the courts. It is, at present, simply inconceivable that the Supreme Court would reverse a legislative choice on an issue as controversial as was contraception in the 1970s. This flexibility and adaptability may partly explain the success, or at least the longevity, of the Constitution. On the one hand, it has underpinned a stable political system; on the other hand, it has imposed fewer and fewer constraints on the sorts of political programmes that can be pursued through that political system.

There are two ironies in this account. First, nearly 100 years after independence, the Constitution of Ireland functions in a manner remarkably similar to the Constitution of the United Kingdom. Both revolve around a bipartite separation of powers between Government and courts. Although the courts in Ireland retain the power to strike down legislation, the introduction of the Human Rights Act in the United Kingdom and the current attitude of non-intervention on the part of the Irish courts has resulted in far greater similarities than was previously the case. At the same time, the political constraints imposed by Parliament, the growth of public administration, and the creation of accountability institutions have progressed on broadly similar lines in both jurisdictions.

The constitutional choices of 1937 engaged in a form of double-speak in relation to Northern Ireland. While the Constitution professed to be enacted by and for the people of an all-island Ireland, it was really made by and for the people of a newly emerged political entity, the 26-county Ireland. National unity was a constitutional imperative, but the ethno-religious features of the Constitution would significantly discourage Northern unionists from feeling any affinity with this new State. The second irony of Irish constitutional development is that, notwithstanding this alignment of the constitutional order of Ireland with that of the United Kingdom, unionists remain as alienated from the 26-county Ireland as ever. The United Kingdom's imminent departure from the European Union, combined with significant demographic change, has brought reunification onto the political agenda for the reasons explored at the end of chapter two. It is questionable, however, what the people of Ireland would be prepared to concede in order to secure reunification. In one sense, this is the ultimate success of the 1937 Constitution: the creation of a constitutional order that will not countenance its own demise, not even to achieve what was first claimed to be a fundamental objective of that constitutional order: national reunification.

Index

www.ingramcontent.com/pod-product-compliance
Lightning Source LLC
Chambersburg PA
CBHW071852270326
41929CB00013B/2202